P9-DIG-922

TY BURR

. . . .

THE BEST

OLD MOVIES FOR FAMILIES

Ty Burr is a film critic for *The Boston Globe.* For eleven years prior, he worked for *Entertainment Weekly* as the magazine's chief video critic and also covered movies, books, theater, music, and the Internet. He began his career at Home Box Office as an in-house "film evaluator." While at *Entertainment Weekly*, Burr wrote *The Hundred Greatest Movies of All Time* and coauthored *The Hundred Greatest Stars of All Time* (with Alison Gwinn). He has also written about film and other subjects for *The New York Times*, *Spin*, the *Boston Phoenix*, and other publications. A member of the National Society of Film Critics and the Boston Society of Film Critics, Burr lives in Newton, Massachusetts, with his wife and two daughters.

WEST GA REG LIB SYS
Neva Lomason
Memorial Library

ALSO BY TY BURR

The Hundred Greatest Movies of All Time

The Hundred Greatest Stars of All Time
(with Alison Gwinn)

The Best OLD MOVIES FOR FAMILIES

A GUIDE TO WATCHING TOGETHER

TY BURR

ANCHOR BOOKS

A Division of Random House, Inc.

New York

AN ANCHOR BOOKS ORIGINAL, FEBRUARY 2007

Copyright © 2007 by Ty Burr

All rights reserved. Published in the United States
by Anchor Books, a division of Random House, Inc.,
New York, and in Canada by Random House
of Canada Limited, Toronto.

Anchor Books and colophon are
registered trademarks of Random House, Inc.

Library of Congress Cataloging-in-Publication Data
Burr, Ty.
The best old movies for families: a guide to
watching together / by Ty Burr.—1st Anchor Books ed.
p. cm.
ISBN: 978-1-4000-9686-2
1. Motion pictures for children—Catalogs.
2. Motion pictures and children. I. Title.
PN1998. B84 2007
791.43'75083—dc22   2006023525

Book design by JoAnne Metsch

www.anchorbooks.com

Printed in the United States of America
10 9 8 7 6 5 4 3 2 1

for

MARJORIE JANE TICE

CONTENTS

. . . .

The Best
OLD MOVIES
FOR
FAMILIES

INTRODUCTION

. . . .

I KNEW WE had passed some twisted point of no return when Eliza announced that she wanted to have a Katharine Hepburn party. With a screening of *Bringing Up Baby*. For her ninth birthday.

My wife, Lori, and I tried to dissuade her. Maybe our daughter could gladly sit through a fifth viewing of the screwball comedy classic, but how many of her schoolmates would make it through their first, conditioned as they were to color, brightness, *Shrek?* Eliza was unmoved: It was *her* birthday, and she argued convincingly for the constitutional right to choose her own party theme.

So out the invitations went, featuring a photo of Hepburn in *The Philadelphia Story* that Eliza personally cut out and pasted on. And in came the phone calls from the parents. To my chagrin, most of them were convinced that her father the fancy-pants movie critic had put her up to it (on a stack of the collected works of Wong Kar-Wai, I did no such thing), but their more pressing concern, which we shared, was that their child would get bored, wander off, play with knives. My wife and I assured them we were laying out a table next to the screening room, filled with books and pencil-based activities to divert those kids

oppressed by the very notion of black-and-white cinematography.

The books were never opened, the pencils never used. We
took a half-hour intermission for cake, but when I asked if the
group was ready to restart the movie, there was a unanimous
roar of assent, and we picked up again with that marvelous
forest-of-Arden sequence where Kate, playing flibbertigibbet
heiress Susan Vance, leads Cary Grant's nerd zoologist David
Huxley through the nighttime wilds of Greenwich, Connecticut. At one point Susan breaks a high heel and teeters up and
down, burbling in delight, "Look, David, I was born on a hill. I
was born on the side of a hill," and the moment feels so sponta-
neous, so magically free, it can make your hair stand on end. (In
fact, the bit was mischievously improvised by Hepburn after the
1938 equivalent of a wardrobe malfunction.) The kids had
never seen anything like it: It felt more unscripted, more *real*
than anything twenty-first-century kid culture feeds them, up
to and including reality TV.

When the parents showed up to collect their children, five
minutes remained—Grant was still stuck in the jail cell with
Hepburn dragging the wild leopard through the door—and
eighteen kids sat mesmerized and giggling. The moms and dads
were astounded. They shouldn't have been, nor should Lori or I.

Great filmmaking trumps all other considerations. This is
even more true if you're nine and every movie still feels like the
first you've ever seen.

Some backtracking may be necessary. I work as a film critic for a
major metropolitan daily newspaper. Before that, I spent over a
decade writing about movies for a national entertainment magazine. Before that, I screened and recommended films for the
acquisitions department of a pay-cable movie network. Before

that, I was a cinema studies major, ran a college film society, and wrote long, impenetrable reviews in the student newspaper. Before that, I was a pale teenage movie ghost who wondered why taking a girl to a double bill of Sam Fuller films never got me anywhere.

This is simply a way of saying that I have seen many, many, many movies. When asked *how* many, I hazard the guess that I average a movie a day, and, since I've been watching seriously for thirty years, the total comes to something on the order of 10,680 films. On a good day, I remember seven thousand of them. On a bad day, maybe five.

I am also now a father to two girls, currently nine and eleven. As any parent understands, this changes *everything*. I once viewed children's films with indulgence, even nostalgia. Today I look at the movie offerings afforded my kids and am stunned into depression at the pandering narrowness. The animation industry has given itself over to the seductions of CGI; live-action kid films have prostrated themselves on the altar of cross-marketing. If you're a girl, the choices are thin: Shall we take in the Lindsay Lohan tweener comedy or the Amanda Bynes tweener comedy or the Hilary Duff tweener comedy? Better to go for the Anne Hathaway tweener comedy; that one costars Julie Andrews, at least. (Oh, wait, Anne Hathaway took her shirt off in a movie about gay cowboys, so I guess she's all grown up now.)

Or maybe we should just head to the video store and choose among the racks of Mary-Kate and Ashley midget consumer fantasies that continue to proliferate like head lice on the shelves. Failing that, there are untold Disney films and imitations thereof, from the pinnacles of *Snow White* and *Beauty and the Beast* to the barely acceptable tedium of *Chicken Little* and *The Wild*. It's worse if you're a boy: Then the choice is between bad American animation, bad Japanese animation, and *Spy Kids 3-D*.

And those are the original concepts. When a film studio takes it upon itself to adapt a prized children's book, the results can be even more grim, since producers feel they have to make the story marketable with fart gags, cooked-up villainy, and pop songs wedged into every conceivable crevice. Some titles survive the treatment, and even prosper, such as *Shrek* or *The Lion, the Witch and the Wardrobe*, or the 2003 *Peter Pan*, a charming film that rescues and deepens the Barrie original. But my older daughter is still steamed at the changes wrought by Hollywood to her beloved *Ella Enchanted*, and I personally would be happy to see Imagine Entertainment brought up on child endangerment charges for what it did to the good and gentle Dr. Seuss with *How the Grinch Stole Christmas* and the genuinely hateful *The Cat in the Hat*.

Some films aimed at children are good—excellent, even. Pixar: I rest my case. But all of them—and I do mean *all* of them—arrive in theaters sold out, prepackaged, and co-opted. A modern family film can't get greenlit for production without marketing tie-ins planned in detail and in-house licensing executives kicking the tires to discern how "toyetic" it is. That's a real word, by the way. Yes, it makes my flesh crawl too.

Today's kids' films are built to cater to and flatter their audience into buying the subsidiary products. That's their job. That bag of "Kelpy Kreme" doughnuts that gets a loving close-up early on in *Shark Tale* isn't there by accident. And because the movie's first order of business is to sell, the story can't afford to challenge children in the slightest degree.

So: A child could go from January to December without having his or her brain interestingly taxed—without seeing a movie that wasn't slavishly geared toward mini-me taste in stars, fashion, music, and flippant attitude. (The moral is applied at the end, like frosting.) Hollywood has become a machine for reflecting a modern American kid's mediated universe right back at him or her; it's a hall of mirrors with no way out except teenage cynicism, when adolescents opt out of the cycle because they start feeling such movies are "just" for kids. Or because they're wising up.

Even then, Hollywood is there to pull them back in with an escalating sensationalism that dulls the brain. The film industry has become adept at creating brilliant CGI-enhanced nightmares and selling them as "family films" that make *Psycho* look like *Dumbo*. The studios and MPAA ratings board collude in helping films that feature rotting zombies avoid the R of death (just as long as there's no nudity, because we know how *that* warps kids), and parents often take the smallest children to see terrifying PG-13 thrill rides like *Van Helsing* or *Pirates of the Caribbean: Dead Man's Chest* because the rating somehow absolves them of having to think for themselves.

But what's the alternative? Drag 'em to *Kill Bill: Vol. 1*? Where's the antidote to the Disneyfied pap and computer-generated overstimulation that passes for children's entertainment these days? Wouldn't it be pleasant to sit down and watch a movie with your kids that wasn't presold on sequels and Happy Meals? Or take them to an action movie that didn't either freak them out or weigh down their little bones with premature irony?

I guess you could lock them in the attic. A better solution might be to vary their media diet, and one way to do that is with old movies. I don't mean *Grease* or *Star Wars*. I mean *old movies*. The kind in black and white or Crayola-surreal Technicolor; the ones that feature stars who were in the grave before Keira Knightley was a zygote. Movies like *The Wizard of Oz* and *Singin' in the Rain*, yes—but also *Some Like It Hot* and *Rebecca* and *Modern Times* and *The Searchers* and *All About Eve* and *I Know Where I'm Going!* and *The Day the Earth Stood Still* and *To Kill a Mockingbird*. Movies that open a door out of modern Hollywood's hall of mirrors onto endless variations in style, behavior, morals. There is so much out there if you have the least idea where to look. If you don't, maybe this book can help.

The first obstacle you'll face is that, in all likelihood, your kids will give you the Blank Stare of Death when you float this idea past them. Why wouldn't they? To parents, old movies represent the recent past, but to a modern child, they're relics from the Dark Ages, mixed up in a vague chronology that sees 45 records, rotary telephones, and granny glasses as so much weird eBay effluvia. The great flicks of the studio days, from the 1930s through the 1950s, are ghettoized on Turner Classic Movies, while other movie channels play "classics" that are fifteen years old—mere babies, with none of the timeless splendor of the real stuff.

How, then, do you get kids into the real stuff? It isn't easy, and the older they get, the harder it becomes. The best and simplest advice, then, is: Start when they're young. Am I advocating screening *The Gold Rush* while your children are still in the cradle? No, because that's when they should be watching the world. Am I saying throw it on as occasional background when they're toddlers, or as part of the eventual kid-TV mix in your house, whatever that may be? Yes.

If a child can watch *Barney*, a child can watch Charlie Chaplin, and in fact, he or she might be better off. As they get older, you can gradually take them to the next level: screwball comedies and women's weepies, war films and issue dramas. They'll follow because they'll have learned that "old" does not necessarily mean "next channel, please."

If you're bringing children between the ages of, say, seven and eleven to classic movies for the first time, you need to pick more carefully, or you'll sour them on the form for good. And if you're hoping to start watching black-and-white films with teenagers, I'm afraid to inform you that the horses have left the barn, gone to *Lost*, MySpace, YouTube, and Ryan Reynolds comedies. And they're not coming back until they find these films on their own.

Which doesn't mean you can't try: This book suggests which old movies retain the power to make even a deeply suspicious adolescent snap his or her head back and say, "*Whoa.*" Scientists call this Going Keanu.

Here's where I should perhaps offer my own test case as proof; I'll let you decide whether it's a brilliant approach that gives you the go-ahead to break out the Bogart or a horrific Skinner-box exploitation of an author's own children.

I introduced Eliza to old movies with *Singin' in the Rain* when she was about three. What's not to like there? It's in color, it's tuneful, Donald O'Connor is a clown for the ages, and even a child can see what makes Gene Kelly such a beautiful ham. She warbled the title song for a good couple of weeks, with strange toddler variations, and then I decided to throw a few more 1950s musicals at her. *Seven Brides for Seven Brothers. Funny Face. An American in Paris. Kiss Me Kate.* She loved them all, even when she had no idea what was going on.

With *Meet Me in St. Louis* she figured out what was going on and cherished the film all the more—and in Margaret O'Brien she discovered the first real child she had ever seen in a movie. When I took her to a revival-theater screening of *It's Always Fair Weather* in New York City, one of the scary old-movie guys in the row behind me leaned forward and whispered, "Is she into Comden and Green?" The funny part is that by then she was, even if she had no idea that Betty Comden and Adolph Green were the ace screenwriters and lyricists behind so many of the movies she was enjoying.

As Eliza got older and her younger sister Natalie grew out of the spud phase and started walking and talking, I began to throw different sorts of old movies at them. I tried silent comedies, seeking some inchoate connection between my children and my own dad, who died when I was young and who was known for his love of slapstick: Chaplin, Keaton, Harold Lloyd. I tried other silents, too—early sci-fi like *Metropolis* and seminal horror like *The Phantom of the Opera* with Lon Chaney. The girls were understandably wary but got sucked in time and again, and the silent-movie format was part of the appeal: those evanescent shadows, the title cards that Dad had to read, the larger-than-life pantomime, all the more dreamlike for not talking.

I tried talkies too, of course: melodramas, comedies, even foreign films. To a few of my acquaintances I am still known as The Man Who Showed *The Seven Samurai* to His Kids. And They Liked It. Some of the movies went over incredibly well. Some tanked. The dirty little secret about classics is that a lot of them have aged poorly and others weren't very good to start with. Still, my daughters came to understand that a DVD with the name Alfred Hitchcock or Frank Capra attached was probably a good deal. They discovered that Harpo Marx could make them laugh as deliriously as SpongeBob. And they found films that scared them pleasurably instead of silly.

They still want to see the latest studio kid flicks and buy the sound tracks and form their generational tastes, and that's as it should be. But classic movies are a regular part of the mix now, and for Eliza, they've become something more—a way into an older America that she finds soul-satisfying on any number of levels. Watching the 1933 version of *Little Women* was for her a revelation that female empowerment doesn't have to come dressed in a belly shirt; discovering Kate Hepburn gave her a role model that will shape her into adolescence and beyond. (On the other hand, providing Cary Grant as a male role model definitely sets the bar too high.)

Not every child is so easily convinced. I have a friend who valiantly tries showing her son classics and he never bites (two words of advice: Three Stooges). My younger daughter, Natalie, still comfortably plonks down in front of the Disney Channel and, for a while, even grabbed shameless straight-to-video sequels—*sequels! the ignominy!*—off our bookshelf. Children develop and things change, though: Natalie always loved her MGM musicals and *The Adventures of Robin Hood*, and if she was skittish about black and white at first, she flipped for Hitchcock's *Rebecca,* a gothic mystery-romance with eternal appeal to girls. Then I caught her riffling through my film coffee-table books, ticking off the movies she had seen and asking about ones she hadn't. Then she wanted to see all six *Thin Man* DVDs in the boxed set. Then she fell in love with Cagney.

Over the course of my daughters' little lives—and, more crucially, over the course of writing this book—I've learned that what speaks to them and what doesn't is a mystery beyond parental prediction. Children are both more and less innocent than we take them for, and we never know what they'll get out of what we hand them: boredom, laughter, ideas that shake the very foundations of their being. Better to risk the boredom for the laughs and ideas, I think.

Still, it can't last. I guess I don't want it to. The girls will soon be lost to their own films, their mother and I won't be invited along, and as long as those films aren't teen slasher movies based on video games, I can live with that. (I understand that merely typing those words ensures they'll come to pass.) Eliza and Natalie will move on to more contemporary role models, and that's okay, too: I knew a few women in college who thought they were Katharine Hepburn, and they were *terrifying.* In truth, my daughters can go away as long as they wish. Kate and Cary and Buster and Harpo and Bette and all seven of the samurai will be there, waiting patiently until they return.

I've noticed something, though: As Eliza starts listening more to her peers than to us, her peers are also listening more to her. And part of what they hear, and learn, is that old movies are okay. Her pals have come to know they may end up watching a classic if they come over—because Eliza's dad is writing this book, but also because that's just what's *on* at the Burr house—and I know there are friends of hers who dread the prospect. Fine. But there are other friends who find the whole thing a curious and interesting pocket of taste, and they appreciate it. Eliza went over to a buddy's house for a rainy Saturday hangout the other week and took Hitchcock's *The Trouble with Harry* along. And they all dug in.

The thing of it is, watching the old stuff changes how kids see the new. My daughters can enjoy *Garfield: The Movie* on its own level—and good for them, because I sure as hell can't—but they inherently understand that it's a short-term investment compared to a movie like *The Producers*, in which Zero Mostel makes a better Garfield than Garfield ever has. On one hand, they're warier of the modern plastics used to build movies these days. On the other, they can better appreciate a gem like *The Incredibles* when it comes along. It's as though they were on the side of a hill—look, David—and able to move up or down through the years and the decades as it suits them.

Here's why this is good: With any luck, my daughters will be able to go through life lacking that fear of old movies—and, much more to the point, old culture—that keeps so many children and their parents locked in an eternal, ahistorical Now. The only way to comprehend Now, of course, is to understand Then. More than almost any other art form, movies show the way back.

HOW THIS WORKS

This is a book for two audiences: people who know and love old movies but aren't sure how to convey that love to their children, and people who don't know old movies from particle physics but want to share a special experience with their kids and be entertained in the bargain.

The first set of readers will find a great many films they know and may already enjoy, arranged in a fashion that hopefully maximizes kid appeal. The second group can take the chapters that follow as homeschooling for the entire family—for, unlike *Monster House*, classics can be enjoyed at all age levels.

A couple of things to note. First, this is not a book to be read from cover to cover. Rather, it's one that should be sampled as you would a buffet. Reach in, pick a title, mull over the comments, decide whether your kids would enjoy the movie. Then go from there.

Second, there are plenty of old movies you won't find in here. Do I really need to add another five hundred words to the million already written about *The Wizard of Oz*? On the other hand, this isn't a textbook, so you won't be reading about *The Birth of a Nation* or other culturally important films that are problematic for kids. I haven't included *Gone with the Wind*, either, for reasons discussed in chapter 2.

Third, when I say "classic movies," I'm referring to *films made during the golden age of the film studios*, from the silent era through the early 1960s. American film went through a major morph in the late '60s and early '70s with the fashionable hippie realism of the New Hollywood; then it morphed again in the late '70s, when *Jaws* and *Star Wars* kicked off the age of the blockbuster, which is only slowly fading now. Those two more modern eras are not the subject of this book. There are many people— probably most people—who hear the words "old movie" and think of *Chinatown* or *Sixteen Candles* or *Field of Dreams*, or, God help us, *Lord of the Rings*. Great films; not on the plate this time. Maybe next book.

Fourth, you're right, I did leave out your favorite film. Sorry. Please write and tell me I'm a pinhead. Better, just rent the thing and show it to your kids.

Last, I willingly confess to a girl-movie bias, since girls is what I got. On occasion I've borrowed one of Eliza's or Natalie's male buddies and hosted a group screening, but whereas watching movies with your own parent is bonding, watching movies with your friend's parent is vaguely weird.

The book is arranged to ramp you up to speed depending on who's living in your house. The first chapter, as the title indicates, should be thought of as a starter kit: fifteen old movies to persuade, respectively, toddlers, tweeners, and teenagers. This is because many classics aren't the right *first* classic. We brought the 1947 gangster movie *White Heat* along to a Saturday dinner with friends, and while Eliza and Natalie were pumped—they'd watched *The Public Enemy* the night before and become immediately hooked on the genre—the other kids drew a blank. They didn't dislike it; they just didn't get it, because it came from Planet Old.

Not all classics do. I've tried to mix color with black and white, musicals with Westerns, so if you can get through all the starter films with a particular child or group of children, they'll have a handle on what constitutes a classic and whether it's something they want more of. Some won't. C'est la guerre.

The next chapter sets out a few parameters describing what, in the author's experience, works and what doesn't, and what ages are appropriate for what sort of movie—why showing *Citizen Kane* to a five-year-old is just plain dumb. Then we're into genres: comedy, drama, action, and so forth, each broken down into its constituent parts (screwball comedy, melodrama, '50s sci-fi, etc.), with representative movies in each grouping. Organization is alphabetical within each subsection. In a few cases—MGM musicals, Universal horror films—it's easier to discuss them as a group with brief paragraphs treating key examples. Finally, there's a separate chapter on foreign-language films that hard-sells the pleasures of "reading" a film to your children.

For each movie, I've tried to convey what makes it special, important, or entertaining, and where the appeal to a child might lie. I've noted appropriate age ranges and provided historical and artistic context, as well as factoids that could increase the cool factor. There are also suggestions for other movies in the same vein. If you're looking for a list of films to appeal to a specific age group—little ones, midsize models, teenagers— check the index at the back of the book; it also includes suggestions for those kids ready to move on to more demanding oldies.

Following the genre chapters is a roundup of the major stars and directors of the Hollywood studio age—nothing overwhelming, but children come out of *The African Queen* wanting to know more about Humphrey Bogart, and here's where you can find the basics of his career and key films. I've tried to address how and why these iconic figures speak to kids (and to the kid in us) as well. Also, there are one or two stars whose work doesn't fall into any convenient category: Shirley Temple was her own genre, and you'll find her movies only in this section.

The directors I've chosen to spotlight are fewer, but you can't avoid Hitchcock, and once you sign up for Hawks, you'll realize the man hardly ever made a bad movie.

For obvious reasons, I've chosen films that are available on video and tried hardest to include those on DVD, with relevant extras noted. Some of these films may be difficult to find at your local Blockbuster but can be dug up at more adventurous video stores, purchased via the Internet, or rented through such online outlets as Netflix. Further information on movies, movie stars, and the availability of old films on video and DVD can be found at the film geek's best friend, the Internet Movie Database, at www.imdb.com.

You may also notice that some of the essays wander pretty far afield, addressing matters tangential to the stated aim of Watching Old Movies with Your Family. The author is of the opinion that reference books should refer to life as well as to their subjects, and that movies, good ones, usually open the door to larger conversations about behavior and meaning and the world's possibilities. Occasionally I've wandered out those doors to see what's in the other rooms. Bear with me; all books are about their author's discovery of the subject at hand, and all these essays hopefully lead back to the things a film, or a person in a film, might give to a child. Children come up for air after watching a classic, and in their first breath is usually a question. You don't have to have an answer. The talking is reward enough.

One final decree: No colorization. Ever.

STARTER KITS: FIRST OLD MOVIES TO WATCH WITH YOUR TODDLER, TWEENER, OR TEENAGER

FIVE OLD MOVIES TO SHOW YOUR TODDLER

BY THE AGE of three, a twenty-first-century American child has logged somewhere in the neighborhood of 1,500 hours of TV viewing, much of which consists of Elmo, Blue the Dog, Shrek the Ogre, Ariel the Mermaid, SpongeBob the Square-Pants, and other simple, brightly colored objects.

Children watch these shows and movies because that's what our culture says they should be watching. You'll find them in the family section at Blockbuster and on TV during times when the networks know kids will be at home. The subtext—one that fits tidily into an era of concerned, fidgety parenting—is that these are the products that are "safe," and that therefore nothing else is.

Hogwash.

Worse than hogwash, actually: culturally stunting. Within this infantilized DMZ of movies and television shows, we limit our children's options while delivering them into the slipstream of the modern media marketplace. By the time they're five, kids have an inherent understanding of the concept of branding: They know they can follow their favorite characters from screen to DVD to CD to action toy to Happy Meal and on to the next sequel, whereupon the cycle starts again.

And that, in a nutshell, is one of the best things about an old movie: It's not selling anything except itself. This is a radical notion to a kid. Freaks some of them out, actually. My daughter's still wondering where she can buy a Bette Davis action figure. I'm afraid to break the news to her that she can actually grow up to be one.

That's not the only reason to stage a jailbreak from the kiddie-video hegemony, though. Toddlers are preoccupied with trying to figure out the mysterious rules by which Large People live, and many old movies answer that need in a manner not overly loud or frightening but, rather, magical and pleasurably confusing. They're writ in bold, iconic strokes that open a window into an adult world where basic problems are posed and solved with resort to song and dance or action. Or even straight-up drama: If *12 Angry Men* doesn't teach children the value of sticking up for what you believe in, don't expect *Shark Tale* to do so.

But *12 Angry Men* will certainly go over the head of any toddler whose parents aren't currently serving jury duty (or time in prison, I guess). What, then, to show them? Historically, *The Wizard of Oz* and Shirley Temple movies have represented the time-honored avenues by which to introduce the youngest kids to classic movies. Neither is without risks. Those mutant-freak flying monkeys have generated several millon nightmares over the decades, and if you're not careful you may end up renting the Temple movie with the subplot about the child molester (seriously: see the next chapter).

So: Following are five alternatives—old movies that are simple without being unsophisticated, plainspoken without

being dumbed down, and that move fast enough to keep toddlers from getting bored. (And if they're still bored, start them
with shorter stuff: the Little Rascals, the Three Stooges, classic
Warner Bros. cartoons.)

A word about presentation: Don't, for pity's sake, let them
know these movies are good for them. If you say it's medicine, it
will taste like medicine. Just throw in the disc, stick in the videotape, let the little yard apes discover for themselves. There's
something to be said for having a Marx Brothers movie running
unannounced when they come back from a playdate, with a
plate of cookies and a glass of milk in front of it. They'll say,
"What the heck is *this*?" And you'll say, "I don't know. Let's sit
down and find out."

THE ADVENTURES OF ROBIN HOOD (COLOR, 1938)

Directed by: Michael Curtiz

Starring: Errol Flynn, Olivia de Havilland, Basil Rathbone,
Claude Rains

Ages: 4 and up

The sell: The original superhero

The plot: Twelfth-century England: King Richard is off at the
Crusades subduing the infidel and has left the country in the
care of his whining, sneering bad-boy kid brother, Prince John
(Claude Rains), who so represses the Saxon minority that
nobleman Robin of Locksley (Errol Flynn) turns outlaw and
gathers his merry men in Sherwood Forest: Will Scarlett (Patric
Knowles), Friar Tuck (Eugene Pallette), Little John (Alan Hale),
and all the rest. The Sheriff of Nottingham (Melville Cooper) is
a useless boob in this telling, but Prince John has a nasty right-
hand hit man in Sir Guy of Gisbourne (Basil Rathbone). Sir

Guy has his eye on pretty Norman damsel Maid Marian (Olivia de Havilland), but Robin woos and wins her first.

Why it's here: Because it's still the most exhilarating version of the legend yet committed to film, with glowing Technicolor photography that's like a Maxfield Parrish painting sprung to life. Flynn is charisma itself: If your children don't know what star quality is, they'll immediately get it when Robin walks into the castle feast carrying a slain deer on his shoulders and flings it down in front of King John. *Grinning.* Under Michael Curtiz's proficient direction, *Robin Hood* is fast-paced and funny (with an undercurrent of brutality to get you sympathizing with the downtrodden Saxons), a delicately headstrong performance from the young de Havilland, an excellent archery contest, a ripely groundbreaking score by Erich Korngold, and a climactic sword fight between Flynn and Rathbone that has been ripped off so many times your kids will probably recognize it from exposure in the womb (especially if you watched *The Princess Bride* during your last trimester). Note: Exposure to this movie will cause an immediate uptick in backyard swordplay. Hide the shish kebab skewers.

Pause-button explanations: There are a few gothic-lettered inter-titles to read, including the opening one that sets up the political context of the tale. It's easy enough to convey to a small person: Good king gone away on business, bad brother running the country into the ground. If your kid has a sibling, it'll make perfect sense.

Useless trivia: The actor playing Little John is not the skipper from *Gilligan's Island*. He is the skipper's father. Maid Marian's horse had a second career as Roy Rogers's Trigger.

What next: If they like Errol Flynn and can handle black-and-white dueling, cue up his two pirate movies, *Captain Blood*, also with Rathbone and de Havilland, and *The Sea Hawk*.

BRINGING UP BABY (B&W, 1938)

Directed by: Howard Hawks

Starring: Katharine Hepburn and Cary Grant

Ages: 4 and up

The sell: *The Cat in the Hat* with a Bryn Mawr accent

The plot: David Huxley (Grant) is a nerdy zoologist just finishing his brontosaurus skeleton and engaged to be married to an uptight lady scientist. Then he meets dizzy heiress Susan Vance (Hepburn), who upends his life, kidnaps him to Connecticut, and sticks him in a lady's dressing gown while her dog, George, buries David's brontosaurus bone, and her tame leopard runs around frightening the bejesus out of everyone, mainly because they've confused him with a wild leopard that escaped from the circus.

Why it's here: It really *is* close to Seussian anarchy: An unstoppably whimsical woman brings down upon the head of a nice young fellow a series of widening disasters that cause kids to go nuts with apprehension and delight. What else can go wrong for the man with the dimple in his chin? Well, this. And this. And, oh yes, this. But the real reason to watch *Baby* with your children is that it's a wonderful introduction to Grant and, especially, the great Kate. Hepburn is not just maddeningly funny here but possessed of an otherworldly enchantment—a couple of times she uncorks a quicksilver laugh that can give you goose bumps. The whole movie seems filmed under moonlight, with Wild Things just over the horizon.

Useless trivia: The movie was an attempt to redefine Hepburn's on-screen persona, which was in a slump after a spate of stodgy costume dramas. It didn't work: The film was a flop on release and had to wait until the 1960s to be rediscovered and recognized as perhaps the greatest screwball comedy of them all.

What next: Any screwball classic—see the "Comedy" chapter—and, when your kids are older, any of the other three films that Hepburn and Grant made together: *Sylvia Scarlett* (1935), *Holiday* (1938), and *The Philadelphia Story* (1940). Kids who love the dog, George, might want to see him as Asta in the *Thin Man* mystery-comedies. For a treat, dig up Peter Bogdanovich's 1972 comedy *What's Up, Doc?*, an affectionate and extremely funny remake of/homage to *Baby* starring Ryan O'Neal and Barbra Streisand.

MEET ME IN ST. LOUIS (COLOR, 1944)

Directed by: Vincente Minnelli

Starring: Judy Garland, Margaret O'Brien

Ages: 3 and up

The sell: How families and little girls lived (and sang) one hundred years ago

The plot: So minimal it's genius. A year in the life of the Smiths, a middle-class family in St. Louis in 1903, the year the world's fair came to town. There are four daughters, including second-eldest Esther (Judy Garland), a dreamy, avid woman-child with her eye on the horizon and a sudden passion for the Boy Next Door. Youngest is seven-year-old Tootie (Margaret O'Brien), whose run-ins with Halloween terrors and snowmen become the stuff of legend. Father (Leon Ames) gets a new job in New York City, a move that threatens the loss of the family's fragile innocence. Will he go?

Why it's here: For the songs, for Judy Garland, for the clear-eyed gentleness with which it parts the curtains on a bygone way of life, and, above all, for Margaret O'Brien, who is so natural and so intense that your kids may watch her scenes with the fascination they reserve for home videos of themselves. *Meet Me in St. Louis* is often wrongly remembered as a quaint period piece, but it contains one of the funniest, darkest, and truest portraits of American childhood ever put on-screen—of playful brutality amid middle-class plenty—and children immediately pick up on it. The Halloween bonfire sequence stands as breathtaking comic evidence of kiddie savagery, and the scene where Tootie destroys the snowmen—and by extension her family—is an emotional killer. And there are the musical numbers: "The Trolley Song," "The Boy Next Door," the title tune, and "Have Yourself a Merry Little Christmas," the latter sung by Garland in that tremulous heartbreak alto that can slay you no matter what your age, gender, or sexual orientation. Tremendous movie.

Pause-button explanations: None, really. You might have to explain what a world's fair is, or point out that the telephone scene shows what it was like when houses first had the device installed, but other than that, just let it roll.

Useless trivia: Minnelli and Garland met on this film, married shortly after, and in 1946 came up with Liza Minnelli. When father Leon Ames sings, that's producer Arthur Freed dubbing his voice.

What next: If this and *The Wizard of Oz* hook your child on Garland, try the little-known but highly enjoyable *The Harvey Girls* (1946) and *The Pirate* (1948), the latter with Gene Kelly. The year they were married, Minnelli directed Garland in the charming *The Clock* (1945), with the star playing a Manhattan office girl who meets and falls in love with a soldier (Robert Walker) in one forty-eight-hour period.

SINGIN' IN THE RAIN (COLOR, 1952)

Directed by: Gene Kelly and Stanley Donen

Starring: Gene Kelly, Debbie Reynolds, Donald O'Connor, Jean Hagen, Cyd Charisse

Ages: 4 and up

The sell: The greatest Hollywood musical of them all—and it costars Princess Leia's mother.

The plot: Kelly plays Don Lockwood, romantic idol of the silent screen who's teamed in a series of hit films with Lina Lamont (Hagen), a vainglorious twit with a voice that could shred sheet metal. This causes problems when the talkie revolution hits and sound films become the rage. Don, his comic-relief pal Cosmo (O'Connor), and his fresh-faced ladylove Kathy (Reynolds) have to come up with a way to save the latest Lockwood and Lamont picture from disaster.

Why it's here: Modern kids are raised with the understanding that people don't spontaneously burst into song at crucial moments in their lives. And isn't that a horrible thing, to remove such evidence of grace on earth from their belief system? Of *course* there are people who start tap-dancing at unexpected moments, or improvise a tune while plucking lyrics from the air. They're called children, and if you spend any time with them, you'll witness life as a musical forty times an hour.

This belief that the wall between existence and performance is porous gets knocked out of kids pretty quickly; by the age of twelve, a musical number in an old movie can evoke only a chilly, knowing smile. All the more reason to stoke the idealism while it's young. You could make the argument that *Singin' in the Rain* should be the first movie *anyone* sees, especially small children. Infectious, colorful, sprightly, funny, tuneful, the movie has a vividly likable hero in Kelly (that Pepsodent smile, that hammy slow turn), a sly goofball in O'Connor (fast-forward to "Make 'Em Laugh" if you need proof), and a dimbulb villainess whose hilariously nasal screeching ("Whaddya tink I am—*dumb* or somethin'?") your kids will imitate until you beg them to stop. As for Reynolds, she's perky, sweet, and, yes, Carrie Fisher's mom. The highlights are endless and all musical: the wee hours pep of "Good Morning," the "Broadway Melody" showstopper featuring Cyd Charisse's endless legs, the vaudeville patter of "Moses Supposes," and Kelly's pas de deux with an umbrella in the justly famous title tune. Your children will imitate *that* scene during the next ten rainstorms, with a mixture of glee and relief: All the world *is* a stage.

Home video notes: If you're looking to buy rather than rent, Warner's two-disc Special Edition is the one to find; it's loaded with documentary extras your kids may appreciate at a later date. The same applies to *The Adventures of Robin Hood* and *Meet Me in St. Louis.*

Pause-button explanations: Yes, it's a chapter of long-ago movie history, but simply tell your kids that movies once were silent and this is what happened when people tried to make them "talk." The farcical scenes involving Lina Lamont and the newfangled microphone come straight from Hollywood history, but it's safe to say that postdubbing wasn't discovered quite this way.

Useless trivia: Kelly filmed the title rain-dance while suffering from a 102-degree fever. A key twist has Debbie Reynolds's Kathy dubbing the singing voice of Jean Hagen's Lina Lamont; ironically, two of Reynolds's singing performances in the film were dubbed by Betty Noyes.

What next: You are in luck: A bazillion MGM musicals are available on tape and disc, and if they're not as unsettlingly perfect as this one, their pleasures are still many. See the "Musicals" chapter, and if your kid develops a thing for Gene Kelly, go immediately to *An American in Paris, The Pirate,* and *On the Town.*

STAGECOACH (B&W, 1939)

Directed by: John Ford

Starring: John Wayne, Claire Trevor, Thomas Mitchell

Ages: 3 and up

The sell: My First Western

The plot: Nine disparate people ride the stage to Lordsburg, New Mexico, through Apache country. Some of them are respectable citizens, including a snooty banker (Berton Churchill) making off with the contents of the vault. Others are outcasts: a "fallen woman" (Claire Trevor), a gambler (John Carradine), a drunken doctor (Thomas Mitchell)—and the Ringo Kid (John Wayne), a cowboy out to avenge his family's murder by the Plummer boys. The social hierarchy is turned upside down when Geronimo attacks, but the stage makes it to Lordsburg in time for a classic Western face-off between Ringo and the Plummers.

Why it's here: The Western has fallen into sad disrepair. You get an occasional big-screen revival like Clint Eastwood's *Unforgiven* or a postironic revision like HBO's *Deadwood*, but the language of the genre is no longer part of our daily speech, as it was when the Old West was still a living memory. Officially announced as closed by Frederick Jackson Turner in 1893, the frontier started dwindling from the pop culture consciousness with the rise of the post–World War II youth audience, which tended to look forward and inward rather than outward and back.

A modern kid can thus go years without seeing a Western, and yet understanding the genre is as important as knowing the Old West itself—it's our national myth, and a child would do well to get his or her arms around its dimensions. The best Westerns, like this one, are great movies, but even a B-level horse opera reflects the process of sifting and resolving our own history, and, yes, lying about it, too.

John Ford consciously designed *Stagecoach* as a Western boiled down to its most basic, almost childlike elements: It plays like an action-filled storybook about how a person's worth is defined by what they do rather than by their place in society. It's also the best introduction to John Wayne, who, whether you love his politics or hate them, is a crucial figure in understanding this country's sense of itself. More to the point, the movie's just really exciting on the cowboys-and-Indians level.

Pause-button explanations: You might have to do some fancy foot-work when Claire Trevor's character is introduced: a prostitute being escorted onto the stagecoach by the town bluenoses. Just tell children the women don't like her because they're mean; they can sort out the rest in years to come. Geronimo and company are old-fashioned movie Indians rather than modern polit-ically correct Native Americans, so do whatever ethnocultural spadework you feel necessary; at the very least, now's the time to point out who got the short end of history's stick in the long run.

Useless trivia: The script was adapted from the 1880 Guy de Maupassant short story "Boule de Suif." Both Wayne and the genre were down on their luck when the film came out: At thirty-one, the actor had yet to become a major star after over a decade in films, and there hadn't been an A-list Western since the early '30s. Director Ford took a gamble that a back-to-basics horse opera would be a hit; with seven Oscar nominations and two wins (one for Mitchell's drunk doctor), he made his point.

This was the first film Ford shot in his beloved Monument Valley.

What next: Many, many Westerns, from the B-level programmers with Roy Rogers to the more mature oaters with James Stewart. The John Ford cavalry trilogy is solid stuff—*Fort Apache* (1948), *She Wore a Yellow Ribbon* (1949), and *Rio Grande* (1950)—and Howard Hawks's *Red River* (1948) features one of Wayne's best performances, but hold off on Ford's powerful and disturbing *The Searchers* (1956) until your kids are older.

FIVE OLD MOVIES TO SHOW YOUR TWEENER

We were having a backyard party, the kind where you invite the neighbors, and it was getting late. Everybody's kids ran around in groups that kept re-sorting themselves into fluid clumps based on age or gender or activity or future political preference, and then they all got bored and wanted to watch a movie. My girls piled them into the study and we mulled over the options: the familiar Disney/Nick/Pixar stuff, plus a stack of oldies. To my amazement, Eliza and Natalie joined forces to convince the others to watch *The Day the Earth Stood Still*. High-fifties sci-fi. Black and white. *Gort, klaatu barada nikto.* On it went.

Every twenty minutes or so, I'd pause from hosting duties and peer through the door. Bernard Herrmann's eerie theremin score kept calling me: *ooo-EEEE-oooo*. It was late summer, the humidity was unbearable, and I could see the cobalt glow of the TV reflecting off the eyes, the teeth, the perspiring faces of twelve children sitting in the dark, ranging in age from six to fourteen. The littlest kids were on the floor, hiding their faces in the knees of the older children on the couch when the giant robot Gort came clomping toward Patricia Neal. Those middle-range kids were rapt, too, but they kept breaking the tension with sarcastic little comments. The oldest two draped themselves on the back of the sofa. Sneering. Asking if they could *please* watch *Starsky and Hutch*.

And there you have it. At the bottom, the smallest and most credulous audience, God love them. At the top, the assured, superior resisters who would only respond to an old movie in one-on-one coaching, never as part of a peer group. And in the middle, as their name implies, the tweeners: one foot in and one foot out, not wanting to give up the innocent enjoyment of simply believing, yet wary of being *caught* believing. Some of them were drawn to the teenagers above them, others hunkered down toward the little kids, and all of them were constantly checking the room's emotional thermostat.

How do you bring such a child into the baroque world of old movies? In a nutshell, killer stories. Plots that have such a well-baited hook that kids can't help biting; films that play children like little trouts until they're wheezing, exhausted, and happy on the living room floor. Cute animals help but not over the long haul; the irresistible stunts of Asta the terrier in *The Awful Truth* (1937) kept my daughters laughing until the divorce-farce plotline kicked in late in the game. (General note: Comedies about divorce are just not funny to children.)

What makes a great plot? They'll know one when they see one, but, basically, a story that places easily grasped characters in situations that start simply and then throw curveballs. *The African Queen*: Slob and priss go down a river together and—surprise!—fall in love. *Some Like It Hot*: Two guys dress like women and turn out to be pretty good at it. Those two are on the list that follows, but there are many, many others. *The Ghost and Mrs. Muir*: Woman moves into haunted house, falls in love with the ghost. *The Producers*: Two idiots try to stage a flop and still manage to fail. *Rear Window*: Man peeks across the way and sees a murder—*maybe*.

That brings up Hitchcock, incidentally. You can start with him now, at least with the easier films. *North by Northwest* is discussed below, and from its outrageous-but-not-scary set-piece scenes (the biplane in the cornfield, the Mount Rushmore climax) to good old Cary Grant to the cameo by the director, it's the most emblematic Hitchcock movie and the best jumping-off point. There's a whole section on his films further on, but it's worth pointing out that Hitch will probably be the first star director your kids know, and his films are an education in and of themselves. Just put off *Psycho* for now.

At this age more than ever, family movie time is the way to go. A child between nine and twelve is probably so self-conscious about what he or she shouldn't be caught dead enjoying that bringing on an old movie during a playdate may result in derision, bed-wetting, costly therapy. All right, derision. At any rate, tweeners—my tweener anyway, and how's that for a sample size?—like the security of snuggling down with the home dog pack for a film, and that's when you can try something different. Then listen to what *they* think.

THE AFRICAN QUEEN (COLOR, 1951)

Directed by: John Huston

Starring: Katharine Hepburn, Humphrey Bogart

Ages: 8 and up

The sell: Queen Priss and King Slob stuck together on a boat going over a waterfall in Africa

The plot: East Africa at the start of World War I. Rose Sayer (Hepburn) is the proper Christian sister of a jungle missionary (Robert Morley) who dies after the Germans torch his church. She hitches a ride downriver in the *African Queen*, a foul-smelling mail boat captained by the fouler-smelling Charlie Allnut (Bogart). Their intense dislike of each other turns to admiration and eventually love when she hatches a demented plan to blow up a German warship patrolling Lake Victoria.

Why it's here: Consider the ways that various types of human beings are portrayed in kiddie media. I'm talking about their staple diet, as purveyed by such keepers of the corporate castle as Nickelodeon, The Disney Channel, UPN, the broadcast networks, the major film studios, the computer animation wings of those major studios, AOL, the whole ball of wax. How are people presented? What do they look like and how do they act? What does that tell your kid about real-life correlatives?

It depends upon the age of the character. Youthful ones—children—fall into four distinct categories: the hero (or heroine), the best friend (a good-hearted dork, often), the mean kid, and the distant love object. Parents are either yammering, well-intentioned fools or thin-lipped martinets who come around in the last act.

And other grown-ups? They barely exist except as two-dimensional objects of fear, ridicule, or blank incomprehension. A cranky next-door neighbor, a dithery old lady, a suspicious shop owner, a sexless teacher, a cretinous middle school janitor—that's about it.

Why such paltry options? Why are kids' movies and TV shows uninterested in adults who are interesting? Because they need to flatter the children who are watching the ads and buying the tie-in toys and, really, paying the bills. Simple as that. The upshot is that your kids get a super-empowering media reality that revolves around them the way the ancients used to think the universe spun around the Earth.

To beat the metaphor into the ground, *The African Queen* is Galileo. John Huston's delightful adventure—perhaps not a great film but undeniably great fun—starts with a pair of characters who are classic kidvid two-dimensional targets: the prim biddy and the creepy slob; the librarian and the janitor. Then it slowly deepens them, in each other's eyes and in ours, until they seem like the only two people on earth—a weathered Adam and Eve floating down a river of possibilities (with leeches).

The movie's a fine, atypical introduction to Bogart (it marked his only Oscar win) and one of Kate's most high-flying spinster roles. But it's the dynamic between the two, as characters and as stars, that makes the movie special—the way his gruff impatience is ennobled by her faith in him, the way he's moved by and then comes to love her crazed gumption. Is this the closest these actors came to playing cartoons of themselves? Yes, but that's what makes it work for children and for many grown-ups. Better, it gives ordinary, unpretty adults—the kind our kids are trained not to see—their own fairy tale.

Home video notes: Why this hasn't yet come to DVD with all the bells and whistles is a mystery—you can get it through Amazon only in a visually unremarkable import version from South Korea. The VHS version from Fox is the one to look for.

Pause-button explanations: None. The World War I setting is mostly backdrop. There's some unpleasantness at the beginning when Rose's brother dies, and Charlie's love of the bottle is played to comic effect. Also: leeches. Even Bogart looks freaked out by them.

What next: If this hooks your kids on Bogey, you may want to move on to *Casablanca* (1942) and *The Maltese Falcon* (1941), but those are rather different movies in feel and sensibility. Really, in all its simplicity, *African Queen* is unlike almost any other classic out there.

THE DAY THE EARTH STOOD STILL (B&W, 1951)

Directed by: Robert Wise

Starring: Michael Rennie, Patricia Neal, Sam Jaffe, Billy Gray

Ages: 8 and up

The sell: We are not alone.

The plot: A UFO lands on the Washington Mall, and two figures emerge: a silver-clad humanoid and a giant faceless robot. The humanoid, Klaatu (Michael Rennie), goes into hiding in the city, posing as an eloquent visitor at a boardinghouse. He befriends a single mom (Patricia Neal) and her young son (Billy Gray) while trying to get through to an Important Scientist (Sam Jaffe) and deliver his message: Stop making war, earthlings, or we'll stop you.

Why it's here: How do you introduce children to science fiction, a genre that can pull the rug out from under their world in all the best ways? You could start with Spielberg, certainly—*E.T. the Extraterrestrial* or, if they're older, *Close Encounters*. And there's *Star Wars*, great fun but really just *Robin Hood* in outer space. Genuine science fiction tells a good story *and* screws with your head. It makes you reexamine preconceptions about yourself, society, our place in the universe. It forces you to ask some of the bigger questions out there, all under the guise of a ripsnorting tale.

Presuming you *want* your children asking questions (and, sorry, they'll do it anyway), *The Day the Earth Stood Still* is an ideal first sci-fi movie. It has an alien who looks like us and a ginormous robot who doesn't. It has a boy who's right at the center of the action, a surrogate for young viewers. The plot widens from the specific (alien craft lands in Washington, D.C.)

to the fetchingly allegorical (Earth must get its act together. Now). The robot needs a catchphrase to come to life, and that catchphrase is one of the great secret handshakes of old-movie lovers. The score is groundbreaking in its use of the theremin, the go-to electronic instrument for '50s sci-fi weirdness and psychedelic Beach Boys songs. The philosophical dilemma of the movie is simple—can't we all get along, and if not, *why* not?—but vast in its implications, and it honors a kid's nascent desire to ponder the Big Ticket Items. And the robot's cool—did I mention that?

Pause-button explanations: A child needs to have a basic understanding of the way the world works—what Washington, D.C., is, why nations fight. More sensitive children may get upset at the thickheadedness of earthlings in their dealings with Klaatu. And the scene where Patricia Neal has to pass along Klaatu's instructions to Gort? Good Christ, it's scary; if your kids are anything like mine, they'll wail like sirens for the five seconds before they realize everything's okay. In other words, not the best time to be out of the room making popcorn.

What next: If they dig it, move immediately on to other '50s sci-fi classics, but watch out for the ones that shade into horror. *The Incredible Shrinking Man*, yes; *Invasion of the Body Snatchers*, no. Good bets: *Forbidden Planet* (1956), *20,000 Leagues Under the Sea* (1954), *The Time Machine* (1960). See chapter 7 for specifics.

NORTH BY NORTHWEST (COLOR, 1959)

Directed by: Alfred Hitchcock

Starring: Cary Grant, Eva Marie Saint, James Mason

Ages: 7 and up

The sell: You are not who you think.

The plot: Roger Thornhill (Cary Grant) is a successful New York advertising executive who has never really grown up. He gets mistaken for another man—a spy named George Kaplan—which eventually leads to him becoming a better Roger Thornhill, but only after almost being machine-gunned by a crop-dusting plane in a cornfield, tangling with a master spy (James Mason) and a shady lady (Eva Marie Saint), and dangling off Mount Rushmore.

Why it's here: Sooner or later, everyone has to come to grips with Alfred Hitchcock. He was, in many ways, the Mozart of movies—a natural storyteller so gifted, so visually clever, so devilishly graceful that we forgive his sadism even as we admit it's one of the major reasons we watch his films. But Hitch is also useful as proof that movies don't just arrive from thin air. A child who sees more than one Hitchcock film understands early that a movie can reflect the distinct personality of its maker, the way books have authors and CDs musicians. He's a star, right down to the goofy cameo appearances he makes in almost every film—but a star of what? Of a *sensibility*. A fairly sick sensibility, true, but an exciting and engaging one—a suspenseful one—and this is salutary in a world where most studio films have the individuality of cloned sheep. Hitchcock says that people, not factories, make movies.

North by Northwest is Hitchcock's greatest wind-up toy and the most playful variation on his eternal theme of "the wrong man." Roger Thornhill isn't George Kaplan (neither is George Kaplan, but you'll have to see the movie to understand why), but everyone thinks he is, and he can only become a living, breathing grown-up by pretending to be someone who may not even exist. Perhaps that's fodder for the graduate thesis, but Grant is in on the joke (it's one of his most delightfully self-aware performances), and so is Hitchcock, and so, intuitively, will be your child. Anyway, the movie moves so quickly they won't have time to reflect. With Hitchcock, meaning is inextricable from narrative—it's in the movie's very bones.

Pause-button explanations: None needed. Some minor, winking bits of adult humor will pass harmlessly over children's heads: a young Martin Landau plays Mason's hit man with a big old gay subtext, and the film's final shot is exactly as metaphorically and campily obscene as Hitch intended it to be.

Useless trivia: Hitchcock wanted to call the film *The Man in Lincoln's Nose*, but the final title is from *Hamlet*, act 2, scene 2: "I am but mad north-northwest; When the wind is southerly I know a hawk from a handsaw." The director's traditional cameo is right at the beginning: he's the portly gentleman who misses the bus. In the Mount Rushmore cafeteria scene, look for the little kid who puts his fingers in his ears *before* Eva Marie Saint shoots Grant—clearly, they'd rehearsed the scene a few times.

What next: See chapter 9, and keep an ear cocked to the individual sensitivities of your children. Best bets to start with: 1940's *Rebecca* (especially for girls) and *Rear Window* (1954).

OHAYO/GOOD MORNING (COLOR, 1959)

Directed by: Yasujiro Ozu

Starring: Koji Shitaru, Masahiko Shimazu

Ages: 7 and up

The sell: Fart jokes are universal. So is parental cluelessness. So is human grace.

The plot: A gently comic snapshot of life in a Tokyo suburb in the late 1950s, focusing on a handful of houses and the people who live in them. A major story line follows the efforts of two young brothers (Shitaru and Shimazu) to get their parents to buy them a TV set, up to and including giving Mom and Dad the silent treatment.

Why it's here: When are your children ready for a foreign-language film? When you're ready to read this one to them.

Yasujiro Ozu was always known as the most Japanese of Japanese directors, especially compared to Kurosawa, who could out-Hollywood Hollywood. An Ozu movie is quiet, contemplative—a saga of ordinary people and their ordinary triumphs and dismays—filmed from the point of view of an observer sitting cross-legged on a traditional tatami mat. Many of his films run together and have soundalike titles such as *Early Spring* and *Late Autumn*. They can also be, if you're attuned to them, among the most transcendently humane movie experiences ever.

To a kid this must sound like dentistry performed slowly, right? So how come my two daughters and their friends watched *Ohayo* in rapt delight and asked for seconds? How come the girls pestered me to buy our own copy?

Well, it's not just because Ozu has made a movie with and about children. It's because he gets their world, especially as it exists in relation to, and in spite of, the grown-up world of their parents. The boys who gaggle together before and after school in *Ohayo* have their local legends and petty cruelties; they're funny and vibrant and, when their folks are around, obedient with a resentment they haven't yet articulated (and which Ozu obviously feels is more honest than the dull timidity of grown-ups in postwar Japanese society).

And, yes, there are the fart jokes. The kids in the movie have a running variation on the old pull-my-finger gag—here it's push-my-forehead—and there's one poor schlemazel who keeps getting it wrong and, in language your sons and daughters would understand, poops his pants. Ozu deals with it in drolly oblique, even poetic, fashion: The kid looks mortified, makes a lame excuse to bolt home, and we cut to a shot of his underwear hanging on the laundry line.

This begs an interesting question: Is there a difference between a fart joke here and a fart joke in a Rob Schneider movie? Ozu might say there isn't, and that's why there is. In a Hollywood stu-com (this is what we called teen comedies like *Porky's* when I worked in pay-cable), a fart is too often an admission that the screenwriters and director have run out of ideas—it's punctuation in an empty sentence, an acknowledgment that kids may not laugh at everything but they'll always laugh at *this*. In *Ohayo*, that acknowledgment is tangled up with a larger point. Cutting a big one is part of the warp and weft of childhood, Ozu's saying, a ritual and intrinsic act of rebellion. It's also plain fun, in no small part because it horrifies the grown-ups. But even putting it that way articulates the enjoyment right out of the movie. Kids love *Ohayo* because it talks directly at them and never, ever condescends.

Home video notes: Available on DVD from Criterion—if you've got an upscale local video store near you, you might be able to find it. Or try Netflix.

Pause-button explanations: You may have to explain some of the adult behavior, the social niceties that Japanese audiences in the 1950s would have taken for granted but that seem a little exotic to us. Also, the boys in the movie eat pumice to fart better; kids, please don't try this at home.

What next: For more Japanese movies, see *The Seven Samurai* (1954) in the next section. Ozu's other films tend to be more grown-up in nature (and are in fact some of the greatest movies ever made *for* grown-ups). Jump ahead to chapter 8 for more ideas on foreign-language classics.

SOME LIKE IT HOT (B&W, 1959)

Directed by: Billy Wilder

Starring: Jack Lemmon, Tony Curtis, Marilyn Monroe

Ages: 7 and up

The sell: Boys will be girls.

The plot: The Roaring '20s. Two Chicago jazz musicians (Lemmon and Curtis) run afoul of local gangsters, witness the St. Valentine's Day Massacre, and have to grab the first out-of-town job available—with an all-girl orchestra. On go the flapper dresses, wigs, and chokers, followed by a lunatic train ride to Florida (played by San Diego). When one of the heroes falls in love with the band's star attraction (Monroe), he poses as a rich twit to woo her, borrowed yacht and all. Then the other guy gets engaged—to a man. Then the gangsters show up again.

Why it's here: It's elemental calculus: (Men) + (Women's clothing) = Funny. I have no idea why this is so, but it goes back a ways. Presumably there was a Cro-Magnon comedian ten thousand years ago who strapped on a pair of coconuts and the Paleolithic equivalent of a housedress and slayed 'em around the campfire one night. The genetic express runs from that to the Monty Python boys and right through this movie.

To children, cross-dressing is even funnier, because it's terrifying. Case in point: Eliza's friend Jerome (not his real name), who came over to play in the yard one snowy day, got his clothes soaked in a drift and had to wear my wife's sweatpants while waiting for his jeans to go through the dryer. Sweatpants:

about as asexual as it gets, right? Only the poor kid sat at the dining room table in a fetal ball of gender confusion, asking, *begging*, every thirty seconds, were his pants ready? He couldn't even make eye contact.

This is someone primed for the great hymn to transvestite embarrassment that is *Some Like It Hot*.

There's a lot to love in this, the comedy many observers feel is the funniest single movie to come out of Hollywood. There's Lemmon at the top of his game as a Nervous Norbert who finds the freedom to be as femme as he wants to be in drag. There's Curtis delivering a pitch-perfect Cary Grant impression once he puts on the yachting cap to win Monroe. ("Nobody talks like that!" snipes Lemmon.) There's old Hollywood ghost George Raft as gangster Spats, and resuscitated vaudeville ham Joe E. Brown as the millionaire with the hots for Lemmon; the latter is especially priceless as he flaps his enormous mouth and gets off the movie's closing gag, a topper that is inarguable and hilarious.

And there's Marilyn. Let this movie be your children's introduction to her, and to the entire concept of the beautiful and the doomed in popular culture. From Monroe they can move on to Judy Garland and James Dean, to Buddy Holly and Janis Joplin and Kurt Cobain, to all the unlucky and unready whose deaths we seem to need. Marilyn was the first moth to the flame of modern celebrity, and all you have to do is mention that she died young, show your kids *Some Like It Hot*, and let her vibrant, uncontainable sadness do the rest.

Pause-button explanations: You'll have to explain what Prohibition was (and speakeasies and the rise of gangsters), and you'll have to do it early, since the film's first sight gag is a hearse with coffins full of bootleg liquor. If this leads into a discussion of the futility of legislating morality—well, good luck.

Useless trivia: The actor playing Spats, George Raft, was coming off a long career in gangster roles; the coin-flipping bit is a parody of his own gimmick in the 1932 classic *Scarface*. Monroe drove her director and costars batty with her inability to remember even the simplest lines of dialogue; a fed-up Curtis reportedly claimed that kissing her "was like kissing Hitler" (and later denied he ever said it).

What next: Depends on which direction you want to go. If your kids crave more Marilyn, head to *Gentlemen Prefer Blondes* (1953), the only other four-star movie she made. More Jack Lemmon, try *The Odd Couple* (1968) and *The Great Race* (1965). If they're jaded enough to handle Billy Wilder's mordantly funny worldview, show them *Sabrina* (1954) and save *The Apartment* (1960) and *Sunset Blvd.* (1950) until they're a little older.

FIVE OLD MOVIES TO SHOW YOUR TEENAGER

There is nothing you can tell a teenager that he or she does not already know. This is not theory, this is fact.

Worse, whatever it is you're trying to hip the kid to, if it's coming from you, it's automatically suspect. If you handed a teenager an interstellar quark, he or she would spurn it as the same old quark you've been foisting on them for years. If one of their friends handed them that same quark, it would be the latest wrinkle in youth culture and *you just don't get it*.

Let's say the quark in question is an old movie, though. Let's say *On the Waterfront* will be on Turner Classics in fifteen minutes and you want to watch it with your son or daughter. Who doesn't like Marlon Brando, at least when the actor was young and still cared and wasn't the size of a small planet? This is the one with the "I coulda been a contendah" speech. Great stuff; a pinnacle of American acting and filmmaking.

A teenager could care less. Actually, the more you insist on the importance of this film, this actor, the more you've lost your case. Anyway, the entire machinery of modern Hollywood is dedicated to providing adolescents—the source of major profits for the studios and an audience whose collective rear end is well worth kissing—with the many diversions they crave. How can a slow, literate, achingly emotive black-and-white film about corruption on the docks of Hoboken compete with the new Johnny Depp movie?

Aha. You can point out that without Marlon Brando there would *be* no Johnny Depp—or Leonardo DiCaprio, or Edward Norton, or Sean Penn, or Russell Crowe, or any actor who works at his craft with sullen charisma. All by himself, Brando changed the language of film acting to a more visceral mode of communication, and he introduced the notion of the rebel star, too. There isn't a serious male matinee idol working today who doesn't owe him, oh, everything.

And that's the trick of bringing a wary teenager into the big tent: Make it personal. Draw the line from his or her passions to the movie you're offering up. Then stand back and let the kid make the decision. You won't get any credit for it, but aren't you used to that already?

Another example: You have a daughter or son who loves teen horror movies, those penny-dreadful dice-and-slicers with interchangeable casts and rococo methods of dispatching them. For a working critic, they're the most predictable and dispiriting genre of them all, but of course they're not made for critics. They're made to give the youth audience a jolt of adrenaline and allow for socially acceptable date-clutching. And they very probably wouldn't exist if Alfred Hitchcock hadn't decided to mess with the mind of America by quietly filming a little thing called *Psycho*—slasher movie ground zero—with the crew of his TV show.

The movies in this section aren't necessarily ones you want to show to younger children. That's part of the appeal. There's a seriousness of purpose to a movie like *Rebel Without a Cause* that can make little kids uncomfortable or bored at the same time that it flatters their older siblings. Also, many of these films are twisted enough to be interestingly cool. Always were, always will be, but your guys don't know that.

Here's a big old caveat, though. All this talk of "teenagers" presupposes a single monolithic group between the ages of thirteen and twenty that walks, talks, thinks, and goes to see the *Saw* movies en masse.

The truth is that the adolescent audience, as with the adults who spawned it, consists of a recognizable mainstream and a jillion overlapping special-interest groups. There are teenagers who are into arcane indie films and outré foreign fare, who can tell you the difference between Takeshi Miike and Takashi Kitano, who have their fingers on the pulse of the digital-video underground. There are teenagers who don't care about movies at all. And, yes, there are teenagers who know more about old films than most of their elders, and certainly more than their peers. As passions go, classic movies can be one of the lonelier ones, but the thing is, you don't pick your passion—it picks you.

It picked me. Up until my early teens I wasn't committed to movies. I enjoyed them, sure, but I also loved riding my bicycle, hanging out with my friends, and playing Beatles records backward listening for Paul-is-dead clues. Still, my father had died when I was nine without my ever really getting to know him, and one night when I was fourteen, my mother saw that *Duck Soup* was playing on late-night TV. (This was back in the pre-video, precable era, when classic films were all over the post-midnight schedule.) "That was one of your dad's favorite movies," she told me, knowing I was hungry for connection on this score. "It's very funny; you should stay up for it."

So I did—and somewhere inside me the tumblers clicked and the door to a fascination swung open. Was it the manic strangeness of the Marx Brothers; their rude, joyful tenement surrealism? Was it a glimpse into a long-ago world I associated with my father? He was a Bostonian, a trial lawyer, a Harvard man, and an older dad—born in 1910, he had a Buster Brown childhood and came of age around the time the movies talked and the stock market crashed. He would have been twenty-three when *Duck Soup* was released, a young man recognizing Groucho's ruthless logorrhea and Harpo's sweet, silent anarchy as the front line of comedy, the way a twenty-three-year-old responds to Jon Stewart or Dave Chappelle today.

I fell in love with it, too. Partly this was because of an unproven link to a dead man, partly because movie comedy in the early 1970s was pathetic, and mostly because *Duck Soup* was just so goddamned wonderful. As were other Marx Brothers movies, as was *Bringing Up Baby*, as was *Dr. Strangelove*, as were all the old films I started catching at downtown revival theaters, and so on and so on, until a passion and a career were born.

I was one of those teenagers, in other words, who found classics on their own. Except that I never would have found them if my mother hadn't pointed, and through her, my father. If they had done more than point—if either of them had at any time lectured, forced, noodged, discussed—maybe I would have resisted. Maybe not; who knows? But I think it's safe to say they're both as responsible for this book as their granddaughters are.

So. Here are five movies. Point at them. Then walk away.

LEAVE HER TO HEAVEN (COLOR, 1945)

Directed by: John Stahl

Starring: Gene Tierney, Cornel Wilde, Vincent Price

Ages: 13 and up

The sell: Beware the ones who cling.

The plot: Novelist Richard Harland (Wilde) meets and marries the gorgeous and slightly spooky Ellen (Tierney), who turns out to be insanely possessive. How possessive? She lets his crippled little brother drown and throws herself downstairs to abort her own baby, all so she won't have to share Richard with *anyone*. As her mother (Mary Philips) says, "There's nothing the matter with Ellen. She just loves too much." *Brrrr.*

Why it's here: Because we're always fascinated with the ones who go bad, especially when they hide it as well as Tierney's Ellen, a gracious, soft-spoken, ethereally beautiful psycho nut-job who contains some of the genetic code that would lead to Glenn Close in *Fatal Attraction*. *Leave Her to Heaven* isn't well known at all (I had never heard of it until I saw it in a college film class), but it's an exceptionally watchable melodrama, and an easy sell to a jaded teenager. It's in color—overripe, eye-popping Technicolor—with outrageous lifestyles-of-the-rich-and-famous sets, and it's enjoyably corny until it suddenly gets very, very weird.

That would be the infamous scene in which Ellen lets her adolescent brother-in-law drown while watching him from ten feet away in a rowboat. When she gets a little bothered by his pleas for help, she puts her sunglasses on. *Brrrr.*

This isn't for small fry, and not just because the heroine kills her own unborn child. Rather, *Leave Her to Heaven* calls romantic love itself into question. Can it be anything but selfish and needy? Is it that intensity that makes love feel so good? Certainly Tierney's Ellen seems more vivid than her handsome, dull husband (played by handsome, dull Wilde), who eventually finds a cardboard sort of Hollywood love with his wife's sensible, dull sister (Jeanne Crain). You barely remember them when the movie's over; your kids may be imitating Tierney's chilly sleepwalking daze for weeks.

What next: See the section on melodrama in chapter 4 for further suggestions on gloriously messed-up heroines.

METROPOLIS (B&W, 1927)

Directed by: Fritz Lang

Starring: Gustav Fröhlich, Brigitte Helm, Rudolf Klein-Rogge

Ages: 7 and up

The sell: The future of the past, and the first Robo-babe

The plot: The city of the future is a massive stone edifice: Think Manhattan compressed into one giant building. Workers toil their lives away underground and plot rebellion while the rich enjoy sunlight and luxury in the upper reaches of the monolithic city-state. Freder (Fröhlich), the spoiled son of the master of Metropolis, wanders into the lower precincts and falls in love with Maria (Helm), a saintly girl who cares for the children of the workers. Hoping to monkeywrench the revolution, Freder's father hires mad scientist Rotwang (Klein-Rogge) to kidnap Maria and replace her with a robot imitation. Not a good idea.

Why it's here: If you want to float a silent movie past your toddler, by all means start with Charlie Chaplin. But if you want to convince anyone older than seven or eight—meaning after modern pop culture has begun to sink its talons into their little psyches—this is the one to go for. As for teenagers? There's a reason disco impresario Giorgio Moroder engineered a rerelease of *Metropolis* in 1984 with a sound track of pop hits by Queen, Loverboy, and Billy Squier. This puppy is the original head movie, and it works just fine without drugs. It's also the movie dystopia that prefigures everything from *Blade Runner* to *Brazil* to *The Matrix*.

The first epic sci-fi film—Lang's original director's cut ran *three and a half hours*—*Metropolis* still packs a punch strictly on the dreamlike power of its visuals. True, Gustav Fröhlich is a little swish in his rich-boy jodhpurs, but the moment the movie heads downtown into the workers' quarters, it's grimly mesmerizing. The character of Rotwang is the original mad scientist (actually, with his metal hand he's the first movie cyborg and Darth Vader's grandpa), and the Moloch and Tower of Babel sequences are impossibly weird. But the scene where the gleaming metallic robot transforms into the False Maria is the part young viewers keep coming back to, as if to the scene of a crime. There's something powerfully resonant about a purely good character having an evil double, and as critic Pauline Kael noted, the bit where Robo-babe does a lascivious little dance is just *wrong*.

We're talking Joseph Campbell territory here: iconic characters behaving in mythic ways that kids and teens immediately grasp and respect. I speak from experience. This is Eliza's favorite silent film and one of her favorite movies, period, and she has shown it to her friends with similar jaw-on-floor reactions.

Home video notes: It behooves you to find the best version of *Metropolis* available. If your local video store has the movie at all, it probably carries the shortened Moroder version—which is fine if you also want to introduce your kids to the glories of Pat Benatar—or one of the various cheapie video transfers that match tinny piano music to atrociously out-of-focus and/or butchered prints. What you're looking for is the restored print released on tape and DVD by Kino in 2003. Accept no substitutes.

Pause-button explanations: There are some biblical references that might need translating. Also, this really isn't for small children, as some of the images are very creepy.

Useless trivia: The film was an enormous flop at the time of its release. Nevertheless, *Metropolis* so impressed the leaders of the nascent Nazi party that in 1933 Minister of Propaganda Joseph Goebbels offered Lang the reins of the state film studio. Lang said he'd think about it and immediately jumped on a boat for America.

What next: Lavish silent melodramas such as *The Phantom of the Opera* (see chapter 7) and *Orphans of the Storm* (see chapter 4), classics of German Expressionism like *The Cabinet of Dr. Caligari* (1920) and (if they're old enough) *Nosferatu* (1922), the original Dracula movie. If you can dig up Lang's other silent master-piece, *Spies* (1928), by all means go for it.

PSYCHO (B&W, 1960)

Directed by: Alfred Hitchcock

Starring: Anthony Perkins, Janet Leigh, Vera Miles

Ages: 13 and up, but it depends on the kid.

The sell: Slasher films 1.0

The plot: Office worker Marion Crane (Janet Leigh) impulsively embezzles money from her boss but comes to regret the deci-sion. She decides to sleep on it while staying at an isolated motel run by the friendly, if jumpy, Norman Bates (Anthony Perkins). Unfortunately, Norman seems to have a rather possessive mother who doesn't like pretty young women taking showers.

Why it's here: *Psycho* is the movie that cut movie history in half. When that knife came sawing through the shower curtain at the forty-five-minute mark, Hitchcock announced that, from now on, all bets were off. A heroine could be randomly murdered halfway through a movie; a nice young man could turn out to have skeletons in his closet and a mummified mother in his basement. The jagged editing of the infamous shower sequence (ninety shots, none of which shows a knife piercing flesh) pre-figured the hurry-scurry pacing of the films we see today and introduced the double-edged notion of the "shock cut." In 1960, *Psycho* was so discombobulating as to seem almost obscene.

Today, of course, it looks quaint. What Hitch wrought with his little TV crew (everyone sworn to secrecy as to the plot) killed off the age of movie sentiment and ushered in the age of sensation in which we still live. In other words, *Psycho* has a lot to answer for: every modern horror movie you wish your teenager didn't watch with his or her friends, every *Ring* and *Saw* and *Scary Movie 37* owes Hitchcock everything. In maliciously playful sensibility and in primordial scares—even in Bernard Herrmann's *eek-eek-eek* violin score, ripped off by so many movies since—this remains the modern horror movie blueprint, so much so that your kids may find it oddly familiar. Tell 'em to shut up and have some respect for the master.

Home video notes: Make sure you don't accidentally rent Gus Van Sant's 1998 nearly shot-for-shot remake, a lab experiment that proves exactly nothing (which, if you're in a semiotic mood, could be construed as the point. Sadly, teenagers are rarely in a semiotic mood).

Pause-button explanations: Give your kids the context: that Hitchcock made this on the quiet and did all he could to keep the ending secret, that it introduced a lot of elements they'll know from movies they see now, that it was a freak-out then and still is. They may get a little bored in the intentionally pokey first half. They won't be bored after that.

Useless trivia: Ghoulish tidbits your audience will appreciate: The "blood" in the shower scene is Bosco chocolate syrup, and Hitch had his soundmen repeatedly stab a casaba melon with a kitchen knife to get the required effect.

What next: *The Birds* (1963)

REBEL WITHOUT A CAUSE (COLOR, 1955)

Directed by: Nicholas Ray

Starring: James Dean, Natalie Wood, Sal Mineo

Ages: 13 and up

The sell: You're tearing me APART.

The plot: Misunderstood teenagers in Los Angeles in the darkest days of the Eisenhower era. Dean is Jim Stark, who can't help but be messed up since his dad is played by Jim Backus (aka Mr. Magoo *and* Thurston Howell III). Natalie Wood is good girl/bad girl Judy, while Sal Mineo is the childlike nerd Plato. The three bond over the course of one very bad night that starts with a fatal chicken race and ends with a showdown at the Griffith Observatory.

Why it's here: Teen movies come and teen movies go, but *Rebel* remains the most emotionally bruised and thus the most honest depiction of what it's like to be young in a bountiful, heedless America. It is to movies what *Catcher in the Rye* is to literature. The reason is not just James Dean but also writer-director Nicholas Ray, who soaks the CinemaScope screen with hyper-real color and swooning camera angles as if to show us what the world looks like through a teenager's eyes. Self-absorbed? Yes, but these are kids who have been given everything except what they need, and that may strike a chord with any disenchanted adolescents in your own house. (I know, your teenagers are fine. Show them the movie anyway.)

They may not be able to see anything except Dean, who plays Jim Stark like an exposed nerve. The actor was twenty-four when he shot the film, but he gets the posture, the little-kid anger, the self-righteousness and self-loathing, the yearning toward absurd nobility of a boy-man convinced the world has it in for him. It is, daringly, one of the least graceful great performances you'll ever see; this is a kid tripping over his own soul. That Dean died in a car crash a month before the film was released is horribly perfect—too perfect if you find the whole Jimmy cult thing a little necrophilic. Still, if your teenager needs someone to worship, isn't this guy preferable to 50 Cent and Slipknot?

Home video notes: *Rebel* has some of the most exquisitely composed camera shots ever, and its cinematography directly corresponds to the psychological state of its young, impassioned characters. Which means you should watch it letterboxed or on a wide-screen TV or not at all.

Useless trivia: Look fast for a very young Dennis Hopper as one of the kids.

What next: Want more Dean? Go for *East of Eden* (1955) or *Giant* (1956). *Rebel* may also serve teens as a springboard to other tortured actors of the era, such as Brando (*On the Waterfront*) and Montgomery Clift (*From Here to Eternity*). If you're ready for more by Nick Ray—everything he made is worth watching— seek out the completely demented Freudian feminist Joan Crawford Western *Johnny Guitar* (1954) or the brooding *In a Lonely Place* (1950), which has what's probably Humphrey Bogart's single finest performance.

THE SEVEN SAMURAI [B&W, 1954]

Directed by: Akira Kurosawa

Starring: Toshiro Mifune, Takashi Shimura

Ages: 8 and up

The sell: Western meets Eastern

The plot: Sixteenth-century Japan. A rural farming village is constantly under assault from a gang of bandits. The farmers pool their resources and hire a motley assortment of wandering samurai to protect them. The leader of the seven (Shimura) understands that the farmers fear them as much as the bandits; meanwhile, a renegade farmer's son (Mifune) tries to prove he's the baddest-ass samurai of them all. The climax(es) comes in three incredibly visceral battle scenes.

Why it's here: Ah, jeez, because it's just a *great movie*: long but consistently engrossing, with tremendous action scenes and characters you root for and care for and mourn for when they die. Because it's the kind of movie you come away from a changed person.

Anyway, what is it in human nature that responds so strongly to ensemble films? Why is there so much pleasure to be had in learning the constituent parts of a team, the disparate individuals that make up the whole? (It's the same motor that propels heist movies such as *Ocean's Eleven* or action groupings like *The Great Escape*.) In *Samurai*, we meet a group of undifferentiated ronin—stern men with topknots and kimonos—and slowly come to know them as men, chief among them Kambei (Kurosawa regular Shimura), the wise Buddhist leader; idealistic young pretty boy Katsushiro (Isao Kimura); stoic master swordsman Kyuzo (Seiji Miyaguchi); and above all, the rowdy, impetuous, tragic clown Kikuchiyo (Mifune), torn between two inimical classes and belonging to neither.

But (you say) it's in Japanese! And it's three and a half hours long! And it's black and white! Inarguable points all. But, look, Kurosawa was consciously working in the tradition of John Ford's Hollywood Westerns, among other American influences—he was considered the least "Japanese" of the holy trinity of classic-era Japanese directors (Ozu and Mizoguchi being the other two). If you have younger kids, break the movie into two parts, and read the subtitles along with them: It's not remotely gory and the story's wonderful. This is how I watched it with Natalie and Eliza when they were respectively six and eight; they clamored to get back to the second half, and the only caveat I offer is that Eliza was pretty busted up when one of the major characters bit the dust at the end.

If you have teenagers, all you really have to do is say "samurai" and let their love of Quentin Tarantino, Hong Kong action flicks, anime, and *Crouching Tiger, Hidden Dragon* do the rest. But you'd better explain that *The Seven Samurai* isn't filmed in the rock-'em sock-'em MTV style they're used to from modern samurai movies. It's comparatively sedate, at least until the action sequences come around. The story more than compensates, though, or it should. Which is to say that if they don't respond to *Samurai*, you may as well throw this book away.

Pause-button explanations: You may have to stop and explain the motivations of some of the characters to younger kids: why the village girl throws herself on the young samurai, why the farmers fear the people they've hired to protect them.

What next: If they're curious about how Hollywood reacted to Kurosawa's co-opting of American studio style, show them the Western remake *The Magnificent Seven* (1960) with Yul Brynner and Steve McQueen. For more Kurosawa, best bets would be *Yojimbo* (1961) and its samurai sequel *Sanjuro* (1962), both starring Mifune and both comparatively bloody. *The Hidden Fortress* (1958) is also fun, especially since George Lucas admits he swiped its story line for *Star Wars*. Older kids ready to absorb more of the master should go to *Rashomon* (1950), *Ikiru* (1952), and *High and Low* (1963). All are available on Criterion DVD.

2

. . . .

THE KONG ISLAND THEORY, OR OLD MOVIES *NOT* TO WATCH WITH YOUR CHILDREN

I DON'T KNOW what I was thinking.

Sometimes being a paid movie geek clouds your reason. You think a classic movie is, by definition, suitable for all ages, by nature of its greatness and its roots in the safe house of the past. The evangelical side of being a critic—which is to say the pushy side, as it relates to parenthood—comes out. You sit your darlings down for a transcendant cinematic experience that ends up making them pee their pants.

In our house we call this *King Kong*.

Natalie must have been about four and Eliza six—I know, shoot me now—and I'd been throwing old movies at them with undoctrinaire regularity. They were receptive, because movies like *Singin' in the Rain* and *City Lights* were good and because they enjoyed spending time with Mom and Dad. In my addled enthusiasm I decided to show them one of the great fantasies of early Hollywood, ground zero for today's CGI special effects, a Beauty and the Beast tale of mythological impact. And it had the Empire State Building, which the girls could just see by craning their necks out of our Brooklyn bedroom window.

It started off well. The opening scenes where the Bar-numesque Carl Denham (Robert Armstrong) outfits a ship and crew to go off and film a "nature documentary" caught the kids' interest, and the bit where he coaches Ann Darrow (the magnificently lunged Fay Wray) to look up and "Scream! Scream for your life, Ann!" gave us all pleasurable goose pimples. But then we got to Kong Island, and all hell broke loose.

It wasn't just the casual Hollywood racism of the way the islanders were depicted. It was the doom-doom-doom suspense that was finally, perfectly broken by the appearance of Kong himself at the village palisades: massive, shambling, poised somewhere between Claymation and nightmare. The girls started fidgeting. After Kong takes Ann into the island's interior and the ship's crew gives chase, there are those vivid, brutal attacks by various dinosaurs, who pick off the shrieking men one by one.

Uh-oh. I'd forgotten about the dinosaurs.

When the brachiosaurus upended the raft and started chewing on the crew like they were beef jerky sticks, Natalie stood up, drily announced she'd had enough, and headed upstairs to find a picture book. Eliza stuck it out, eyes growing to the size of soup tureens until the climactic fight between the Tyrannosaurus rex and Kong—you know, the one that ends with the giant ape *bloodily ripping the T. rex's jaw off its face*. At which point she starting screaming like an air horn: one note, top volume.

My wife ran out from the kitchen, shot me a vicious look that said she'd be using this as evidence in any subsequent divorce proceedings, and turned off the TV with a sharp blow of her palm. Eliza stopped screaming, stared at her in shock, and bellowed, "WHAT ARE YOU DOING? TURN IT BACK ON!"

Now, this is an interesting thing. My daughter had just discovered the pleasure principle that drives scary movies—the idea that you can be terrified and still, on some level, have an incredibly exciting time. Granted, she discovered this in a way for which I may yet have to pay therapy bills. My bad. But still.

For better or worse, we finished the movie. Eliza wept bitter, bitter tears over Kong's plummet from the Empire State Building—she had also just learned you can empathize with a monster—and then informed me that she never wanted to see the movie again. So, basically, I cheated my children out of discovering one of the great movie classics on their own.

There are two lessons here. The first is: Don't turn it into school. I showed the girls *King Kong* because I was getting off on the notion of exposing them to the breadth and depth of the classic movie canon, the way some dads play Bob Dylan CDs until their kids retaliate by going over to Kelly Clarkson. Sometimes it works—viz, the *Seven Samurai* experiment in the previous chapter. With *Kong*, it bit me on the ass.

I've learned—slowly, and the lesson's still sinking in—that the only way to watch old movies with my daughters without being pedantic about it is to keep in mind what they might *want* to see, as opposed to what they *should* see. Translation: I was never all that into *Seven Brides for Seven Brothers* or the fairly obscure Judy Garland musical *The Harvey Girls*, but Eliza and Natalie have watched them both repeatedly if not obsessively. By contrast, I'm not going to even think about showing them legendary Universal horror movies like *Frankenstein*, *Dracula*, *The Mummy*, *The Invisible Man*, and *The Wolf Man* until and unless they ask. No, not even the resplendently wiggy *Bride of Frankenstein*. (See chapter 7 if you're curious.)

But your kids might love *Frankenstein*. Or they might be bored stiff by *King Kong*. (They'll definitely be bored stiff by *Dracula*, the most dated of the Universal bunch and a movie that creaks like a coffin lid.) You have to know them and be one step ahead of them, just as you do for modern multiplex movies.

That leads into the second lesson: Do your homework. Watch

the movie yourself beforehand or (more realistically) read up on the plot and check out other people's comments at Web sites like the Internet Movie Database (www.imdb.com) and Amazon. Take your best guess and err on the side of caution. Who would think a Shirley Temple movie would have anything objectionable in it? Here's *Poor Little Rich Girl* (1936), in which the adorable tyke is shadowed throughout the movie by a sweaty, nervous pedophile who keeps trying to lure her away with him. (Jack Haley eventually busts him on the button.) It's a freaky little bit, and should your children watch it? Would it be useful in case you want to have "the talk" about strangers? Or would it give them nightmares? Only you would know, since you know your child. Better you know the movie, too.

Most oldies don't spring funky surprises like *Poor Little Rich Girl* or *King Kong*, but there are plenty that won't fly because they've dated badly or because they deal with grown-up themes or because the pace is too slow—well, *all* old movies are slowly paced by modern standards; that's their curse and blessing—or just because. Why didn't Eliza and Natalie get into *It's a Mad, Mad, Mad, Mad World*, a splattery epic farce featuring every comedian working in 1963? We turned it off at the halfway point and never looked back, and not because they had no idea who Milton Berle and Buddy Hackett and Sid Caesar were. They bailed because the movie was noisy without being particularly funny, other than the occasional random cameo: When Jerry Lewis tootled by in a convertible, making his hey-lady face but not saying a word, the girls immediately wanted to know who *that* guy was, and so I made plans to someday bring home *The Nutty Professor* (see chapter 3), which paid off in spades. On the other hand, one of my fellow Boston-area movie critics has an eight-year-old daughter who splits a gut watching *It's a Mad* (etc.) *World*. Go figure.

If other children besides your own are involved, then you really have to be ahead of the curve. This isn't just to avert legal action (although that's not necessarily a bad idea; no one wants to be the one to explain that little Olivia's coming home in clinical shock because you let the kids watch *Freaks*). Also because a roomful of bored kids is a societal meltdown waiting to happen.

Case in point: Eliza's tenth birthday party. Remember her ninth birthday, the Katharine Hepburn party described in the introduction? The one that maybe got you to buy this book? Here's the dark flip side, and there's a reason it's buried in the middle. Since the Kate birthday had been such a hit, E. wanted to do another movie party, this time using *Blue Hawaii* as the centerpiece of a luau theme. Lori and I hadn't seen the movie in years and Eliza hadn't seen it at all, but an Elvis flick? Can't go wrong.

Except it did. First, there was entirely too much kissing going on for a bunch of ten-year-olds to countenance. More to the point, the movie was corny in a way that we grown-ups understand as kitsch or camp or a guilty pleasure and that kids understand as . . . corny. To appreciate Elvis in the twenty-first century, I suddenly realized, you need to have irony installed. According to the user manual, that's scheduled for seventh grade.

So the *Blue Hawaii* screening devolved into wriggles and giggles and wrestling, and Eliza got a little teary about it, the way a hostess does when the guests get drunk and say rude things about the furniture. We switched the movie off after thirty minutes; we might have never turned it on in the first place if we had just prescreened it.

Sometimes a child's rejection of a movie is hard to figure out initially—it goes against all prevailing critical wisdom. That, of course, is what's good about it. Does the name Jacques Tati ring a bell? French comedian/director from the 1950s onward, dry and droll and the creator of nearly silent exercises in precision slapstick that were rapturously received at U.S. art houses back in the day. The common scholarly consensus is that Tati was a genius on a rung just below Keaton and Chaplin, but my daughters are not scholars, and they found both *Monsieur Hulot's Holiday* (1953) and *Mon Oncle* (1958) tedious and only fitfully amusing. Seeing it through their eyes, I had to agree. But I have a friend whose nephew's obsession with *Mon Oncle* verges on the fanatic, and he's right too. Watching old films with children backs you into honesty simply because they know no other way to behave. Am I a better movie critic thanks to Eliza and Natalie? I think so. I *hope* so.

Sometimes seeing a classic from a child's viewpoint can give you an entirely different angle on it. We watched *Gone with the Wind*, or most of it; the girls never fully took to the movie. They had trouble with the wimpiness of Leslie Howard's Ashley Wilkes (Eliza acidly noted that both the actor and his character had *girls'* names), and they were too young for Gable to work his hoodoo on them. I think they thought Scarlett was pretty much a pill. But they had the hardest time with the black characters— with Hattie McDaniels's Mammy and Butterfly McQueen's Prissy. The girls knew, by this point, the historical basics of slavery and the Civil War, and they correctly sensed this movie wasn't telling them the truth. "Why is she so silly?" asked Natalie about McQueen in dismay, and I could have said, well, because that's how 1930s Hollywood portrayed black people: with cutesy, derisive condescension. I've said as much with other old movies, trying to put the era's accepted cultural bigotry into context so the girls can see a shuffling comic-Negro train porter for the ruinous little cartoon he is while still enjoying the rest of the movie. But I couldn't do it this time. Previously I had given *GWTW* a free pass because of its its pop-culture impact and importance to film history, but seen through the Natalie filter, racism was encoded in the film's very DNA—in the nostalgia both it and Margaret Mitchell's original novel felt for a vanished world built on the backs of the unwilling. My daughter has irrevocably tainted *Gone with the Wind* for me, and someday I'll get around to thanking her for it.

Natalie wasn't ready for *Citizen Kane* either, and again she put her finger on its essence, as children can do. (Warning: If you haven't seen *Kane,* skip this paragraph.) I was revisiting the Orson Welles landmark for an article I was writing, and Eliza plopped down to watch it with me (she was around seven or eight, I think). Her younger sister pottered around on the carpet, playing with toys and not appearing to pay attention. The subtleties of the film went over Eliza's head, but she was into figuring out as much as she could, and there was some pausing as I explained the details of turn-of-the-century newspaper publishing and why the real Marion Davies wasn't as bad as Susan Foster Kane. We got to the end, the newshounds dispersed, and Rosebud was fed to the flames. Eliza choked back a little *snurf*—and suddenly Natalie let out a wail from the corner. "It was his *sled*," she wept inconsolably. "All his life, he missed his *sled*." Which is the uncomplicated reaction of a normal five-year-old, but one that also honors both the depth and the glibness of Welles's conception. Among many other things, *Kane* is about how we pay for our youth with the rest of our lives, through the loss of things that only we know, and Natalie got that by barely looking up from her own toys.

Now, of course, she says she'll never watch that terrible movie again. Jesus, give me the Bad Dad medal and retire it already. Maybe she'll stick to that promise. More likely she'll find herself watching *Kane* again someday—in a class, on TV, who knows?—and she'll remember that it once spoke to her very core.

3

. . . .

COMEDY

THE FIRST OLD movie your child watches should always be a comedy, on the Pavlovian theory that we repeat what we find pleasurable. So, yes, the films in this chapter may be cinematic monuments, but they are first and foremost absurdly enjoyable and they should be offered to your children as such. If they want to know why they're important, they can find out later. The films are roughly organized according to subgenre: silent comedy, screwball comedy, great comedians, etc. But, really, the best argument is the movies themselves—that and the joy of watching a seven-year-old pass milk through his nose.

THE HOLY TRINITY OF SILENT COMEDY: CHAPLIN, KEATON, LLOYD

THE GOLD RUSH (B&W, 1925)

Directed by: Charlie Chaplin

Starring: Charlie Chaplin, Georgia Hale

Ages: 3 and up

The sell: No need to sell it. Just put it on.

The plot: The Klondike Gold Rush of 1898. The Lone Prospector, aka The Little Tramp, aka Chaplin, arrives to make his claim but ends up in a shack teetering on the edge of a cliff, chased by a hunger-crazed prospector (Mack Swain) who thinks Charlie is a roast chicken, and spurned by the dance hall girl (Georgia Hale) with whom he's in love.

Why it's here: Before Mickey Mouse, Marilyn Monroe, and Michael Jackson, there was Charlie Chaplin, the first global superstar and the first mass icon of the age of cinema. With *The Gold Rush* he peaked; like that house on the precipice, the film balances on the point between his early slapstick work and his later, increasingly sentimental films. There are comedy bits here so classic they've been endlessly recycled, ripped off, and homaged: This is the movie with the deft little dance of the dinner rolls that Johnny Depp imitated in *Benny and Joon* (1993). There's also the marvelous scene where Charlie, starving in a blizzard, dines on his boiled shoe as if it were the finest filet mignon in Paris.

What Chaplin did better than any comedian before or since—

and kids pick up on this—is alternate the absurdly refined gesture (a tug of his waistcoat) with moments of broad, canny aggression. He's an artist who's a street fighter, the former by temperament, the latter by necessity. Again, that's a duality that's just plain human, and when we and our children laugh, it's out of both surprise and recognition. George Orwell lauded Chaplin's ability "to stand for a sort of concentrated essence of the common man," which is just a fancy way of saying he feels like one of us.

But you don't read things like that and not have them go to your head. As with many great artists, Chaplin started going downhill the moment he realized he was important. To watch his later movies—stubbornly silent in the early sound era, then gravely giving in to chatter—is to see him draw the blueprint for every comedian since who has struggled to be serious in spite of the greater depth of his comedy. Jerry Lewis, Woody Allen, and Robin Williams are just three examples of people who owe Charlie everything, for better and for worse.

But all your kids have to do is watch the epic *Gold Rush* to get what made him unique: the nose-thumbing resistance to authority, the stolen moments of acrobatic finesse, and the flinty self-pity that comes with believing the world is stacked against you. Chaplin could simultaneously blow a raspberry and break your heart, and never better than here.

Home video notes: The version to get is Warner's two-disc Special Edition DVD, which puts Chaplin's 1942 rerelease of the film— with a musical score and the director's plummy narration in place of title cards—on disc one and a restored version of the original 1925 release on disc two. Disc two is the one you want to watch.

Useless trivia: The shoe was made of licorice; after sixty-three takes, the perfectionist Chaplin was taken to the hospital suffering insulin shock. The dancing dinner-rolls sequence was such a hit that some theater owners stopped, rewound the film, and played it again.

What next: From here, proceed directly to—in order—*City Lights* (1931), *Modern Times* (1936), *The Kid* (1921), *The Circus* (1928), and any of the shorts compilations you can lay your hands on. Save the darker, more weirdly maudlin later films like *The Great Dictator* (1940), *Monsieur Verdoux* (1947, and cynically brilliant in its way), and the goopy *Limelight* (1952) until they're older. Avoid the exceedingly strange final two, *A King in New York* (1957) and *A Countess from Hong Kong* (1967), unless you've been drinking heavily.

SAFETY LAST! (B&W, 1923)

Directed by: Fred Newmeyer and Sam Taylor

Starring: Harold Lloyd

Ages: 3 and up

The sell: See the man hanging from the clock tower? Please don't try that.

The plot: A young man (Lloyd) journeys to the city to make his fortune, writing back to his girlfriend (Mildred Davis, Lloyd's real wife) that he's a success when he's actually only a department store clerk. When she arrives in town he has to make money in a hurry, which somehow results in his climbing the side of a tall building in a "human fly" act.

Why it's here: Harold Lloyd is usually considered the least important of silent comedy's "big three," but it's worth remembering that he was almost as popular as Chaplin in his day and much more popular than Keaton. Look at Lloyd's movies and you'll understand why: They're *funny*. Not great works of pathos, not stone-faced technical marvels. Just . . . funny. The comic got some newfound respect starting in 2005, when his films were at last released on DVD with appropriate bells and whistles, but the ultimate test audience is your children. They'll enjoy *Safety Last!* just fine for the first two-thirds: the prototypical Lloyd character, a glasses-wearing go-getter, is both amusing and surprisingly mean, and the department store gags are as inspired as anything in Chaplin or Keaton—less poetic, perhaps, but just as effective in earning straight-up belly laughs.

It's when the star has to climb the twelve-floor "skyscraper" that the movie lifts off into a masterpiece of theme-and-variation comedy. Pigeons, mice, cops, dogs, painters, flagpole, ropes—every floor has a maddening new obstacle, as if in a weird way *Safety Last!* prefigured the world of video games. Except that it's real, and Harold Lloyd is genuinely hanging from the hand of a clock a hundred feet off the ground. Natalie loved the movie, but by the end she was prostrate in front of the TV, completely wrung dry.

Pause-button explanations: There's a "comic" Jewish pawnbroker that could use some context from a parent. Nobody in Hollywood was particularly ethnically sensitive at the time, but Lloyd, originally from Nebraska, seemed to have slightly more than his share of this kind of thing in his movies.

Useless trivia: The star had blown off part of a hand in an on-set accident a few years earlier, so consider this: He's climbing that building with only eight fingers. Lloyd remade the film for sound as *Feet First* (1930), but it bombed: Audiences became uncomfortable when they could hear the hero gasping for help.

What next: *The Freshman* (1925), *Speedy* (1928), *Grandma's Boy* (1922)

SHERLOCK JR. (B&W, 1924)

Directed by: Buster Keaton

Starring: Buster Keaton

Ages: 5 and up

The sell: Ever want to be in a movie? I mean really be *in* a movie?

The plot: Milquetoast movie theater projectionist (Keaton) has hopes of being a great detective and winning the girl, but luck goes against him. He falls asleep on the job and literally dreams his way into the film he's projecting, which becomes a comic mystery about the brilliant Sherlock Jr. and his hairbreadth escapes.

Why it's here: There are those who love Chaplin and there are those for whom Buster Keaton is the greater artist: more modern, more rigorous, less sappy. And, yeah, funny. As a die-hard Keatonian, I felt it my duty to throw some of the man's films past the girls: his acknowledged pinnacle, *The General* (1927), and *The Navigator* (1924), the feature that convinced me of the man's worth back in high school. They enjoyed them well enough but the deal was hardly closed. The films were slow by current standards and I realized that one of the things I loved about Keaton—that he doesn't let you in close, often in literal, visual terms—was exactly what prevented Eliza and Natalie from connecting with him. Then, too, it may be a boy thing; Buster was fascinated with machines and systems, and it shows in his movies, which often use him as one bemused cog in the comic Rube Goldberg contraption of life. Chaplin offers plenty of emotional toeholds; Buster, by contrast, has to be met partway (but, oh, the rewards).

Then one afternoon I threw on *Sherlock Jr.*, and the girls fell in love. The movie's an anomaly in Keaton's career: forty minutes in duration, it's longer than his short films and shorter than his features. This turned out to be the perfect length for E. and N., because the pace was fast enough while still giving them the leisure to get to know his character.

But what really sold them was the film's concept—of a man walking into a movie screen and entering a looking-glass alternate world. I could get all pointy-headed here and talk about the metafictional construct of *Sherlock Jr.*, how it explores and explodes the theory of montage, and how it prefigures postmodern media irony by a good sixty years. And my children would look at me like the overeducated gasbag that I am. For them, it's simple. Buster climbs into the screen and the movie decides to mess with him by editing around him: He dives into the ocean and it turns into a snowdrift. And so on. Your kids intuitively understand why this is so.

Later, when the detective-mystery plot kicks in, there are a few stunts that are simply not to be believed and that children demand to see a second time, if only to figure out what just happened. Example: Buster's trapped in the villain's shack, but earlier we've seen him place a mysterious drum in the window. He dives through the window and instantly lands on his feet disguised as a little old lady; the bad guys dash past. It's not a trick shot.

Likewise the bit where Keaton somehow jumps *through* the middle of his assistant, or rides at top speed on motorcycle handlebars unaware that the driver has fallen off, or sidles up to a pool table and with one shot sinks every ball except the one the villains have loaded with explosives. Again, movie trickery isn't involved. Keaton delighted in doing his own stunts and making the impossible look real. That's what puts children on the edge of their seats—the sense that someone is playing around with the laws of the physical world itself. The emphasis should be on the word "play," because *Sherlock Jr.* is just that—a daydream, a doodle, an idle riff on the way movies intersect with the waking world.

Home video notes: The film's available on video only as a package with *Our Hospitality* (1923), Keaton's Hatfield-and-McCoys feature comedy. It's not his best work but it makes a fine follow-up to *Sherlock*.

Useless trivia: The scene where Buster jumps off a train and grabs a water tower spout that opens up and splatters him to the ground? He fractured his neck while filming the shot but didn't realize it until years later, when a routine X-ray revealed the damage.

What next: Save *The General* until they're older, unless you have a train freak in the house; it's epic in scope and the slightest bit stodgy. Go for *Steamboat Bill Jr.*, *The Navigator*, *Seven Chances*, and all of the shorts. Everything Keaton did is on DVD thanks to Kino, so there's no excuse.

SCREWBALL COMEDY

It arose in the Depression out of a number of interrelated developments: the arrival of sound and the concomitant need for snappy dialogue; a combined resentment for and fascination with rich people as portrayed by swank Hollywood stars; a desire to see them brought down a peg or two; the pleasure of seeing fancy clothes and Art Deco sets for audiences struggling to make ends meet. At its best, screwball comedy mashes the social classes and sexes together until someone cries uncle and everyone goes to bed. The stars are beautiful and zany, obviously, but there's also enjoyment to be had in getting to know the lumpen faces and personalities of the studio stock players:

Eugene Pallette of the bowling ball body and froggy voice, swishy Franklin Pangborn, ditsy Alice Brady, grumpy William Demarest, snide Roscoe Karns, exasperated father figure Walter Connolly, and on and on. See *Bringing Up Baby* in chapter 1 for the author's favorite in the genre; see the films below for further dementia.

HIS GIRL FRIDAY (B&W, 1940)

Directed by: Howard Hawks

Starring: Cary Grant, Rosalind Russell

Ages: 10 and up

The sell: The fastest comedy ever

The plot: Hard-nosed Chicago newspaper editor Walter Burns (Grant) was married to his best reporter Hildegaard "Hildy" Johnson (Russell), but she divorced his sorry ass and is now retiring from the game to marry a dull but good-hearted insurance salesman (Ralph Bellamy, who else?). Walter sets his hat on (a) postponing the wedding by framing the fiancé for anything he can think of and (b) getting Hildy to cover the case of condemned (and innocent) murderer Earl Williams (nebbishy John Qualen), who somehow ends up hidden in a rolltop desk in the courthouse press room.

Why it's here: Young people sometimes complain that old movies are slow. Show them this one; they'll get whiplash. The newspaper comedy to end all newspaper comedies—and, yes, this is *exactly* what life is like at a major metropolitan daily—*Friday* was adapted by screenwriter Charles Lederer and director Hawks from the classic stage farce *The Front Page*. Which was about two *men*. It had been filmed once before, but when Hawks was working out the script for a remake, he had a secretary read Hildy's lines and the lightbulb clicked on over his head. The second stroke of genius was to hire Cary Grant and let the actor expand on his rarely expressed streak of nasty glee—he is indeed "wonderful, in a loathsome sort of way," to quote Hildy. The third bright idea was to have the actors step on each other's lines, starting to talk before the other person had finished.

The result is a film with no fat on it whatsoever, one whose happy cynicism can still take a viewer by surprise (and perhaps shock the more tenderhearted children). It's not what happens to poor, sweet Ralph Bellamy that's so funny; it's that the schmo deserves it for being a nice guy in a world of sharks. Your kids may as well learn this sooner than later.

Pause-button explanations: You'll probably have to rewind a lot just to catch all the dialogue.

Useless trivia: Remade twice more, once by Billy Wilder in 1974 as *The Front Page* with Walter Matthau and Jack Lemmon and once in 1988 as *Switching Channels*, with Burt Reynolds and Kathleen Turner at a cable news station.

What next: Any of Hawks's comedies with Grant: *Bringing Up Baby* if you haven't already been there, the triumphantly silly dragfest *I Was a Male War Bride* (1949), or the criminally underrated *Monkey Business* (1952), where Grant drinks a youth potion and ends up acting like a teenager and horsing around with a young Marilyn Monroe. Cary's also in *The Awful Truth* (1937), a very funny screwball about d-i-v-o-r-c-e costarring Irene Dunne, Ralph Bellamy again (and again as a boob), and Asta the dog from *Bringing Up Baby* and the *Thin Man* comedies.

IT HAPPENED ONE NIGHT (B&W, 1934)

Directed by: Frank Capra

Starring: Clark Gable, Claudette Colbert

Ages: 7 and up

The sell: The first movie to win all five major Oscars

The plot: Spoiled heiress Ellie Andrews (Colbert) has eloped with a rich flyboy, to the consternation of her moneybags father (Walter Connolly), who kidnaps her onto his yacht. She escapes and, on her way back to shallow hubby, meets Peter Warne (Gable), a cynical newspaperman who teaches her how to hitchhike and ride the bus with the common folk. He thinks he has a great story; what he has is her.

Why it's here: Kids learn early the clichés of Hollywood story-telling, one of which is that the prissy princess and the saucy commoner will be forced to hit the road together and eventually fall in love. *It Happened One Night* gives your children a chance to see the formula fresh from the mint, starring the actors who set the archetypes that still pay dividends for today's stars.

The best way to convey Gable's impact to your children is to tell them he was the Brad Pitt, Russell Crowe, Tom Cruise, and Will Smith of his day. Combined. Times ten. Seriously, in the swamp of the Depression, Gable was proof of the ongoing existence of the American male.

It Happened One Night catches him at his peak and pairs him with Colbert, ladylike but with a neurotic spitfire wit to go with her elegance. The director is Frank Capra, coming off a sterling career making silent comedies and early sound melodramas and about to embark on the series of "Capracorn" classics for which he's remembered: *Mr. Smith Goes to Washington, Mr. Deeds Goes to Town, It's a Wonderful Life* (see chapter 9 for details).

Happened is a road movie for much of the running time, with such set pieces as Gable trying to teach Colbert how to hitch a ride (leg beats thumb in the end) and the famous "walls of Jericho" scene in which the two share a cramped motel room with only a blanket hanging between them. I know—in movies today the stars are shagging from frame one, but this was mighty titillating in 1934 and may still seem so to your easily shocked darlings. That's the wonder of old movies, that they can seem so innocent and so worldly at the same time.

Useless trivia: No one wanted to make the film except Capra. Gable was loaned from MGM as punishment for not taking roles; Colbert accepted the part after everyone else had turned it down and only because they doubled her salary. The film went on to win the Oscar grand slam (best picture, director, actor, actress, and screenplay) and turned Columbia Pictures from a B-level studio to an industry heavyweight overnight. The scene where Gable takes off his shirt to reveal a bare chest famously crippled the men's undershirt industry; some manufacturers unsuccessfully tried to sue the studio. And the bit where Gable munches a carrot? Warner Bros. animators have claimed it was a crucial element in the birth of Bugs Bunny.

What next: You might try *Midnight* (1939), another Colbert winner from the underrated Paramount director Mitchell Leisen. Gable never made another screwball comedy per se, but many of his early MGM films are on video. Try 1933's wiggy *Dancing Lady*, which pairs him with Joan Crawford and throws a young Fred Astaire and the Three Stooges in for support—it's as if all the levels of early-'30s Hollywood stardom had collapsed into one ground-floor pig-pile.

THE LADY EVE (B&W, 1941)

Directed by: Preston Sturges

Starring: Henry Fonda, Barbara Stanwyck, Charles Coburn

Ages: 8 and up

The sell: Screwball reversed: Rich nincompoop meets sassy lady

The plot: Charles Pike (Fonda), the naive heir to a beer fortune, loves snakes more than anything else. On a ship back from a South American herpetological expedition, he meets Jean Harrington (Stanwyck) and the "Colonel" (Coburn), a father-daughter pair of con artists. Will Jean fleece the rube or fall for him?

Why it's here: And so we come to Preston Sturges, the writer-director who perfected his own ribald, literate version of screwball and mined it for all it was worth. *Sullivan's Travels* (1941) is his acknowledged classic, but I'll take this farce from earlier the same year as a personal favorite. It makes the best introduction to Sturges for kids too, if only because Henry Fonda is so good at playing simpleminded that he seems like an actual child. The fun children have with this movie is knowing that no one—not even they—could be as clueless as the man one character describes as "that tall backwards boy always toying with toads and things."

How else to explain that Charles Pike falls in love with Jean not once but twice, convinced she's two different women? The first time's on shipboard, the second is when she shows up in New York to exact revenge and passes herself off as the titled heiress Lady Eve Sidwich, and if you're thinking this is a heyday for Stanwyck fans, you're right. The actress specialized in making brassy common sense seem attractive, and here she's in control of the situation throughout, making this a rather interesting film for tweener girls. When she tells Fonda that "the best [girls] aren't as good as you think they are and the bad ones aren't as bad," that's more food for thought than a year of Lindsay Lohan movies.

And, as always, there's the Sturges supporting company: dithery old Coburn, Eugene Pallette as Fonda's blustering dad, prissy Eric Blore as a fellow con artist, William Demarest as Fonda's street-smart babysitter. The fun in a Sturges movie is often on the sides of the frame, as these reprobates comment on and cackle about everything the leading players are doing wrong.

What next: More Sturges: *Sullivan's Travels* (1941) is about a Hollywood comedy director who wants to make a serious film called *O Brother Where Art Thou* (a title later stolen by the Coen brothers). *The Palm Beach Story* (1942) is as seriously wack as only a movie with a character called the Weenie King can be. Sturges's wartime farces *The Miracle of Morgan's Creek* and *Hail the Conquering Hero* (both 1944) are noisy and a little obvious by comparison, but a little-known gem is *Easy Living* (1937), written by Sturges and directed by Mitchell Leisen, in which working-class gal Jean Arthur is elevated to the penthouse life after a fur coat falls on her head while she's riding a double-decker bus down Fifth Avenue. For more screwball Stanwyck, check out Howard Hawks's *Ball of Fire* (1941): It's a sharp, sarcastic redo of *Snow White and the Seven Dwarfs* with the actress as a brassy showgirl and Gary Cooper leading a crew of twittery etymologists. Go ahead, look it up.

MY MAN GODFREY (B&W, 1936)

Directed by: Gregory La Cava

Starring: William Powell, Carole Lombard

Ages: 7 and up

The sell: What happens when you bring a homeless person home?

The plot: Scatterbrain Manhattan rich girl Irene Bullock (Lombard) and her idiot friends host a scavenger hunt where one of the items is a "forgotten man"—a homeless victim of the Depression. Irene "wins" when she brings home Godfrey Smith (Powell) after she finds him in an East River shantytown. He gleefully insults her and her entire social set, and since no one has ever talked back to her, she hires him as a butler, to the horror of her family (dad Eugene Pallette, mom Alice Brady, snooty sister Gail Patrick). To the further horror of her family, Irene falls in love with him.

Why it's here: You could introduce small children to the Great Depression by showing them *The Grapes of Wrath*, but they'd probably end up hiding under their beds for a week. Save it for the follow-up and start with this genial, snappy bit of high goonery starring the suavely cynical Powell and the great Carole Lombard.

How best to describe Lombard? For a start, try imagining Robin Williams in the body of Cameron Diaz. The studios kept sticking the actress in dramas because they couldn't think outside the box, but Lombard was unquestionably at her best in comedies, where her frazzled energy and delight in horseplay rendered her a superior being. (Offscreen she was known for swearing like a sailor and making film crews fall in love en masse;

she married Gable, who never seemed to recover after her 1942 death in a plane crash.)

The Depression in *Godfrey* is a harmless, Art Deco thing. The dialogue has bite, especially when Powell is telling Lombard off, but no one really gets hurt—it's significant that Godfrey turns out to be a Harvard man down on his luck. But this is fine for kids, and the supporting players are rich. When Mischa Auer, as mother Bullock's pet *artiste*, does his gorilla imitation, the laughs are both screwball and socially penetrating.

Pause-button explanations: If your kids are young enough, you'll have to clue them in on the basics of the Great Depression. Also, let them know what a scavenger hunt is.

What next: So much to choose from. For more Powell, head straight to the series of *Thin Man* comedy-mysteries—the first two are best (and the second stars a young Jimmy Stewart in a surprising role), but there's an awful lot of martini-sozzling going down; see chapter 6. *Libeled Lady* (1936) stars Powell, Myrna Loy, Spencer Tracy, and Jean Harlow and alternates side-splitting physical comedy (that fishing sequence) with dull patches. For more Lombard, dive into the manic *Twentieth Century* (1934), in which the actress goes head to head with John Barrymore at his most juicily hammy; director Howard Hawks referees. Follow up with *Nothing Sacred* (1937), in which she plays a girl *not* dying of radium poisoning. Lombard's final film, 1942's *To Be or Not to Be*, is terrific, but it rather daringly makes fun of the Nazi Third Reich ("What you are doing to Shakespeare, we are doing to Poland," says one of the Germans to the hambone actor played by costar Jack Benny), so you may want to save it until the kids can appreciate black comedy.

NONSCREWBALL COMEDY CLASSICS

ADAM'S RIB (B&W, 1949)

Directed by: George Cukor

Starring: Katharine Hepburn, Spencer Tracy, Judy Holliday

Ages: 10 and up

The sell: Kate and Spence as married lawyers on opposite sides of the same case

The plot: Doris Attinger (Holliday) tries to kill her philandering husband (Tom Ewell), and attorney Adam Bonner (Tracy) is assigned to prosecute the case. His firebrand lawyer wife Amanda (Hepburn) decides to defend Doris in the interests of cheated-upon wives everywhere.

Why it's here: Because your kids really need to see one Tracy-Hepburn movie, and because this is the one to see. Written by Ruth Gordon and Garson Kanin, it's expertly tailored to the two stars' personalities and to the affection they had for each other and we have for them. Plus, the film was the first to showcase the dizzy charms of Judy Holliday, who so impressed the stars that they campaigned for the actress to re-create her starring role in the Broadway hit *Born Yesterday* when the studio wanted to cast someone more well known.

But it's the Tracy-Hepburn dynamic we're here to see, and of their nine films together, this is the one that best captures their prickly mutual adoration. Too many of the other pairings are turgid dramas like *Keeper of the Flame* (1942) or comedies in which Tracy and the filmmakers take a little too much delight in bringing Hepburn down a peg (the kitchen scene in 1942's

Woman of the Year being the best example). Spence playfully slaps Kate's rear in this one, but for once she calls him on it. For imprinting the ideal married relationship in your children's heads, it beats Britney and Kevin Federline any day.

Pause-button explanations: Not that it has to come up, but in talking about the stars' long offscreen relationship your kids may learn that Tracy, a devout if seriously conflicted Catholic, never divorced his wife. This gave Eliza a hiccup in her Kate worship; you could see the gears turning in her head as she balanced what she knew to be wrong with a person she deeply felt to be right. She came out of it realizing that people are complicated, which may be the only possible lesson. There's also the irony of Hepburn's character, Amanda, trashing her client's husband for the same sin her lover was committing in life. Live with it; Hepburn did.

What next: Despite the above caveat, *Woman of the Year* should be the next Tracy-Hepburn on your list, followed by *Pat and Mike* (1952). *State of the Union* (1948) and *Guess Who's Coming to Dinner* (1967) are too talky; *Desk Set* (1957) is cute but klutzy; *The Sea of Grass* (1947) is just bad. *Without Love* (1945), however, is a nifty, mature little wartime romantic comedy that's a good bet for grown-ups and older Kate devotees.

DR. STRANGELOVE, OR: HOW I LEARNED TO STOP WORRYING AND LOVE THE BOMB (B&W, 1964)

Directed by: Stanley Kubrick

Starring: Peter Sellers, George C. Scott

Ages: 14 and up

The sell: A comedy about nuclear war?

The plot: An insane general (Sterling Hayden) gives the order for bombers to drop nuclear weapons on Russia; scrambling to call back the planes are, among others, a British army major (Sellers), the president of the United States (Sellers), and the president's mad-scientist advisor (Sellers).

Why it's here: At some point—and you and they will know when it is—your kids will be ready for satire. Not the awful *Saturday Night Live* kind (that's parody, and bad parody to boot) but the genuine article: dark and uncompromising, the sort that rearranges the moral fault lines in your head. *Dr. Strangelove* is the movie to show a teenager who has begun to understand that grown-ups have no idea what they're doing. It will confirm his or her paranoia at the same time that it introduces the radical and liberating idea that paranoia can be funny.

The character names in *Strangelove* are silly—General Jack D. Ripper, Buck Turgidson, President Merkin Muffley—and the double-talking dialogue is priceless ("You can't fight in here—this is the War Room!"), but the stakes are as high as they get, and the film ends, shockingly, not with a whimper but an apocalyptic, end-of-the-world bang. Because Mutually Assured Destruction is logical within the context of Cold War realpolitik while remaining disturbingly illogical for a commercial movie, this is not for younger kids (mine don't even know it exists yet). It is, however, for adolescents who like to challenge themselves and everyone around them by thinking about the unthinkable.

Home video note: Look for the recently released 40th Anniversary Edition from Columbia TriStar: the print is remastered and the extras are a notch above.

Pause-button explanations: Ah, well, yes, you'll have a lot of sociopolitical 'splaining to do unless your kid has been boning up on the Cold War in school. Not that the nuclear threat doesn't exist now, but it's of a different sort than when the United States and Russia were staring down each other's barrels and my older sister was duck-and-covering under her desk during school drills. It's probably easiest to relate your own memories than go for a historical PowerPoint presentation, since there's a chance your adolescent may know more about the era than you do.

Useless trivia: Kubrick wanted to end the film with a custard pie fight in the War Room and even shot the sequence, but decided against using it.

What next: *The Manchurian Candidate* (see drama chapter), the only movie even more politically deranged than *Strangelove*. *Fail-Safe* (1962) is a serious treatment of the same idea. For more Sellers social comedy, dig up *Being There* (1979). For more Sellers idiot comedy, find the *Pink Panther* movies: The 1963 original is a tad too dry for kids, but *A Shot in the Dark* (1964) is priceless, and 1975's *The Return of the Pink Panther* leaves the recent Steve Martin silliness in the dust.

GENTLEMEN PREFER BLONDES (COLOR, 1953)

Directed by: Howard Hawks

Starring: Marilyn Monroe, Jane Russell

Ages: 8 and up

The sell: Are diamonds really a girl's best friend?

The plot: Lorelei Lee (Monroe) and Dorothy Shaw (Russell)—"two little girls from Little Rock"—are gold-digging gals looking for millionaires on shipboard. Scatterbrain Lorelei is engaged to a rich boy but can still smell a diamond a mile off. Dorothy is romanced by the down-on-his heels Ernie (Elliott Reid), who's actually a private detective hired to keep an eye on Lorelei. Musical numbers like "Diamonds Are a Girl's Best Friend" and "Anyone Here for Love" intrude—the latter astoundingly and intentionally gay, not that your kids will pick up on it.

Why it's here: You could say that *Blondes* purveyed Do Me Feminism about forty years before the Riot Grrrls got around to it. Or you could say that it offers your daughters the radical notion that women can be powerful and sexual at the same time—that the two might even be linked. Or you could say it's a movie made by dirty old men that exploits America's breast obsession and the female stars most identified with it.

Eliza and Natalie would say it's just a very, very funny movie.

Monroe plays Lorelei Lee—the creation of Anita Loos in her novel and play—as a proudly superficial ditz who aims to marry the richest man she can find; money, in her view, can and will buy her love. To that end, her big production number, "Diamonds Are a Girl's Best Friend," is a declaration of independence. Such a character would be heinous if not for two things: It's Marilyn and she's adorable, and her comic lust for loot is tempered by Russell's Dorothy, just as assured in her sexual vitality but looking for Mr. Right rather than Mr. Rich.

That said, Hawks is probably more on Lorelei's side, since most of the men in the movie are only after one thing. Fair trade, no? Especially since the movie plays the transaction (never actually consummated in the film; it's the '50s, after all) for absurdist laughs. The men available to these women aren't an impressive lot: Lorelei's rich fiancé (Tommy Noonan) is a dweeb, Ernie's a liar, and the best catch Lorelei can come up with on the boat is a dirty old man named Sir Francis Beekman, nicknamed "Piggy" (Charles Coburn, popping his monocle with relish). She's also fascinated to hear that the wealthy Henry Spoffard II is aboard but disillusioned to learn he's six years old (and played, to my daughters' utter delight, by the gravel-voiced George "Foghorn" Winslow). In this playground, the women beat the men every time—and they sing and dance better, too.

What next: Monroe in *Monkey Business* (1952) or *Some Like It Hot* (1959), if you haven't got to them already. The same year as *Blondes*, Monroe appeared with Betty Grable and Lauren Bacall in the similar-sounding *How to Marry a Millionaire*, but it's a mean-spirited farce with none of the ribald pizazz of the Hawks film. Avoid.

THE PHILADELPHIA STORY (B&W, 1940)

Directed by: George Cukor

Starring: Katharine Hepburn, Cary Grant, Jimmy Stewart

Ages: 10 and up

The sell: Whom will Kate marry—her ex-husband, her fiancé, or the nosy reporter?

The plot: Rich snob Tracy Lord (Hepburn) is about to marry an up-and-coming industrialist (John Howard) and isn't happy to have her ex-husband, C. K. Dexter Haven (Grant), hanging around the edges of the upcoming nuptials. Dex has been forced by unscrupulous gossip-rag editor Sidney Kidd (Henry Daniell) to bring along reporter Macaulay Connor (Stewart) and photographer Liz (Ruth Hussey), and Connor the cynical newsman finds himself falling for the ice queen. There's a drunken scene by the pool, a priceless morning-after sequence, and a wedding that leaves the identity of the groom up in the air until the last minute.

Why it's here: Because it's yar; see the movie and you'll understand. For Eliza, the self-designated Hepburn freak in our house, this one's on a par with *Little Women* and *Bringing Up Baby*; to a grown-up, it's just one of the most intelligently elegant social comedies Hollywood has ever turned out. Maybe your children won't understand this (or maybe they will), but it's a story about *bending*, about how fatal it can be to hold yourself and others to impossibly high standards—about how "the best time to make up your mind about people is never." Tracy can't forgive her errant father (John Halliday) or her ex-alcoholic ex-husband until she forgives herself for being human, and *Story* is the story of how she finds her way there. This should resonate with any small perfectionists you may know, as well as big ones.

Philip Barry's dialogue is expertly turned—glittering and deep at the same time—and Hepburn is at her peak. It was a comeback role, one she had commissioned Barry to write for the Broadway stage, and she takes full advantage of it; when Macaulay Connor tells Tracy she's "lit from within," you know what he means. For all that, this is a movie about humility, and that was a new thing for Hepburn.

Stewart won his only Oscar here and he's marvelous, especially in a sly, beautifully played late-night drunk scene with Grant. But it's the latter who makes an impact out of all proportion to his meager screen time. C. K. Dexter Haven's the mature conscience of Tracy Lord and of this movie, and if your children don't get that now, they will later.

Pause-button explanations: Younger kids might need some of the interrelationships spelled out for them—it's a pretty sophisticated movie and best saved for the tweeners.

Useless trivia: Remade in a musical version, *High Society* (1956) with Bing Crosby, Frank Sinatra, Grace Kelly, and Louis Armstrong as himself. It's not bad but not a patch on the original.

What next: *Holiday* (1938) is Hepburn and Grant in another Philip Barry play adaptation directed by Cukor, and it's comparably swell, though a little stagy next to *Philadelphia*.

PILLOW TALK (COLOR, 1959)

Directed by: Michael Gordon

Starring: Rock Hudson, Doris Day, Tony Randall

Ages: 9 and up

The sell: Phone tag, 1950s-style

The plot: Career gal Jan Morrow (Day) shares a telephone party line with songwriter/bachelor/ladykiller Brad Allen (Hudson), whom she knows and loathes by voice alone. The feeling's mutual until he gets a look at her, at which point Brad pretends to be a gentle Texas millionaire to win her over. Jan's client (and Brad's neurotic best friend) Jonathan Forbes (Randall) threatens to spoil the charade.

Why it's here: The girls didn't know *what* to make of this one, but it hooked them as soon as Day started singing that inanely catchy title tune. Prude that she is, Eliza approved both of Dodo's power-virgin persona and her character's distaste for Rock Hudson—his character *is* an unrepentant cad and, worse, his taste in women is lame. Once the plot machinery kicked in, though, the girls were in for the duration, if only to see how Hudson could wriggle out from under such a breathtakingly obvious tower of lies. (He can't; the tower comes crashing down.) *Pillow Talk* gets a bit of a bum rap as smarmy high-'50s fluff, but it's tartly written (the script won an Oscar) and visually playful (all those split screens, including the famous bathtub duet, which had Natalie hooting).

It's interesting to note, though, that Rock didn't win either of my daughters over. The character's too much of a jerk by modern standards, no matter that the star portrays him with the same sweet, limited gentleness with which he played all his roles. They didn't buy Brad's third-act change of heart, and they especially didn't buy Jan's final capitulation—not after she had given his apartment that screechingly hideous makeover (big belly laughs there).

It's not that the whole corny, repressed calculus of 1950s romantic comedies didn't work for them—for preadolescent girls, that pretty much makes sense. It's that, by 2005 standards, Dodo chooses the wrong man. "She should have married Jonathan; he's smart and he's funny and he treats her well," said Eliza about the smart, funny best pal played by the smart, funny Tony Randall. Natalie agreed, and is there some strange irony to the notion that they opted for the fussbudget straight guy (Randall being one of the first modern metrosexuals as we know them, here and on TV's *The Odd Couple*) over the handsome closeted gay man chasing the Virgin Queen of the Eisenhower era?

Perhaps. In ten years, I'll ask them.

Pause-button explanations: Unlike most of the romantic comedies of the preceding decades, this one's more about S-E-X than love. Hudson's character has it—a lot of it—and Day's character at one point is clearly ready to have it with him. If that bothers you, go with *Lover Come Back* (see below). My girls raised their eyebrows when they twigged to the subtext, but they rolled with it; in any event, *Pillow Talk*'s winking but essentially deeply moral attitude toward the subject is doubtless shared by many tweeners. Also, the great Thelma Ritter (*Rear Window*) plays the heroine's alcoholic maid, and much comic sport is made of her crippling hangovers and ability to drink Hudson under the table. This was amusing back in the two-martini-lunch days and just seems strikingly callous now, like making fun of a burn victim.

What next: Day, Hudson, and Randall re-upped for 1961's enjoyable *Lover Come Back*—many fans think it's better than *Pillow Talk*—and Day played opposite Clark Gable in *Teacher's Pet*

(1958), Cary Grant in *That Touch of Mink* (1962), and James Stewart in Hitchcock's *The Man Who Knew Too Much* (1956). (Her best role, though, may have been opposite James Cagney in the emotionally brutal 1955 gangland romance *Love Me or Leave Me.*) *Down with Love* (2003) is an awkwardly sweethearted remake/homage to the *Pillow Talk* genre starring Renee Zellweger, Ewan McGregor, David Hyde Pierce in the Tony Randall role, and . . . Tony Randall.

THE QUIET MAN (COLOR, 1952)

Directed by: John Ford

Starring: John Wayne, Maureen O'Hara, Victor McLaglen

Ages: 10 and up

The sell: Ireland, the beautiful cartoon

The plot: Sean Thornton (Wayne), an American boxer who has killed an opponent in the ring, returns to the small Irish village of Innisfree to reclaim his family homestead and escape his demons. He's immediately taken with the lovely colleen Mary Kate Danaher (O'Hara) and she with him, but her pugnacious brother (McLaglen) is spoiling for a fight. Thornton would rather do anything *but* fight.

Why it's here: Nearly perfect and (as shot in Technicolor by Winton C. Hoch) gob-stoppingly beautiful to behold, *The Quiet Man* is also one of the most maddening, retrograde movies ever to come out of Hollywood, and among the most problematic films in this book. If you're a parent who has a stiff back when it comes to relations between the sexes—or if you have a daughter who's a firebrand feminist in the making—don't expect the scene in which a colorful Oirish villager says to Wayne, "Here's a good stick to beat the lovely lady" to go over well.

At that point, Wayne's dragging O'Hara across the green fields of Galway by her hair, so you may already be throwing things at the screen. O'Hara's character understands that this is a form of love, so she doesn't really protest. What *planet* are we on?

The Quiet Man, in other words, is not for the doctrinaire, the politically correct, or anyone who gags on high Irish corn. The film was a labor of love for John Ford and it shows—he won best director that year at the Oscars—but while there are those who think it's a grand fairy tale of the auld country that should be watched as often as possible, there are others who find it a clichéd embarrassment and the closest thing to greenface imaginable.

Here's what I think: On its own terms, the movie is comic, two-dimensional, and intensely charming, and its take on the battle of the sexes is more nuanced and less prehistoric than humorless viewers might want to admit (it's no less piggish than *The Taming of the Shrew*, but no more, either). Maureen O'Hara has never been more gorgeous in a movie and John Wayne has never been gentler, right up until the point where he gets fed up with the villagers and his wife urging him on to beat the sweet Jesus out of Squire Danaher (who after all has been sticking his chin out the entire film). *Quiet Man* says there are some fights that can't be avoided if you want to be a functioning member of a society—if it takes a village to raise a child, it takes this village to urge Sean to claim his birthright by pounding his brother-in-law.

What's refreshing about Frank Nugent's script is that it lets us see Sean and Mary Kate both through their own eyes and each other's. A kid watching this movie understands what Mary Kate's withheld dowry means to her—freedom—and understands, too, why Sean loathes money and won't fight, and also why he has to. There are insights into one's parents here, perhaps: the sources of their arguments and the sources of their love. Far from being a Neanderthal take on a man's right to drag his wife wherever he pleases, *The Quiet Man* is fairly evolved about how two proud people who are nuts about each other have to broker *some* sort of peace if they're ever going to live together.

The fight, when it comes, is a comic donnybrook, with stops for beer and bets placed on all sides. By that point we know everyone in Innisfree, from the old gaffer to the squire's toady to the priests (Catholic and Protestant) to the pleasant young man who we learn in one throwaway line is the local IRA representative. That's how rosy *Quiet Man* is, and how deluded. But perhaps it's the point of movies to convince us briefly of their two-hour worlds and then send us out to see where they fit—or don't—into the world in which we live.

Useless trivia: What does O'Hara whisper into the startled Wayne's ear during the "curtain call" finale? Only she, he, and John Ford knew, and O'Hara, still going strong at this writing, ain't talking.

What next: *How Green Was My Valley* (1941) is Ford's other visit to the British Isles, although it's set in Wales and was shot in Malibu. Maureen O'Hara's in it, too, but she really wasn't made for black and white—she may only truly exist in color.

THE SHOP AROUND THE CORNER (B&W, 1940)

Directed by: Ernst Lubitsch

Starring: Jimmy Stewart, Margaret Sullavan

Ages: 11 and up

The sell: What happens when the pen pal you love turns out to be the coworker you hate?

The plot: A delicate comedy-drama set among the employees of Matuschek's, a small gift shop in Budapest, Hungary. Stewart is the headstrong young clerk and Sullavan is the new girl who takes an instant dislike to him, and he to her, no matter that they're writing passionate anonymous pen-pal letters to each other.

Why it's here: Director Ernst Lubitsch was famed for "the Lubitsch touch," which in some films meant he could suggest erotic sub-texts in a way that audiences instantly comprehended or, as here, convey the complexities of the human heart with a simple, elegant camera shot. *Shop* is a wonderful film, not corny at all, about how easily love can get away from us when we hide our secret selves. The two central characters' astonishment when they realize who each other are—*really* are—is funny but, more than that, terribly moving; it's as if they see they can no longer fall back on pettiness and it scares them. In a sense, they echo the way older boys and girls work out their attitudes toward each other, veering from intense dislike to unspoken crushes and slowly coming to understand the two are intertwined. Or maybe I just say that because I've got an eleven-year-old at home. At any rate, one of the primary pleasures of this movie is watching the two main characters grow up before our eyes and in each other's.

But Lubitsch extends humanity to everyone in the shop: the timid middle-aged clerk (Joseph Schildkraut), the mousy stock-lady (Sara Haden), especially the blustery shop owner, who's played by Frank Morgan—the Wizard of Oz himself—and who has an achingly fine few scenes toward the end. This one's for older kids who can grasp its nuances. And for you, of course.

Useless trivia: Remade (and rewired) as the 1998 Tom Hanks–Meg Ryan film *You've Got Mail*. Eh.

What next: More Lubitsch? *Ninotchka* (1939) gave Garbo her only comedy; it's dated but effective. *To Be or Not to Be* (1942) is great but your kids really need to appreciate the black comedy of poking fun at the Nazis to get the most out of it. *Trouble in Paradise* (1932) is just too damned sexy.

STAGE DOOR (B&W, 1937)

Directed by: Gregory La Cava

Starring: Katharine Hepburn, Ginger Rogers, Lucille Ball, Eve Arden, Ann Miller, Andrea Leeds

Ages: 9 and up

The sell: "The calla lilies are in bloom. . . ."

The plot: Terry Randall (Hepburn) is a rich girl who so wants to prove herself as an actress that she leaves Kansas City and moves anonymously into a Broadway boardinghouse with other starving actresses. Her roommate, Jean (Rogers), doesn't trust this princess, but they bond over the perfidy of double-dealing men like producer Tony Powell (Adolph Menjou). Terry gets her break at the expense of hopeful starlet Kay (Leeds) and comes to regret it when Kay commits suicide, but ends up older and wiser.

Why it's here: A comedy? With that plotline? Actually, *Stage Door* is one of the more sparkling comedy-dramas to come out of Hollywood, adapted from a play by Edna Ferber and George S. Kaufman and filled to the brim with smart young actresses. Yes, that's *I Love Lucy* Lucy in her youth, cracking wise with a cat around her neck, and that's a young Eve Arden keeping perfect snide pace with her. There's a teenaged Ann Miller years before she tap-danced through all those MGM musicals. And there's the salt-and-ginger pairing of Hepburn and Rogers, the snob and the sassy gal.

That's what drew Eliza and Natalie to this film, since they knew the two stars from other movies and couldn't quite conceptualize their being in the same frame at the same time. And they looked forward to hearing Hepburn actually say, "The calla lilies are in bloom again," as their dad and countless other lousy impressionists have done over the years. She says it a number of times—it's a line in the play Terry Randall is rehearsing—and the gag is that it came from a Broadway flop Hepburn had actually been in the previous year.

This one's good for the girls, obviously—it's a sisterly empowerment film with an unusual frankness about the gender wars. One of the actresses (Gail Patrick's Linda) is clearly sleeping with the producer, and his expectation is that both Terry and Jean will, too, if they want to get ahead. You might want to make sure your kids are old enough or sophisticated enough to handle the subtext, and that they can deal with the death of the character played by Leeds, a little-known actress who gives a spooky (and Oscar-nominated) performance here.

Pause-button explanations: See above, and hope they don't ask too many questions.

Useless trivia: Hepburn's career was in a tailspin after too many stuffy costume dramas, and pairing her with Rogers was the studio's idea of goosing her image.

What next: If this is your first stop with either Hepburn or Rogers, off you go to *Bringing Up Baby* and any of the Astaire-Rogers musicals.

GREAT COMEDIANS

Following are a handful of representative films from the singular funnymen who flourished during the studio era and who, because they were under contract for extended periods of time, built bodies of work that function as bizarre parallel universes sealed off from the rest of Hollywood. Because these stars were so unique, their films don't fall into any category other than, say, "Marx Brothers movies" or "W. C. Fields movies," which should be good enough for your purposes. If your children respond well, there are plenty more to choose from.

Not included here but also highly recommended are any video shorts compilations featuring either the Little Rascals or the Three Stooges (the ones with Curly or Shemp, please, not fake Stooges Joe and Curly Joe). Same goes for Warner Bros. cartoon "comedians" like Bugs Bunny and Daffy Duck (by which we mean Mel Blanc); DVD compilations of classic, uncut *Looney Tunes* are available and recommended. I've left out Bob Hope movies, though, including the Hope-Crosby *Road* films. The reasons for this are twofold: The extremely topical nature of Hope's comedy style renders it almost incomprehensible to a twenty-first-century child, and, to this writer at least, Hope is not now nor has he ever been funny.

THE COURT JESTER (COLOR, 1956)

Directed by: Melvin Frank and Norman Panama

Starring: Danny Kaye, Basil Rathbone, Angela Lansbury, Glynis Johns

Ages: 5 and up

The sell: The pellet with the poison's in the vessel with the pestle.

The plot: Merrie Olde England, except a not-so-merrie usurper has taken power while rebels led by the Black Fox plot to return the rightful infant king to the throne. Royal babysitter Hubert Hawkins (Kaye) wants to be in the thick of the action and gets his chance when he pretends to be Giacomo, king of jesters and jester to kings. A pretty fellow rebel (Johns), a hot-to-trot princess (Lansbury), and a lady-in-waiting (Mildred Natwick) with a knack for hypnosis complicate proceedings.

Why it's here: As the studio years recede into the past, Danny Kaye is becoming forgotten, and, truth to tell, his movies are the reason why. They're high-spirited but awkward mixtures of patter songs and pep, and Kaye's appeal doesn't translate across the decades. He's sprightly and likable and he tries awfully hard, but there's nothing about him that's interestingly unique as there is with, say, Groucho or Fields or Curly Howard. Danny Kaye is not insane, and it hurts.

The Court Jester is the great exception, even if it's not a Great Movie. An inspired *Adventures of Robin Hood* knockoff—to the extent of hiring Basil Rathbone to effectively reprise his role as sneering Sir Guy—*Jester* is triumphant silliness that piles on the plot: Kaye has to protect the baby king; no, now he has to pose as the new jester; no, the jester is actually an assassin hired by Rathbone to kill his rivals, so Kaye has to pretend to be an ice-cold killer; no, wait, the princess's maid hypnotizes Kaye into being a great lover; no, wait, Kaye's midget acrobat friends assault the castle (did we mention he used to be in a circus?). Oh, and there are songs, yappy little ditties written by Sylvia Fine, Kaye's wife.

The part everyone remembers, though, is the scene where Kaye has to battle a sneering black knight and is told that one— and only one—of the ceremonial prejoust cups has been slipped a Mickey Finn. Which led to Natalie obsessively chanting, "The pellet with the poison's in the vessel with the pestle; the chalice from the palace has the brew that is true" until I threatened to take away her allowance. She also went big-time for the baby king's heinie, which has a flower birthmark that gets a number of close-ups—the height of elegant, Noël Coward–style comedy to an eight-year-old. Older kids may resist this colorful, corny fable at first, but if they're anything like Eliza, they'll be in by the time Kaye and Rathbone are dueling all over the cardboard-castle sets.

Pause-button explanations: You might want to point out that the woman playing the princess was the voice of Mrs. Potts in *Beauty and the Beast* and she played that old lady detective on TV, too—I guess if your kids are Sondheim fanatics, you can tell them she also originated the role of Mrs. Lovett in the Broadway production of *Sweeney Todd*. Don't hit them with *The Manchurian Candidate* until they're older, though, or they'll freak.

What next: There's a lot of Danny Kaye out there—best bets are *Wonder Man* (1945) and *The Inspector General* (1949). *The Secret Life of Walter Mitty* (1947) has its fans, but lovers of the James Thurber short story are not among them.

DUCK SOUP (B&W, 1933) AND A NIGHT AT THE OPERA (B&W, 1935)

Directed by: Leo McCarey/Sam Wood

Starring: The Marx Brothers: Groucho, Harpo, Chico, and sometimes Zeppo; Margaret Dumont

Ages: 5 and up

The sell: You think you and your brothers are nuts? Watch these guys.

The plot: *Duck Soup*: Rufus T. Firefly (Groucho) is elected president of the republic of Fredonia and all hell breaks loose. *A Night at the Opera*: The brothers get behind the scenes of a production of *Il trovatore* and all hell breaks loose.

Why they're both here: I'm opting to include two movies because the bros had two distinct phases to their career and these are the best films from each period. In the five they made for Paramount, they had writers like George S. Kaufman and *New Yorker* humorist S. J. Perelman; the comedy was more aggressive, absurdist, East Coast intellectual. When the Marxes jumped ship to MGM after the commercial failure of *Duck Soup*, production head Irving Thalberg softened them up with romantic leads and musical numbers. He mainstreamed them, in other words, and while it worked in spades for *A Night at the Opera* and the follow-up *A Day at the Races* (1936), the comic returns diminished over time. Try both films with your kids and head backward or forward in the Marx filmography as it suits them.

One thing that should be noted is that younger children—my daughters at least—respond far more strongly to Harpo than to any of the others. And that makes sense, since he's a silent buffoon working in the tradition of Chaplin and Keaton. He's also the most kidlike himself, both in innocence and in anarchy. Groucho leaves Eliza and Natalie in awe, but he's so logorrheic he's a little scary; he double-talks too fast for them to keep up. And Chico? Chico, I hate to say, was never funny except in those set-piece scenes where he ties Groucho in knots of illogic. (Zeppo was the straight man—though reputed to be the funniest of the bunch in real life—and when the team switched to MGM, he threw in the towel and became a highly successful Hollywood agent.)

Duck Soup, of course, is the movie that endeared the Marxes to 1960s hippies, and its surreal political calculus still smarts today—when Groucho, as the newly installed president, sings, "If you think this country's bad off now, just wait till I get through with it," the line could apply to any politician you care to think of. This is also the one with the ongoing battles between Harpo and the lemonade vendor (the great slow-burner Edgar Kennedy) and the famous mirror sequence, which has been swiped countless times and which my daughters demanded to watch again immediately.

The comparable classic bit in *Night at the Opera* is the stateroom scene—twenty people in a room the size of a steamer trunk—which added the phrase "and two hard-boiled eggs (HONK)" to our family lexicon. It's a friendlier movie than *Duck Soup*, with Allan Jones and the young Kitty Carlisle easy to take as the singing lovers. What really matters is the gleam in the brothers' eyes as they contemplate both the opera they're about to dismantle and its human correlative, the magnificently bosomed dowager Margaret Dumont. Bonus for lawyers: the entire "party of the first part" contract scene, which had my wife the attorney turning purple with all-too-knowing laughter.

Useless trivia: *Duck Soup* was banned in Italy by dictator Benito Mussolini. This made Groucho very happy.

What next: The Paramount and MGM films are all available separately or in two boxed sets. If your kids like *Duck Soup*, bring on *Horsefeathers* (1932, the brothers at college) and *Monkey Business* (1931, the brothers as shipboard stowaways) and skip the creaky first two films, *The Cocoanuts* (1929) and *Animal Crackers* (1930). If they go for *Opera,* proceed to *A Day at the Races* (and marvel at or fast-forward past the unfortunate "All God's Chillun Got Rhythm" production number) and the underrated *A Night in Casablanca* (1946).

IT'S A GIFT (B&W, 1934)

Directed by: Norman McLeod

Starring: W. C. Fields

Ages: 8 and up

The sell: How can a man who looks so funny *be* so funny?

The plot: Harold Bissonette (pronounced "Bissonay," please) runs a small-town grocery store and is henpecked by his wife and ordered around by his children. Chaos rules his store when blind Mr. Muckle reduces the inventory to rubble. Sleeping on the porch is impossible when a random insurance salesman comes looking for Carl LaFong at 6 AM: "Capital *L*, small *a*, capital *F*, small *o*, small *n*, small *g*—*Carl LaFong!*" Harold buys an orange grove in California and transports the whole family across the country only to find the land is a dust bowl. Somehow, though, he triumphs.

Why it's here: Kids are usually flummoxed by W. C. Fields at first because he fits no known category. He's not young and hip; he doesn't have a gimmick, like Chaplin's cane or Groucho's mustache. He's just a strange old guy who mutters.

Yet halfway through *It's a Gift*, during the wonderful, over-long sleeping-porch sequence, the girls started shaking with laughter, realizing that it wasn't this man who was funny so much as the things that *happened* to him—a parade of indignities to which the only response is a sigh and an insult no one else can hear. Someone once wrote that Fields did what no other comedian has managed: He despised amusingly. True enough, but *Gift* may be the gentlest of his comedies. He's not a drunk or a dirty old man or a con artist here, just a hardworking stiff who knows that wherever he puts that stack of lightbulbs, Mr. Muckle the blind man will run into it.

This is an achingly funny comedy of disappointment, in other words, and that daunted Eliza, who as adolescence approaches is getting wary of movies that are "depressing." (Natalie, by contrast, will watch anything up to and including a test pattern.) But Fields is so beguilingly odd that you can't look away, and the film's kind enough to land with a gracefully preposterous happy ending. If nothing else, the girls have learned something about the humor of inference, while the name Carl LaFong, a handle of mysterious staying power, has been installed into their root folder.

Home video notes: Only on VHS as of this writing, not on DVD—home video has yet to do right by Fields.

Useless trivia: The screenplay writer, one Charles Bogle, is Fields himself. Other favored aliases were Otis Criblecoblis and Mahatma Kane Jeeves.

What next: *The Bank Dick* (1940), the completely twisted (not to say metafictional) *Never Give a Sucker an Even Break* (1941), *International House* (1933). You might want to try to dig up Paramount's exquisitely strange all-star *Alice in Wonderland* (1933), in which Fields plays Humpty Dumpty.

THE MUSIC BOX (B&W, 1932)

Directed by: James Parrott

Starring: Stan Laurel, Oliver Hardy, Billy Gilbert

Ages: 4 to 10

The sell: The never-ending playdate

The plot: Stan and Ollie have to deliver a piano up an endless flight of steps. What goes up must come down.

Why it's here: Laurel and Hardy are the great big babies of classic slapstick, and that's their source of delight for young children: that ostensible grown-ups could play by the rules of toddlerhood and get away with it. Or perhaps they're two eternal siblings: Stan the younger brother teetering between giggles and panicky tears, and Ollie the elder, patiently explaining the rules and looking out at us in the audience with exasperation, as if to ask, "Can you believe what the child has done now?" Kids *love* to be put in this position.

The Music Box is the 1932 short—about thirty minutes—that won an Oscar for best short subject, and it is an elegant, slightly padded variation on a theme: Two Idiots with Piano Meet Steps. It's not the duo's most perfect short (that would be *Big Business*, also known as Two Idiots Selling Christmas Trees in July, on the hard-to-find "Slapstick Masters" DVD), but it may be the best introduction for very young viewers. *Music Box* is elemental and exquisitely silly in ways that flatter a four-year-old's intelligence, and if your children like it, they can proceed to *Sons of the Desert* (1933), Laurel and Hardy's best feature film, on the same DVD.

In general, you have to be young enough or old enough to appreciate these guys: young enough to laugh at them uncomplicatedly or old enough to groove on their rigorous, Zen-like infantilism. Tweeners and jaded teens who just don't get it may be bored, but the hell with them. Watch the bit with the switched derby hats in *Music Box*: schtick that's older than God yet played so straight and with such demonic precision that it becomes both art and running commentary on art. This is comedy with no wasted gestures, and something for your kiddies to consider before they start inhaling Rob Schneider movies on a regular basis.

Home video notes: Hallmark's 2003 Laurel and Hardy DVD compilation puts *Sons of the Desert* plus *The Music Box* and three other shorts onto one disc. Aficionados are ticked off that the restored prints available on European DVDs aren't on the U.S. releases, and they have a point, but your kids won't care. If you want to go the L&H whole hog, buy a region-free DVD player and score the twenty-one-volume collected works from Amazon UK.

Useless trivia: Stan Laurel (born Arthur Stanley Jefferson) was the comic brains of the duo, writing all their gags and working with the directors. The universally adored "Babe" Hardy just showed up for work.

What next: *Sons of the Desert* and *Way Out West* (1937), the two best Laurel and Hardy features

THE NUTTY PROFESSOR (COLOR, 1963)

Directed by: Jerry Lewis

Starring: Jerry Lewis, Stella Stevens

Ages: 7 and up (depending on their capacity for scary stuff)

The sell: I'm sorry, kids—the video store didn't *have* the Eddie Murphy version.

The plot: College chemistry professor Julius Kelp (Lewis) is the nerd of all nerds until he concocts a potion that turns him into a suave ladies' man and full-time jerk who bears a suspicious resemblance to Dean Martin. Unfortunately, the potion has a nasty habit of wearing off at inopportune times.

Why it's here: Lewis is a love-him-or-leave-him proposition, but children seem to love him. As mentioned in chapter 2, the only part of *It's a Mad, Mad, Mad, Mad World* that got Eliza and Natalie's attention was Lewis's ten-second cameo, and on the strength of that I brought home *Nutty Professor* a few months later. It's considered the best film of his solo, post-Dean years, and the one that comes closest to making good on all the claims the French have made for him.

It's also one freaky movie—a blat of Technicolor comedy and neurosis that's both idiotic and very funny. The centerpiece is the transformation scene, and the scary music, odd angles, and weird *teeth* unnerved Natalie so completely she made me fast-forward through to the next bit. At the end of the movie, she shrugged and said it was okay—and then she asked to see *Professor* the next day, and watched it four more times before the week was out, and began to cough up bits of dialogue at odd times. To hear a seven-year-old doing a pitch-perfect imitation of Jerry Lewis saying, "What'll it *be*, HMMMM?" is an unsettling experience. So clearly it made an impression.

The gag is that Lewis's alter ego in this movie—the Hyde to his Jekyll—is a hateful lounge singer whom many have interpreted as the comedian's revenge on his former partner, Dean Martin. Lewis has always denied this, maintaining instead that Buddy is modeled after "every unkind, nasty SOB" he ever met. To which I say . . . maybe. Anyway, to a kid, there's an entirely different subtext at work here: the notion that inside every kindhearted person is a self-absorbed jerk itching to get out. And vice versa. What'll it be, *HMMM?*

Home video notes: Go for the Paramount Special Edition DVD— you want to watch this cinematic Rorschach test in all its gaudy wide-screen splendor.

What next: Try *The Disorderly Orderly* (1964) or the engagingly plotless *The Bellboy* (1960). If you want to test out Jerry with Dean, look for the funny *Nothing Sacred* remake *Living It Up* (1954).

4

. . . .

DRAMA

ON ONE LEVEL, our current pop culture throws far too much at children's heads: casual violence, glittering coarseness, crude language, kiddie sexuality, the cynicism of the constant sell. On another level, it overprotects them from the things that are supposed to hurt and that we learn from. It has been years since the movies felt comfortable offering young audiences—any audiences, for that matter—endings that were anything but triumphant, regardless of how far they have to distort plot and character. If *Old Yeller* were made today, the dog would live; in a remake of *To Kill a Mockingbird*, Tom Robinson would walk out the courthouse door a free man and Boo Radley would be on Xanax. And some idiot parent would approve of the changes because their children wouldn't be challenged by unhappiness, however briefly.

The films in this chapter do not offer unrelieved gloom. To be honest, most of them are enjoyable and engaging. Some of them are nearly comedies, others are earnest social dramas, still others romances, epics, period films, thundering melodramas. But some are tragedies that will, in fact, make your children shed tears at the unfairness of life and of the movies. And my point is that this is not a bad thing, because drama is how we process life when it's not actually happening to us.

From cavemen dancing in the firelight through Shakespeare to *Chinatown*, tragedy is how we explain things going wrong—in a very real way, it's an act of communal dreaming in which we sit in the dark and work out the kinks and troubles of the day. If a movie like *Mockingbird* or *Queen Christina* or *Imitation of Life* or even *Casablanca* helps a smallish person rehearse the disappointments that certainly lie in store, then they may be better prepared for life than kids who've watched nothing but Pixar. And I *love* Pixar. Even if these films don't end badly, they often provide grist for a child's mental mill. I can't tell you how many times E. or N. will pop up with a comment regarding a movie she saw a week, two weeks, three months ago. These things can take a while to percolate before they get compressed into hesitant conclusions. On the other hand, the discussion we had immediately after watching *To Kill a Mockingbird* was one for the record books.

As noted above, the movies I've chosen for this chapter cover a lot of ground, and I've tried to include most of the appropriate four-star classics while making sure important stars and directors are covered. (For a fuller treatment of these personalities, see chapter 9.) Melodrama—or rather, the unrepentant women's weepies that held sway from the 1930s through the 1950s—has its own subsection, because the kids who go for these films are a very special breed (there's one living under my roof). Silent dramas are tucked in at the end, but don't think they're mere exotica: I've seen a roomful of children watch the original 1925 *Phantom of the Opera* in a hushed rapture. As always, story trumps format.

ALL ABOUT EVE (B&W, 1950)

Directed by: Joseph L. Mankiewicz

Starring: Bette Davis, Anne Baxter, George Sanders, Celeste Holm, Marilyn Monroe

Ages: 9 and up

The sell: Be careful who your friends are.

The plot: Margo Channing (Davis) is a Broadway diva, addicted to the grand gesture and fretful about getting old. Into her life comes Eve Harrington (Baxter), a mousy would-be actress with a knack for being in the right place at the right time. Is Eve to be trusted? Margo's friends think so and are sure the star is just pitching another hissy fit. However: Just because you're paranoid etc., etc.

Why it's here: How well do we know people? How wide is the gulf between social mask and root personality? At a certain point, around the age of nine or ten, these questions become more than idle speculations. They turn into a kind of daily Rubik's Cube of social life and death—a matter of identity itself. Why is my best friend acting differently all of a sudden? Why is that boy a good kid when we're alone and King Jerk when we're with friends? Can I trust this girl? If not, *why* not? If I pretend to be confident, does that make me confident?

Kids at the edge of middle school are constantly engaged in exploring the way stations between being true to oneself and playing a part. They are slowly learning that we all play parts—a hundred different parts every day, depending on whom we're with and what we want from them and what they want from us and what we had for breakfast. It's daunting, scary, empowering all at once. It's a thrill and a dirty lie.

All about Eve is a movie about acting, the kind we do onstage and in life. It explicitly addresses where one might become the other, and why that might be a very bad thing in the long run, for one's friendships and for one's soul. And it does so in a way that is supremely well written, funny, touching, and—for the right kind of kid—eye-opening.

Eliza and Natalie watched the movie because Eliza had already been sold on Bette Davis (see *Now, Voyager* in the "Melodrama" section below) and because Marilyn Monroe has a small but pungent role as a sweetly numb wannabe. But they stuck around because of the central social mystery: Is Eve Harrington in fact a conniving backstabber? Anne Baxter plays her with such genuine sweetness that it seems impossible, and, really, Margo is a pill, with a drama-queen ego most kids natively recognize.

So when the mystery is resolved and Eve's true colors are revealed, my daughters let out a gasp of shock: The extent of her goodness is suddenly matched by the depth of her treachery. They felt personally betrayed: Eve has been *acting* all this time! But wait: Isn't that what Margo does? So when does the performance stop? When it hurts someone?

So much food for thought here. As a bonus, there's George Sanders playing theater critic Addison DeWitt, the first interesting on-screen cynic the girls had encountered.

Pause-button explanations: You'll have to help them sort the characters out according to what they do in the theater. There's the easily bruised playwright (Hugh Marlowe) and his trouper wife (Celeste Holm), the director (Gary Merrill) in love and exasperated with his star, the roughneck producer (Gregory Ratoff), the star's seen-it-all dresser (Thelma Ritter, crassly perfect as always).

Useless trivia: Davis, whose career was in trouble at the time, got the role only after Marlene Dietrich, Claudette Colbert, and others hadn't worked out. She later admitted the movie resurrected her from the dead. She also got her next husband out of the production—Gary Merrill. The film shares with *Titanic* the record for most Oscar nominations (fourteen). It won six, including best picture, director, supporting actor (Sanders), and screenplay (Davis lost to Judy Holliday in *Born Yesterday*).

What next: For more backstage intrigue, dig up *Stage Door.* More Davis? *Now, Voyager*; *Dark Victory*; and—if they can handle a star playing a dazzling bitch—*The Little Foxes* and *The Letter*. See chapter 9.

CASABLANCA (B&W, 1942)

Directed by: Michael Curtiz

Starring: Humphrey Bogart, Ingrid Bergman, Paul Henreid (Zzzzz . . .), Claude Rains, Dooley Wilson, Peter Lorre

Ages: 9 and up

The sell: Sacrifice is cool.

The plot: Wartime Casablanca, in German-occupied North Africa. Everyone comes to Rick's Café including a lot of European refugees literally dying to escape the Third Reich and sail to America. Among them are Ilsa (Bergman), an old flame of Rick's (Bogart), and her husband, freedom fighter Victor Laszlo (Henreid). Will Rick help Victor get out of town or hand his rival over to the French cops (led by Rains) and German Gestapo (Conrad Veidt)?

Why it's here: This one needs so much setup for a kid that it may not seem worth it. Even with the corny/cool Warner Bros. stock map at the beginning, you'll have to lay out the basics of World War II: who the Germans are, why they took over France, what everyone is doing in Morocco, whether Claude

Rains's Capt. Renault is a good guy or bad guy (he's both, and that's a hard nut to crack), where the Americans are (not in the war yet), why your children should care. When I first watched *Casablanca* with Eliza, there was so much pausing, explaining, restarting, that I was sure none of it registered.

And yet. About six months later, we came across *Casablanca* again on Turner Classics, just as it was starting. She yelped, "I *love* this movie!" and begged me to let her watch it again. "You do?" I asked, recalling her furrowed brow the first time around. She did, and now that she had the story straight, she could sit down and actually enjoy it. She could groove on all those wonderful supporting roles—"Cuddles" Sakall waggling his jowls, Sidney Greenstreet swatting flies and stopping just short of eating them, Peter Lorre shrieking "*Reeck! Reeck!*" as the Nazis cart him away and Bogey sits there stone-faced, a dead soul, not lifting a finger. Man, he's cold, but you can see what a sap he really is as soon as Bergman walks into the room, and so will your kids. *Casablanca* works today because of Bergman and Bogart— her woozy emotionalism and the way his tough-guy act completely falls to pieces in her presence.

The ending throws children the first time they see it. Rick doesn't get the girl! He lets her go off with the boring guy who's going to save the world! In fact, Rick gets the *guy*, Capt. Renault, and strides off into the night for the beginning of a "beautiful friendship" (and, yes, there probably have been doctoral dissertations on coded gay motifs in *Casablanca*, but save that for after your kids have seen a few Rock Hudson movies).

Here's the thing, though: It's a happy ending for the world if not for Rick, so doesn't the fact that Rick knows it make it a happy ending for him too? In other words, can giving something up make you a better person? The great thing about *Casablanca* is that you don't have to spell this message out for your children—it's right there in gorgeous black and white.

Home video notes: Warner's 50th Anniversary DVD Edition and more recent two-disc Special Edition are both visually the best out there, but the twofer has more extras, including the Bugs Bunny parody *Carrotblanca*.

Pause-button explanations: See above and spend a little time explaining the basics—and I mean the basics, unless they're history nerds—of the early days of World War II.

Useless trivia: The movie won the Oscar for best picture, but it came close to falling apart during the shoot. The screenwriters worked barely one day ahead of the production, so when it came time to shoot the scene where Bogart nods at the club orchestra to play "La Marseillaise," the actor had no idea what he was nodding *at*.

What next: It's all downhill from here.

FEAR STRIKES OUT (B&W, 1957)

Directed by: Robert Mulligan

Starring: Anthony Perkins, Karl Malden

Ages: 10 and up

The sell: Sports dads suck.

The plot: Jimmy Piersall is a kid who likes baseball and is good at it but whose father (Malden) wants him to love it and be perfect. Jimmy grows up to be played by Anthony Perkins, gets drafted to play with the Red Sox, and eventually cracks under the pressure of his assimilated work ethic. Thank goodness for those saintly '50s-movie psychiatrists.

Why it's here: To make you look good. Unless, of course, you're worse than Karl Malden in this movie. *Fear Strikes Out* speaks volumes to the fears that all kids—even the talented ones, *especially* the talented ones—have about organized sports. A field full of unpressured children playing to the limits of their abilities is a marvelous thing to behold, but all it takes is one grown-up with . . . issues to turn a game into a psychological obstacle course at Quantico.

Which is to say that children will instinctively recognize poor Jimmy Piersall's twitchy, neurotic drive to be better than his father's hopes for him as a sad impossibility. And they'll recognize Malden's John Piersall as the kind of bullying grown-up they know from life and learn to walk blocks out of the way to avoid.

More likely, you'll both flinch as Piersall père plays catch with his son until the latter grimaces in pain (and takes it), groan as the father talks about "our" career with the Sox, and goggle at the scene in which young Piersall snaps and climbs the fence behind home plate, trying to crawl out of the nightmare ball field in his head. Everything that comes after is reassuring Eisenhower-era Freudianism, and the dad quietly gets his comeuppance, but *Fear* still puts the unspoken angst that can come between a parent and child right out there on the coffee table. Look at it this way: If your son or daughter is a little *too* quiet after this movie, maybe you want to look in the mirror before the next practice.

Useless trivia: The real Jimmy Piersall did have a nervous breakdown on the field and came back to have a solid career (lifetime batting average of .272, not bad at all). That said, the outfielder distanced himself from this movie, deeply displeased with the way the relationship with his father was simplified and Hollywoodized. It's still a good and potent movie, if not an especially factual one.

What next: This was director Robert Mulligan's first feature film; he'd go on to make *To Kill a Mockingbird* (see below). If your little baseball fan wants a less emotionally taxing true-life diamond flick, try *Pride of the Yankees* (1942, with Gary Cooper as Lou Gehrig; see below), *The Stratton Story* (1949, Jimmy Stewart as one-legged pitcher Monty Stratton), and *The Jackie Robinson Story* (1950, with Jackie Robinson playing himself). Or you could try the more recent *Field of Dreams*. If you screen it, they will come.

THE GRAPES OF WRATH (B&W, 1940)

Directed by: John Ford

Starring: Henry Fonda, Jane Darwell

Ages: 10 and up

The sell: America is hard.

The plot: Tom Joad (Fonda) gets out of prison and returns to the Oklahoma dust bowl and a family farm blowing away in the wind. He loads up with his family and they head for California, just another bunch of despised migrant Okies pinning their hopes on an impossible dream of orange groves and employment.

Why it's here: Your children can learn about the Great Depression in school or from older relatives or by surfing the Web, but nothing socks it home with high Hollywood effect like John Ford's adaptation of the John Steinbeck novel. It's a measure of how cosseted kids are in early twenty-first-century America that the images in this movie have the power to shock them into silence, and yet it's still a candy-coated, nobly romanticized version of reality.

Director John Ford and cinematographer Gregg Toland consciously tried to re-create the documentary photographs of Walker Evans and Dorothea Lange, and the sense of despair, even panic, is palpable. These people are destitute, Third World, and they're our grandparents. They would not begin to recognize our current land of plenty. (But they would recognize the poor who still live between the cracks, noticed even less by a media addicted to good news unless a Hurricane Katrina forces them into view.)

Henry Fonda is our stoic, poetic hero, and his speech at the end—"wherever there's a fight, so hungry people can eat, I'll be there. Wherever there's a cop beatin' up a guy, I'll be there"—is an emotional killer and a precise distillation of the populist socialist argument of the 1930s. The softening of the edges—the sentimentality of Jane Darwell's Ma Joad, for instance—is what makes this both bearable for children and an excellent beginner's history lesson. Given how obsessed today's kiddie movies are with immediacy—how a Lindsay Lohan movie doesn't look any further back than the film it's remaking—*Grapes* is a revolutionary experience. It broaches the notion that there was a yesterday that led up to today, and that it was hard as hell. And it introduces the idea that for some people it still is.

Home video notes: The 2004 Fox DVD is the one to get; Toland's images have never looked starker and more unyielding.

Pause-button explanations: The Depression and the dust bowl are topics that should be sketched in prior to viewing.

Useless trivia: A hugely controversial movie in its day, based on a book that is still regularly banned from school libraries. Why? Because it puts the blame on bankers who foreclosed on farms and other big-money interests, and it inherently advocates revolution. Neoconservatives still hate the film and the Steinbeck source novel; less doctrinaire viewers can take it as a moving saga of all-American resiliency.

What next: Look for any of the other socially concerned dramas Fonda appeared in: the antilynching *The Ox-Bow Incident* (1943) or *12 Angry Men* (1957).

GREAT EXPECTATIONS (B&W, 1946)

Directed by: David Lean

Starring: John Mills, Jean Simmons, Alec Guinness, Martita Hunt

Ages: 7 and up

The sell: Other people matter.

The plot: Young orphan Pip (Anthony Wager) lives out on the moors with his adult sister and her easygoing husband. He briefly helps an escaped convict (Finlay Currie) and is occasionally sent to the mysterious mansion of Miss Havisham (Hunt), a crazed old woman with a beautiful but coldhearted young ward named Estella (Simmons). Eventually grown (and played by Mills), Pip learns a benefactor has arranged for him to become a London gentleman. He moves to town, befriends an amiable young lad named Herbert Pocket (Guinness), and lives the life of a young toff. Eventually Pip learns that his benefactor is not Miss Havisham, as he'd assumed, and that there are people and causes worth sticking one's neck out for.

Why it's here: Which should be a child's first Dickens movie? Some will argue for *Oliver!* (1968), but allow me to point out that as great as "Food, Glorious Food" is, the movie's a Broadway filtering of Dickens, and a kid arguably deserves to get Boz straight from the bottle. *A Tale of Two Cities* and *David Copperfield* (both 1935) are high-water marks of early Hollywood Dickens, the first with Ronald Colman as an effectively cynical/doomed Sydney Carton, and the second with—joy—W. C. Fields as Micawber.

Yet those movies pull their punches and David Lean's two Dickens films don't, in ways that younger viewers understand as a sign of respect. Lean made the definitive *Oliver Twist* (1948), with Alec Guinness as a still-controversial Fagin, and that one's dark enough to make the musical remake look like the faint-hearted color photocopy it is. Lean's *Twist* may in fact be the single best Charles Dickens adaptation of all, but it is unrelent-ing, and if your kids are younger, you probably want to start them with *Great Expectations*, made two years earlier.

Just understand that the opening sequence, with Pip coming across the fearsome convict Magwitch on the lonely marshes, has the potential to wet small pants. I'd actually read the first few chapters of the book to Eliza and Natalie, so they knew what was coming, and part of the creepy pleasure of the movie for them was how closely the opening scenes matched up with the printed words—how the grown-up characters retained the car-toonishness the author wrote into them and how horror was always just kept at bay by Pip's resourcefulness.

Estella was for them a figure of concern—how could a girl be such a brutal snip?—and Miss Havisham and her mouldering wedding cake a creature of eerie fascination. They liked seeing Obi Wan Kenobi as a young man. But *Great Expectations* truly came alive for them in the midsection, as they followed Pip into a wealthier, shallower, and vainer youth than he was meant for and as he slowly comes to understand the primacy of people over class. Pip very nearly turns into a snob, reviling the poor convict Magwitch who—spoiler alert—has bankrolled the young boy who once showed him kindness. But because both Dickens and children believe that character is constant, Pip's goodness must resurface and does, tempered and rather shamefaced. You know the expression your kids have when they've learned a hard lesson? That's what John Mills looks like here.

So, yes, there are morals in *Great Expectations*, but your children will probably be too caught up in the final scenes to realize they're being inculcated. This one blew Natalie away: She fully identified with young Pip and allowed herself to be swept along from there, falling back in happy exhaustion when the end credits rolled, a Dickens fan for life.

Home video notes: Look for the Criterion DVD—the print is rich and atmospheric, which counts with this movie.

What next: Lean's *Oliver Twist*, if you think they're up for it—it's brilliant but unforgiving. Then on to *A Tale of Two Cities* and *Oliver!*

HOW GREEN WAS MY VALLEY (B&W, 1941)

Directed by: John Ford

Starring: Roddy McDowell, Maureen O'Hara, Donald Crisp

Ages: 8 and up

The sell: Love your family while you have them.

The plot: Life in a tiny Welsh mining village, centering on the Morgan family. Crisp plays the terse, loving patriarch and unofficial leader of the miners, Sara Allgood is his long-suffering wife, and twelve-year-old McDowell is Huw, the youngest of six sons and the one his family hopes will go to university. Depression hits the village and a number of the Morgan sons emigrate to other lands, seeking work; their sister (O'Hara) marries the mine owner's coldhearted son despite her love for village minister Mr. Gruffydd (Walter Pidgeon). Young Huw weathers a cruel teacher and a bout of paralysis to work in the mines, but his father's death in an accident convinces the boy that his fortunes lie in the wider world.

Why it's here: Shot on location in the Welsh mountains of, uh, Ventura County, California, *How Green Was My Valley* may be the best introduction for a young child living in America the Bountiful to notions of poverty and toil. Older kids can handle the picturesque agonies of Ford's *The Grapes of Wrath*, teenagers can digest Holocaust dramas and whatever sobering documentaries you can get them to sit still for, but this rigorous yet fundamentally sentimental adaptation of Richard Llewellyn's autobiographical novel offers as beautiful an image of abject poverty as Hollywood was able to muster. Not surprisingly, it won the best picture Oscar of 1941, famously beating out *Citizen Kane*.

How Green Was My Valley is a child's garden of despair and thus a provocative, emotional, and reassuring piece of work. The paralyzed child walks again; the abusive teacher is summarily dealt with by the lovable town drunk; the beautiful sister stands to gain her forbidden love at last. Father and the old ways die that the child may live.

This last scene is, oddly, not as distressing as you might think, since the writing has been on the wall for most of the movie. As soon as Eliza understood that mine accidents occur here, she said, "The father's going to die, isn't he?" and that's less a sign of tweener world-weariness than an ability to read classic movie plot conventions from far down the road.

Valley is pitched perfectly for younger children, balanced as it is between Dickensian grime and rough, rural prettiness. Natalie watched this movie intent as a scholar, partly because the presence of young Roddy McDowell offered her a way into the tale but also because she recognized how brutally unfair the miners' lives were, and how warm and comforting their hearths. Family is all you have, says Ford, and it can get picked apart until the only thing left is the memory. And memory is to be treasured, even when it turns golden with the years.

What next: Similar stories of family nostalgia viewed through a child's recollections: *Meet Me in St. Louis* is the acknowledged champ.

I KNOW WHERE I'M GOING! (B&W, 1945)

Directed by: Michael Powell and Emeric Pressburger

Starring: Wendy Hiller, Roger Livesey

Ages: 10 and up

The sell: Don't be so sure.

The plot: Ambitious Londoner Joan Webster (Hiller) knows where she's going—to the isle of Kilorney in the Hebrides of western Scotland to marry a wealthy, older industrialist she doesn't love. But a fog creeps in and strands her for days on the mainland with a crew of locals and the island's impoverished young laird, who's just back from World War II.

Why it's here: This was my mother's favorite movie, and not just because she bore a resemblance to Wendy Hiller. All right, perhaps because of that, but also because Hiller in this movie acts in a way my mother and many women of her generation may have admired but were too cautious to try for themselves. Joan Webster is headstrong, a control freak, a middle-class girl determined to better her lot by marrying well. And she blows it, totally, for a penniless Scottish nobleman, because the Hebridean voodoo gets to her and shows her that the lived life is more important than the planned life.

That's a movie conceit, of course, but maybe this is close to why we go to the movies in the first place—to dream variations on the ways we have to live. My mother was a middle-class girl who married well, to a Boston lawyer thirteen years her senior; they loved each other convincingly but, looking at it in a way we should never look at our parents, there *was* the whiff of the contractual about it, on both sides. *I Know Where I'm Going!*—that title, down to its exclamation point, gets ready to knock the heroine on her rear end—says that if you treat life as a series of places to reach, you may be just lucky enough to get stranded across the water from your goal. When my mother watched this film, letting the magic of the island mist and bewitching regional music get to her like it does Joan Webster, perhaps she could pretend she had never made it to her own island and that a modest young laird was still waiting in the wings.

A girl's daydream. Actually, a son's daydream of what his mother might have daydreamed. But we need daydreams, if only to properly value what we end up with. *I Know Where I'm Going!* is a lovely, important movie for a child of the right age to see—a daughter, perhaps, who has begun to feel sure *she* knows where she's going. Michael Powell and Emeric Pressburger, the British writing-directing team known as the Archers, always set dreaminess against their countrymen's stiff upper lips, and the dreams always won, sometimes shockingly so (see 1947's *Black Narcissus* for that). In this film, it's the illogic of the place and people that drives Joan Webster crazy with frustration until she has to give in: the whirlpool off the coast, the look on the face of Catriona Potts when she enters windswept with wolfhounds, the brain-cramping response of Torquil when Joan comments on the poverty of the locals ("Not poor. They just haven't got any money").

A character refers in one scene to "intelligent female nonsense," and the movie itself comes close to a working definition of same. Show it to your most hard-hearted child, to the realist, before it's too late.

Home video notes: The Criterion Collection version has the best print and lots of interesting bells and whistles, including home movies Powell took of the Scottish locations, narrated by his widow (and Martin Scorsese's longtime editor), Thelma Schoonmaker Powell.

Pause-button explanations: The film is made under the shadow of World War II, which remains safely offscreen but which deeply informs the characters' lives. The 1945 audience took this for granted; you might have to do some setting up.

What next: More Powell and Pressburger, please: *The Red Shoes* (1948), *Stairway to Heaven* (1946), *The 49th Parallel* (1941), *One of Our Aircraft Is Missing* (1942), and *The Thief of Bagdad* (1940) are all good choices depending on age and gender. See chapter 9 for details.

IT'S A WONDERFUL LIFE (B&W, 1946)

Directed by: Frank Capra

Starring: James Stewart, Donna Reed, Thomas Mitchell

Ages: 6 and up

The sell: Appreciate what you have, little one.

The plot: George Bailey (Stewart) is a small-town boy whose big dreams of seeing the world are confounded by the usual compromises of life. He marries, has children, takes over the family business, finds himself in sudden middle-age despair, and decides it would be better if he had never lived. This being a Frank Capra movie, there's an angel—a fuddy old coot named Clarence (Henry Travers)—who shows George how connected each person is to everybody else.

Why it's here: *It's a Wonderful Life* has become so familiar after decades of Yuletide airings that its cultural sprocket holes have all but worn off. There's a lot to be said for watching the movie through a child's fresh eyes.

On the surface, it carries a profoundly reassuring message— *you matter.* Even if you're stuck in some Podunk backwater, even if your dreams have been smashed and laid aside one by one, the world would be a far worse place if you didn't exist. That this is not true is demonstrable, and Capra knew it—he had just returned from heading a documentary field unit in World War II and had seen much to testify to man's inhumanity to man. *Life*, then, is agitprop for optimism, and more than willing to resort to angels and back-lot meanies like Lionel Barrymore's Hiram Potter to get its point across.

That said, it's the shadows at the edges that keep the film interesting to modern grown-ups and children. Who hasn't fantasized about what the world would be like without us? This movie's terrifying answer is that things would roll on, heedless, our good deeds not undone but *never* done. And if Capra contemplates total negation from his catbird seat high in the Hollywood corn, Jimmy Stewart gets right down there in the rows and starts shucking. This is the actor's most naked, despairing performance—he, too, was newly back from World War II and had seen death firsthand—and his anxiety grounds the film and makes it matter. If Capra is able to turn such gnarly subjects as unhappiness and suicide into palatable kid's food, it's Stewart who ensures the meal sticks to the ribs.

Still, only this director could make the sentimental scenes so homespun and fresh. George's wooing of Mary (Reed) has an aching sincerity to it that's partly the actors but mostly Capra, who embraces small-town Americana and its values with a grip of sweet relief. Call it sappy if you like, but it's a movie made by people who've seen things they'd give anything to forget.

Home video notes: Look for the remastered print DVD released by Republic in 2002; the film has been in the public domain for so long that many inferior copies exist on video.

Pause-button explanations: If this movie doesn't prompt a discussion about suicide, it should.

Useless trivia: The movie was a flop in 1946, considered an overdone fantasy in rather poor taste. The studio even let the copyright lapse into the public domain, which is why local TV stations started showing the film around the holiday clock in the '60s and '70s. Within years *Life* was the beloved classic it never had been and millions of people knew the meaning of the phrase "Zuzu's petals!"

What next: Crank up the Capracorn: *Mr. Smith Goes to Washington* (1939), *Mr. Deeds Goes to Town* (1936), *It Happened One Night* (1934).

JANE EYRE (B&W, 1944)

Directed by: Robert Stevenson

Starring: Joan Fontaine, Orson Welles

Ages: 11 and up

The sell: The original Goth chick

The plot: Jane Eyre (Peggy Ann Garner) is an orphan child living with her nasty aunt (Agnes Moorehead), who ships her off to a cruel boarding school where Jane grows up to be played by Joan Fontaine. Finding a position as governess at Thornfield, Jane meets the moody, tortured Rochester (Orson Welles) and comes to love him. But who—or what—is he keeping in the attic?

Why it's here: Eliza was torn about this one. She'd read and loved the book—it was the first grown-up classic she'd tackled—and she was *not* pleased at the violence done to Charlotte Brontë by Darryl Zanuck and the folks at 20th Century Fox: the kindly Miss Temple gone missing from the scenes at the Lowood Institution for orphan girls; the entire St. John subplot and the revelation of Jane's inheritance neatly excised. Eliza missed the final scene of Jane bringing the water to the blinded Rochester, and I could hear her quietly harumphing throughout as we watched.

But there were also the things that worked: Joan Fontaine as Jane with her carefully unplucked eyebrows, a mouse with a spine. Orson Welles as Rochester with some kind of magnificent fake nose and high-key lighting on his eyes to make them glimmer with noble dementia (or was that disappointment over his stalled Hollywood career?). A very young Elizabeth Taylor, her character dead before fifteen minutes are up, and Margaret O'Brien the same year as *Meet Me in St. Louis* but somehow seeming much, much younger. Agnes Moorhead as Mrs. Reed and Henry Daniell as Brocklehurst, the pair of them despicable in ways to warm the heart of a child.

All wonderful things, and then there's the mystery of the maniac in the attic. Natalie hadn't read the book, but those cackles and wayward candles kept her reeled in, even when Welles's Rochester yammered on in the sort of flowery, cynical speeches that turn to porridge in your ears.

It's a film with lumps in the batter, in other words, and Robert Stevenson isn't much of a director (although he had a healthy and strange career, bouncing from this to 1949's *I Married a Communist* before settling in as Disney's house director on everything from *Mary Poppins* to *The Love Bug* and *That Darn Cat!* His last film was *The Shaggy D.A.*, directed when he was seventy-one). *Jane Eyre* finds its grim, brooding equivalents to Brontë's unyielding prose in cinematographer George Barnes's images and Bernard Herrmann's score; on a scene-by-scene basis, it's full of fog and madness. That was enough to keep the girls going.

That, and Jane herself, who is plain but regal, who dares to speak her mind to her social betters/moral inferiors, and who, more than anything, views herself as a perversely unlovable outsider. Right there is the missing link between Gothic fiction and modern Goth: the will to self-exile. There are teenagers who perceive the falsity of the everyday world and choose not to participate in it, and there are younger kids, too, who are beginning to sense as much. Maybe they haven't yet broken out the black nail polish and emo CDs (among other keepsakes of mass iconoclasm), but they're open to suggestion. *Jane Eyre* insists that the DNA of Goth is 150 years older than *The Cure's Greatest Hits*.

Home video notes: Not available on DVD at this writing and out of print on video—but adventurous stores should stock it.

Pause-button explanations: You might want to briefly stop during the scenes at Lowood and point out how good your kids' own school looks in comparison.

Useless trivia: Rumors abound that Welles in fact directed a number of scenes.

What next: More Brontës? Try *Wuthering Heights* (1939), directed by William Wyler and shot by the great Gregg Toland (*Citizen Kane*). It stars Laurence Olivier as Heathcliff and Merle Oberon as Cathy, both of whom have their defenders and detractors. No one denies they look great, though the movie cuts as many plot corners as *Jane Eyre* (more harumphing from E.). Also, try Hitchcock's *Rebecca* (1940) if you want good fake Brontë with a fine Fontaine.

LITTLE WOMEN (B&W, 1933)

Directed by: George Cukor

Starring: Katharine Hepburn

Ages: 8 and up

The sell: The *real* American Girls

The plot: Massachusetts during the Civil War, and times are tight for the March family. Father is off at battle and Marmee (Spring Byington) holds her family of four daughters together, reminding them to help those worse off than they. Jo (Hepburn) is the impetuous writer; Meg (Frances Dee) the sensible eldest; Amy (Joan Bennett) the slightly spoiled youngest; Beth (Jean Parker) the beloved and doomed. There are marriages and deaths, disappointments and quiet triumphs—life occurs.

Why it's here: This is the movie that sold Eliza on the classics, on Katharine Hepburn, on Louisa May Alcott—on the old America that popular culture does its best to erase daily. It's not for every girl (or for every boy); a 1933 film, slow in some places, stiff in others. If Hepburn weren't in it, *Women* would be a dusty piece of lacework.

But Hepburn *is* in it, impossibly young and full of a rakish tomgirl energy that can only be called Alcottian. I can't think of any other actress who would have been right as Jo—impetuous dreamer, tough-minded artist, sisterly bully and bully-for-you sister, coming to value her family all the more as it grows and spreads and frays. Kate was born to the role: The Connecticut daughter of a wealthy doctor and a suffragette mother, she came as close to the entitled, idealistic social conscience of the New England Transcendentalists as a twentieth-century woman could. She is the cameo in the attic chest made vibrant and alive. Audiences of the time knew it—the film was easily the biggest

hit of Hepburn's early years—and the actress knew it, reaching
back to the nineteenth century to base her performance on her
aunt Edith Hooker, the Jo of her mother's side of the family.

Children know it, too. Eliza did, anyway. All girls play with all
dolls, drawn to whatever fantasy projection is in the playroom at
the time, but there are those who are drawn to Barbie, those
who feel kinship with Groovy Girls, and then there are the kids
who go for the American Girls line—who, however young,
sense value and comfort in an older, even unfashionable way of
doing things. (This, of course, is what the dolls are selling.)
They're the ones who read Laura Ingalls Wilder as evidence of a
continuum of girlhood and who perhaps find tougher meat
there than in the choices modern kid culture offers.

Here, the young Hepburn is that continuum made flesh—or
at least living, breathing, black-and-white celluloid—and she
honors Louisa May Alcott's self-portrait. Jo doesn't marry the
boy next door, even though he's in love with her. Rather, she
goes her own way, moves to New York to become a writer
(blazing a trail that is now a freeway), suffers doubts about her
art, her family, her own pigheadedness, and then finds a quiet
sort of love with her intellectual equal.

The Jos of today live in Brooklyn and start Web sites, and
their every move is encrusted with all-knowing irony. The
women of *Little Women* are pre-irony, though, and some kids
will find that corny. The ones who don't—who are naive or
mature or some admixture of both—will recognize the artless
sincerity here as a thing to be emulated, even if the world
doesn't always honor it.

Pause-button explanations: The Civil War looms in the background
and may need some introduction.

What next: Hepburn fans will probably want to avoid the other
costume dramas she made in her youth—with the exception of

Quality Street (1937), they're tony, high-flown, and excruciatingly dull. Go for the modern-dress Kate: *Bringing Up Baby*, *Stage Door*, etc. There have been two other film versions of *Little Women*: I can't vouch for the 1949 edition, other than to marvel at a cast that includes perky June Allyson as Jo, shady lady Mary Astor as Marmee, Margaret "Tootie" O'Brien as Beth, and a young Liz Taylor as Amy. The 1994 Gillian Armstrong film, by contrast, is a lovely piece of work, with strong performances by Winona Ryder, Susan Sarandon, Kirsten Dunst, and Christian Bale, and a score by Thomas Newman to make you weep with nostalgia.

LUST FOR LIFE (COLOR, 1956)

Directed by: Vincente Minnelli

Starring: Kirk Douglas, Anthony Quinn

Ages: 8 and up

The sell: Art is lonely.

The plot: The life of Vincent Van Gogh (Douglas), from his early years as an unsuccessful preacher to his struggles with painting. Always poverty-stricken and riddled with doubts, Van Gogh relies on his brother Theo for financial and emotional support and on the blustery Paul Gaugin (Quinn) for friendship and advice. Distraught when Gaugin moves on, Vincent mutilates his ear. In the end, after painting his final canvas, *Wheatfield with Crows*, he shoots himself. He has sold one painting during his life; today his work is among the most valuable on the planet.

Why it's here: Cheery little story, huh? Yet for kids who are into art and famous painters, it's a fascinating film—the equivalent of the illuminated life of a saint. And for anyone who thinks the creative process is one of romantic (i.e., "fun") torment, *Lust for Life* offers the cautionary note that it can be absolutely miserable. Worth it? Maybe. You decide, kid.

It happens that we have one of those art freaks in Natalie, the rare child who likes to go to museums and who collects famous painters the way some kids collect baseball cards. It started with an interest in Jackson Pollock, who splattered paint everywhere just like she did and somehow became famous for it; she then moved on to the Impressionists, Warhol, Picasso, Rembrandt, Vermeer, the whole gang, abetted by a neat series of kids' books by Mike Venezia titled *Getting to Know the World's Greatest Artists*—nice work, Mike.

Van Gogh held special interest, though. The paintings are spooky and childlike, the self-portraits doubly so. The story about the ear—well, what kid wouldn't want to know more? So one day I rented Vincente Minnelli's acclaimed biopic, knowing it was going to be harsh but trusting in my eight-year-old's interest to see us through.

For Natalie, I think it was a transformative experience. She recognized the seriousness of the film, but the idea that beauty could somehow come out of such grinding loneliness was a new one on her, this most sociable of kids. She knew the art arose from the same place as Vincent's inability to fit in. I think she was relieved other artists didn't have to be the same way— Gaugin, for instance. (Quinn won a supporting Oscar for his role here, and it's a bluff, smart piece of work; he and Douglas work together like mismatched roommates driving each other crazy.)

The film is beautifully shot, with intense colors and an agonized performance from Douglas (who should have won an Oscar too; the best actor award went to Yul Brynner for *The King and I* that year), and it feels as hyperreal as a Van Gogh painting itself. Natalie was worried they'd show the ear-cutting, and I assured her it happened offscreen; she watched the film soberly and steadily, as if it were a case study of someone for whom she cared deeply.

A few weeks later, we wandered over to the Fogg Museum of Art in Cambridge, across the river from where we live. It's a pocket-sized place with a tidy assortment of Great Works, and when we walked into one gallery there was a Van Gogh on a wall: the 1888 self-portrait, in which the artist looks almost Asian. I heard the intake of Natalie's breath as she caught sight of it, and we walked up close, examining the thick brushstrokes and the distant, hollow look in his eyes. For her, the movie was proof of the life, and the painting was proof of the movie. The art, of course, needed no proof.

Home video notes: *Lust* finally got the proper wide-screen DVD treatment from Warner Home Video in early 2006. Avoid the VHS version that crops the exquisite CinemaScope frames almost in half—it's like looking at great artworks through a picket fence.

What next: Other famous-artist movies? The best ones are more recent. Forget about *Pollock* (2000) until they're older—you want depressing? *The Girl with the Pearl Earring* (2003) is surprisingly kid-friendly, though; Lori watched it with the girls to applause all around. *Frida* (2002) is great to look at and well done, if long; again, for when they're more grown-up. If you can get your hands on the 1956 documentary *The Mystery of Picasso*, though, grab it—it consists of a spry Pablo hanging sheets of translucent paper between himself and the camera lens and creating painting after painting right on the spot. It's available on DVD from Amazon and other outlets.

THE MANCHURIAN CANDIDATE (B&W, 1962)

Directed by: John Frankenheimer

Starring: Frank Sinatra, Laurence Harvey, Angela Lansbury

Ages: 14 and up

The sell: Don't trust *anybody*.

The plot: Not to give too much away, but: Returning Korean War vet Ben Marco (Sinatra) can't shake the nagging feeling that his fellow soldier Raymond Shaw (Harvey) is not the hero everyone claims he is but rather something more sinister. Digging deeper, Marco unearths a viper's nest of brainwashing, political assassination, and deadly mother love.

Why it's here: Whether you bring them up Republican or Democrat or civil libertarian or Whig, at some point children start to sense that leaders can lie. That what a president says does not necessarily equal what he knows, and that political discourse is often a diversionary tactic to cover a world of compromise, strategic screwing over, and occasional straight-up greed. Because so much of this happens out of sight, it's easy and, in a queasy way, entertaining to imagine worst-case scenarios and then amp them up by a factor of a thousand.

This, class, is called political paranoia, and *The Manchurian Candidate* is one of its earliest and most baroque examples. Unhappily, thirteen months after its release came the real-world sequel, the Kennedy assassination, which is a primary reason the film was pulled from circulation for years by star/coproducer Frank Sinatra (whose friendship with JFK was complicated enough to be worth a book of its own). When *Candidate* resurfaced in the 1980s, in a world in which no conspiracy theory was too bizarre to consider, a movie about a woman who makes a pact with Korean Communists to turn her own son into a brainwashed assassin so her boob of a husband can advance to the presidency seemed perfectly reasonable.

Not for the toddlers, obviously, and they'll be confused, if not bored, long before the film starts hinting that mommies may not always be nice. (If you only know Angela Lansbury from *Murder She Wrote* and *Beauty and the Beast,* by the way, this movie makes an excellent corrective.) It might even be too disturbing for sensitive older kids. It's a genuinely strange film: The tone falls in the gray area between drama and satire, occasionally drifting into the blackest of comedy, and while Lawrence Harvey's Raymond Shaw may be an ice cube of a hero, you have to feel for a guy who's forced to shoot the girl he loves because the Queen of Hearts told him to.

No, *Manchurian* is for teenagers who are convinced they've seen everything and don't mind being proved wrong. It's appealingly cynical about politics, too; asked how many Communists have been identified, a senator glances at a Heinz ketchup bottle on the table and announces "fifty-seven." Mostly, the movie's sick in a way both you and they will understand is a compliment.

Home video notes: Go for the remastered wide-screen MGM DVD released in 2004, and make sure you don't take home the Denzel Washington remake of the same year by accident; while it's actually pretty good, it's not the masterpiece this is.

Pause-button explanations: If you try to explain the political background of the movie, you might end up using a whiteboard. Throw it on and field the questions as they come up.

Useless trivia: Lansbury was only three years older than the man playing her son.

What next: *Dr. Strangelove, or: How I Stopped Worrying and Learned to Love the Bomb* (1964).

MR. SMITH GOES TO WASHINGTON (B&W, 1939)

Directed by: Frank Capra

Starring: James Stewart, Jean Arthur, Claude Rains

Ages: 8 and up

The sell: The system works.

The plot: When a senator from a large midwestern state dies unexpectedly, a wide-eyed Boy Scout leader named Jefferson Smith (Stewart) is appointed to replace him. The corrupt industrialist and his backroom cronies who control the state are convinced the kid is too naive to spoil their graft, but with the help of a devoted assistant (Arthur) who knows the ropes, Smith makes his stand on the floor of the U.S. Senate.

Why it's here: On the theory that you have to believe in something before you can be cynical about it, *this* is the political movie to show kids too young for *The Manchurian Candidate*. Idealistic, wholesome, and hugely entertaining, it's the peak of prewar Capracorn, with Stewart in the role that epitomizes his appeal. There's also the endearing, squeaky-voiced Arthur—I had a major teen-geek crush on her after seeing this back in the 1970s—and the foolproof Thomas Mitchell. And Rains, who sometimes seems like he was in every classic movie ever made; here his hair's dyed white, and he looks like Ted Kennedy on a good day.

Yes, the ending's a stretch—Jeff Smith is saved only because his corrupt mentor (Rains) discovers a conscience at the last minute. I bet the boys in the pressroom had a good laugh over that one. But, so what, it's a fairy tale, with Stewart a child's own stand-in as he takes his faith in the rightness of things to the Capitol, where it dovetails with the ideals of the Founding

Fathers. The Lincoln Memorial scene is the linchpin; Eliza and Natalie had been there years before seeing this movie, but it brought back the place in all its spooky, reverential hush. The film draws the finest of correlations between personal decency and U.S. history, making the former as attractive as the latter is inevitable.

Pause-button explanations: If you have younger kids, you may be called on to distinguish governors from vice presidents from senators. Luckily, Arthur's character will do a lot of the job for you as she squires Smith about town.

Useless trivia: Not surprisingly, the movie didn't go over well in D.C., with politicians denouncing it as a caricature (yes, but an *effective* caricature) and the press offended by the notion that they were drunks (yes, but *effective* drunks).

What next: *Mr. Deeds Goes to Town* (1936), which is to Gary Cooper what *Smith* is to Stewart.

MUTINY ON THE BOUNTY (B&W, 1935)

Directed by: Frank Lloyd

Starring: Clark Gable, Charles Laughton, Franchot Tone

Ages: 9 and up

The sell: You're stuck on a boat with a jerk. Do you fight back?

The plot: HMS *Bounty* sails for Tahiti to trade for breadfruit. On board are first mate Fletcher Christian (Gable), midshipman Roger Byam (Tone)—and Captain William Bligh (Laughton), a cruel sadist who flogs the men and cuts their rations for the bloody pleasure of it. After a bit of paradise on Tahiti, the crew of the *Bounty* mutinies and puts Bligh and his supporters in a longboat to drift to their doom. Astoundingly, Bligh makes it back to England and some of the mutineers make it to trial.

Why it's here: Well, certainly not for historical reasons. The only *Mutiny* that's reasonably close to the facts as they're known is the 1984 Anthony Hopkins/Mel Gibson version, and that was a box office flop, if a fairly good movie. The 1935 version, by contrast, is a rousingly entertaining best picture winner that's politically incorrect and about as close to fiction as you can get.

The real William Bligh was reportedly a not unpleasant chap and actually may have been one of the more enlightened captains in the Royal Navy. All of which is nothing next to Charles Laughton's portrayal of him as a brilliant thug—one of those schoolyard bullies who have mysteriously been given the power of life and death over other children.

Kids are fascinated with Bligh because he's a grotesque, and a charismatic one. The girls and I were channel surfing one afternoon, and when we came upon *Mutiny*, all activity screeched to a halt. The allure wasn't Gable—he's minus his mustache here (they couldn't wear them in the Royal Navy) and minus his shirt most of the time. It wasn't Franchot Tone, who's actually quite excellent in the concocted role of the film's upper-class moral conscience, and it certainly wasn't the white actors in Tahitian blackface or the passive, personality-impaired Tahitian women the mutineers elope with.

No, it's all about Laughton here: Just the way he bites off the words "*Mis*-tah Christian" gives you the willies. The depiction of life at sea is pretty tough for a Hollywood film and may even put it off-limits for the squeamish: Eliza says she's glad she saw *Mutiny*, but that keelhauling scene was just too much. So save it, perhaps, for the kids who are into pirates and blood-and-thunder. And have a nice little talk over your grog and biscuits that night: Was Christian right to mutiny? Would he have been right if Bligh wasn't as bad, as was the case in real life? Where's the line between duty and morality—between what you've been told to do and what you *should* do?

All interesting subjects for debate. One thing, though: If you're the kind of parent who likes to lay down the law, maybe you should watch your back.

Pause-button explanations: See above. Telling the kids the events really occurred (although not in quite this way) is an effective hook.

Useless trivia: All three leads were nominated for best actor—the only time it has happened in Oscar history. (Not surprisingly, they canceled each other out; Victor McLaglen won for *The Informer.*)

What next: Derring-do on the high seas: *Captain Blood* (1935) and *The Sea Hawk* (1940) are excellent Errol Flynn vehicles, and *The Crimson Pirate* (1952) features Burt Lancaster at his most youthfully athletic. There are two good *Treasure Island*s: a 1934 version starring Jackie Cooper and Wallace Beery, and a 1950 Disney production with the incomparable Robert Newton as Long John Silver. For more Laughton, look for *The Hunchback of Notre Dame* (1939), *Ruggles of Red Gap* (1935), or *The Canterville Ghost* (1944), and—only if your kids are older and can handle scary movies—*The Night of the Hunter* (1955), which Laughton directed but doesn't appear in.

NATIONAL VELVET (COLOR, 1944)

Directed by: Clarence Brown

Starring: Elizabeth Taylor, Mickey Rooney, Anne Revere, Donald Crisp

Ages: 6 and up

The sell: A girl and her horse, and the rest of the world disappears.

The plot: Velvet Brown (Taylor) lives in the English countryside, the youngest child of a large and boisterous family. She wins a horse named Pie in a local lottery and comes to realize the animal has the potential to be a great racer. With the help of a footloose young trainer (Rooney) and ultimately the blessing of her parents (Crisp and Revere), Velvet enters the unheralded steed in England's biggest race, the National.

Why it's here: Because it's a horse movie, silly. But also because it's a gorgeous Technicolor paean to Hollywood England and Elizabeth Taylor's eyes, and a warm, vivid family film about family. Neither of my girls is a horse freak—is this a selective gene, like boys with dinosaurs?—but they responded to *National Velvet* because the milieu is so specific and familiar and inviting. In particular, Crisp and Revere as the parents are more three-dimensional than in modern Hollywood family movies. Revere won a best supporting actress Oscar here, and you understand why; her Mrs. Brown breathes both sorrow and wisdom and deals the latter out sparingly, like jam on Sundays. The women I know who love this movie are fascinated either by the horse or by Revere; my mother was one of the latter, in no small part because her own mother had no interest in measuring up.

Not that Taylor's a slouch. Among many other things, *National Velvet* is a story about individuation—about carving your own identity in the endless sibling rumpus. Velvet is lost in the Brown throng until she comes upon Pie, at which point Taylor starts vibrating with an intensity that's almost sexual (and would be, soon enough). Horse movies are always more about the owner than the horse, and Pie doesn't really have much of a personality, to be honest. It's Velvet's identification with him, and the fierce generosity with which she bestows it, that make the story worth telling. This is a movie about loving something hard enough for the rest of the world to see it too.

Useless trivia: Taylor got to keep the horse.

What next: The 1946 *Black Beauty* doesn't bear much resemblance to Anna Sewell's classic book but is worth catching nevertheless.

ON THE WATERFRONT (B&W, 1954)

Directed by: Elia Kazan

Starring: Marlon Brando, Eva Marie Saint, Rod Steiger, Karl Malden, Lee J. Cobb

Ages: 12 and up

The sell: To tattle or not to tattle?

The plot: Terry Malloy works on the docks of Hoboken, across the river from New York, and he isn't a bright guy. A former boxer—"I coulda been a contendah, Charley"—he runs small errands for his corrupt lawyer brother (Steiger) and powerful union boss Johnny Friendly (Cobb). Indirectly responsible for the murder of a witness at the hands of Friendly's goons, Terry finds himself falling for the dead man's sister (Saint) and urged by the local street-tough priest (Malden) to stand up and be a man.

Why it's here: A few reasons. It's a chance to see Brando at the absolute pinnacle of his powers—this was his first Oscar, one out of eight for the film—and he is transfixing. You feel as though you're watching a man articulating himself for the first time, astounded at the thoughts that come, and Brando makes each of Terry's baby steps toward dignity immediate and surprising. The celebrated glove scene is often cited as an example of the actor's seizing the moment; when Terry first meets Saint's Edie Doyle, he impulsively picks up her fallen glove and absentmindedly toys with it throughout their shy, halting conversation. Brando was winging it, but the bit keeps us in suspense, and Edie too (and presumably Saint as well).

The more interesting conversation to be had, if your children are older, is whether the movie lionizes the moral courage to stand up for what's right or defends ratting out your friends. Both screenwriter Budd Schulberg and director Elia Kazan had "named names" before the House Un-American Activities Committee during the McCarthy-era witch hunts—they identified acquaintances and coworkers as Communists—and *On the Waterfront* has been interpreted as an allegorical rationalization for squealing. Both men denied any intentional connection between their testimonies and their film, and Schulberg, in his nineties, continues to do so. In a way it's a moot point, since the two sides, deed and film, reflect upon each other so provocatively. Ask the kids what they think.

Oh, and Brando takes a hell of a beating at the end of this movie, and the black-and-white blood and Christian imagery flow forth with abandon. Not for the little ones, who doubtless wouldn't be interested in the first place.

Useless trivia: The characters are all based on real-life figures, and much of the script background came out of the Waterfront Commission hearings and Malcolm Johnson's Pulitzer-winning reporting on the same for the *New York Sun* in the late 1940s.

What next: *A Streetcar Named Desire* (1951) is too adult for young kids, but *The Wild One* (1953) is okay—not a very good movie, but iconic Brando nonetheless. *Viva Zapata!* (1952) is pretty terrific, with Kazan and Brando joining forces for a live-wire bio of the Mexican rebel leader.

THE PRIDE OF THE YANKEES [B&W, 1942]

Directed by: Sam Wood

Starring: Gary Cooper, Teresa Wright, Babe Ruth

Ages: 8 and up

The sell: Heroes can be fragile.

The plot: A biopic of the life of Lou Gehrig, Hall of Fame first baseman for the Yankees in their 1920s and 30s' heyday. We see young Lou grow from his Bronx tenement beginnings into a young man (Cooper) playing for Columbia and eventually quitting college against his immigrant mother's wishes. He becomes part of the famed "Murderer's Row" of Yankee sluggers and befriends players like the legendary Babe Ruth (played by himself), eventually building a record of 2,130 consecutive games that would stand until the 1990s. Happiness comes with marriage to Eleanor Twitchell (Wright); tragedy arrives with his physical degeneration from ALS—amyotrophic lateral sclerosis, now known as Lou Gehrig's disease. In a moving day of honor at Yankee Stadium, the Iron Horse bids the world farewell and calls himself "the luckiest man on earth."

Why it's here: I'm getting weepy just typing that last sentence. Watched it with the girls last night and, strangely, they were less choked up than I was. Eliza, usually a pushover, commented with surprise on how she *didn't* cry for once; Natalie sat there in her softball uniform—she had just come from a game; two hits, one run, one RBI, thanks for asking—and asked why sad movies about real people, like this and *Lust for Life*, always end with a flourish of mournful-yet-triumphant music. Gotta send the audience home with something to hold on to, I said, despite all evidence to the contrary.

Their fascination with this movie—and they had been clamoring to see it—was that it presented them with firsthand evidence of the mythical world of Old Baseball. I should probably explain that we're a house divided: Boston-born and raised, I have rooted for the Red Sox through endless existential toil and unexpected payoff. In this, Natalie is my mostly companion. My wife Lori is a Long Islander, the daughter of New Yorkers, and she's a Yankees woman all the way. Eliza, forcibly relocated from Brooklyn to Boston at age seven, holds tight to the Bronx Bombers like a frayed blanket from childhood.

In my two decades in New York, however, I never had any problems with the Yanks. Don't get me started on the Mets, but Steinbrenner's boys were fine by me unless the Sox were in town. They had the history and they had the legends, and by honoring two of them, *The Pride of the Yankees* honors the entire run by extension.

And there is, quite simply, Babe Ruth playing Babe Ruth. Natalie had just finished reading a book about the Bambino—a kid's book, but good enough that the rest of us kept picking it up whenever she was out of the room—and as far as she was concerned, it was as if someone had coaxed George Washington out of the grave and onto the screen. This isn't just a cameo, either; Ruth has a fair number of scenes, including a very funny one in which Gehrig is tricked into eating Babe's hat. Ruth had been retired from the player's life for seven years when the film was shot, and you can feel his joy at being back in a uniform. He's a big old bear—the real deal, with the stink of the locker room on him instead of the sheen of Hollywood pomade.

Cooper as Gehrig is just as stoic and decent as the man himself was said to be, and Wright is more mischievous than you'd expect as his wife. The film spends a good amount of time on their relationship, too much so for Eliza and Natalie, who drifted a bit during the domestic scenes and snapped to attention the moment Yankee Stadium came back into view. Whether or not Gehrig was a saint, that's how Coop plays him, and the movie's happy to enforce the cliché. Perhaps my children didn't weep because they understood going in that this man was doomed—that his legend is inextricable from a death that was early and wrong. The entire purpose of *Pride*, released as it was almost a year to the day after Gehrig's death, is to eulogize. But it was the signs of life my daughters came away with.

Pause-button explanations: You'll probably have to explain what's medically wrong with Gehrig, since the movie is extremely coy about it (presumably audiences in 1942 didn't need a recap). Per the ALS Association Web site (www.alsa.org), it's "a progressive neurodegenerative disease that affects nerve cells in the brain and the spinal cord." Cinematically translated, this means Cooper stares at his hands a lot with a puzzled expression and, in one quietly awful scene, topples over in the locker room while his fellow Yanks look on, not wanting to shame him by helping him up.

Useless trivia: Gehrig was a lefty; Cooper was a righty and by all accounts a lousy baseball player. The filmmakers solved the problem by reversing everything—including the lettering and numbers on the uniform—having Coop bat right, then flipping the film over in the editing room.

What next: See *Fear Strikes Out* below. If they're older and can handle more doomed athletes, *Brian's Song* (1971) or *Bang the Drum Slowly* (1973) should make their macho cup runneth over.

QUEEN CHRISTINA (B&W, 1933)

Directed by: Rouben Mamoulian

Starring: Greta Garbo, John Gilbert

Ages: 10 and up

The sell: How much would you give up for love? A throne?

The plot: The seventeenth century: Young Christina is crowned Queen of Sweden upon the death of her father on the battle-field. She grows up a wise, beloved, and benevolent ruler who slowly becomes disenchanted with the imprisonment of royalty and yearns to live as a normal woman (since she's Garbo, this is a tragic impossibility, obviously). While traveling disguised as a man, Christina meets the Spanish ambassador Don Antonio Pimentel de Pradol (Gilbert), and the two embark on a love affair after a snowbound evening in an inn. The country is roiled by the news of her desire to marry a Catholic Spaniard, and Don Antonio is challenged to a duel. He dies, upon which Christina abdicates and sails off to an unknown future.

Why it's here: There are people who live closer to the wellsprings of unhappiness than the rest of us. They sense things, or they have seen things, and they know better than to talk about them.

Greta Garbo is their elected representative to the cinema. Everyone knows and imitates her signal phrase—"I vant to be alone"—because to do so is to turn her unyielding doubt into a joke, to shave the edge off it and make it bearable. But still we're drawn to her the way we are to a dark room.

In childhood, if we're very unlucky, we have a person like this in the house: a depressed parent, an impossible-to-please older sibling, an uncle given to black fits. But to know someone like this outside the family circle yet within arm's reach is less hurtful. It teaches sympathy and knowledge of struggle, and it helps us build a framework for our own disenchantments, when they come, which they do.

The fall after my father died, when I had just turned ten, a family friend took it upon himself to become my makeshift dad. He would stop over after school and ask if I wanted to throw the old ball around, and there was always relief on both parts when I'd say no. Instead we'd read comic books together—Carl Barks's fiendishly detailed Donald Duck adventures—and talk about this or that, and then he'd have drinks with my mother, three of his to one of hers. He'd take her out to dinner occasionally, too, and then come sit on my bedside afterward and solemnly ask me about my day. There wasn't any intimation of romance between them (he wasn't offering, she wasn't asking), and I certainly felt safe with the man, yet he leaked a sort of constant silent sadness about his own home life, and when his wife left him for the next-door neighbor a few years later, it wasn't at all surprising. More like the rent coming due.

He was the first drunk I knew—rather, my first awareness of a real, human alcoholic instead of a hiccuping movie cliché. Some of those bedside visitations were a suspense of bleared words, increasingly off-topic conversations about his own misfortunes, and occasional tears. At other times he would just sit there with the glooms while I nattered. Once in a while we would both be quiet; either nothing to say or nothing that could be said, each of us honoring the other's unhappiness. After a while he stopped coming around; I'm not sure why.

I loved him for it, though—for his gentleness and good intentions, and also for his weakness, which was proof to me of something I hadn't even known I was looking for. He was the chink in the armor of adulthood, evidence the grown-ups were as screwed up as I felt, even though most of them acted otherwise as if their lives depended on it, which they did. Not him, not Bobby—he was a basket case. And he latched on to my innocence as surely as I used his haplessness. Our misery was symbiotic.

With Garbo, that relationship became a consensual mass affair between star and audience. Moviegoers flocked to her to watch everything go wrong and for Garbo to smile sadly as if she'd expected it all along.

And yet, in all her films, there's always one short window of bliss, unexpected and wondrous, before everything goes to hell, forever. For people like Bobby, I think, this window is childhood; for others, perhaps, a love affair. In *Queen Christina*, it's the few days at the snowbound country inn during which the disguised queen and the Spanish ambassador begin their romance, and its brevity is very much the point.

Garbo, of course, began as a sensation of the silent screen, and the sequence in which she moves about the cloistered room, touching objects in a kind of rapture, is allowed to play out noiselessly and at daring length. "I have been memorizing this room," she finally tells the bewildered Gilbert. "In the future, in my memory, I shall live a lot in this room." Already the remembrance is more precious than the actuality. So much of the beauty lies in its loss. This is the urge behind nostalgia, poetry, drinking, and the adoration of dead movie stars.

The final shot of the film. Christina has abdicated, her lover has died. She sails away from Sweden and stands at the bow of the ship, looking into the middle distance, not at her approaching future but at some invisible universe of sorrow and resignation. The shot seems to go on for an eternity; the face growing bigger until it fills the screen. Mamoulian, famously, told Garbo to think about nothing: "I want your face to be a blank sheet of paper. I want the writing to be done by every member of the audience."

Well, we always project ourselves onto people in movies, but usually their personas provide a handhold or two: Cary Grant's moral slyness, Bogart's sour humor, Kate Hepburn's certainty. In this moment—and pretty much this one moment in the totality of Hollywood cinema—we are invited to fill Garbo's face with only the darkest depths of our hearts. It's enough to make you shrink in fear, or, if you're the sunny sort, blink and press rewind.

Eliza burst into tears. She was watching the movie with my sister, who was visiting, and the two of them had to calm down with tea after the end credits. Again, it wasn't the loss of love that undid my daughter. To tell the truth, she found Gilbert mannered in a way that barely had currency in 1933 and certainly has none seventy years later. It was, I think, the emptiness in Garbo's eyes as they reflected the void, and, behind that emptiness, a serenity completely without reassurance.

For myself, when I saw the film at age fifteen, in a now long-gone revival house in downtown Boston, I recognized in her face something of Bobby, wobbling in profile on the edge of my bed five years earlier. What does an intimate acquaintance with disaster look like? All I know is that Garbo made a career out of it, and he made a life.

Useless trivia: There was a real Queen Christina and she did *possibly* have an affair with the Spanish ambassador, but most of the film is Hollywood hokum rather than history. She abdicated over her conversion to Catholicism, not for love.

What next: Lighten the kids up with Garbo's only comedy, *Ninotchka* (1939), or, if they really want more tragedy, hit 'em with *Camille* (1936) and *Anna Karenina* (1935). Get ready to explain about courtesans and adultery, though, and prepare for consumptive cries of "Armand . . ." throughout the house.

THE RED SHOES (COLOR, 1948)

Directed by: Michael Powell and Emeric Pressburger

Starring: Moira Shearer, Anton Walbrook, Marius Goring

Ages: 10 and up

The sell: Do you want to be a dancer? Or do you want to have a life?

The plot: Boris Lermontov (Walbrook) rules the Lermontov Ballet in Paris like a brilliant dictator. He discovers Vicki Page (Shearer), a wealthy girl with the soul of an artist, and grooms her for stardom in a ballet of the Hans Christian Andersen fairy tale "The Red Shoes." Upon achieving fame, Vicki falls in love with the company's young composer (Goring), but Lermontov treats this as a betrayal of both him and of art. Torn between love and her need to dance, Vicki takes the hard way out.

Why it's here: *The Red Shoes* is a movie for those special children who are gifted natural performers and whose intensity and immersion in their chosen medium borders on the creepy. It's a celebration and it is a warning, both in allegorical terms and as practical, nuts-and-bolts news you can use.

The Hans Christian Andersen fairy tale "The Red Shoes" is about a young girl who puts on a pair of magic dancing slippers that cause her to dance forever, or until her clothes turn to rags and she dies. Britain's Michael Powell sets his ballet version within a larger story about a dance troupe and the young star who rises to fame under the tutelage of a stern master. It's realistic but it has the undertow of a Freudian daydream. The choices facing Vicki Page are as stark and as heartless as those in the fairy tale—dance or die, and you can forget about love. Fantasy constantly bleeds into the film's reality, especially in the long "Red Shoes" ballet, which is ostensibly staged for a paying audience but whose special effects mark it as the most extreme of movie dance numbers. Powell doesn't care. This is where obsession takes you. This is where *art* takes you.

But art is also planning and funding and other people, and one of the reasons I love *The Red Shoes* as a parent is that it doesn't pretend this stuff just happens. For any child dreaming of stardom—which in our culture is all of them—Powell and his company say: Yes, but it takes *work*. *The Red Shoes* is inside baseball, and for certain women who may or may not grow up to be dancers, it is transformative. Watch your daughters as they watch this movie.

Home video notes: Look for the Criterion Collection DVD, with its lush color restoration.

What next: Ballet videos, perhaps, or more Michael Powell: See chapter 9.

ROMAN HOLIDAY (B&W, 1953)

Directed by: William Wyler

Starring: Audrey Hepburn, Gregory Peck

Ages: 8 and up

The sell: The original Princess Diaries

The plot: Princess Ann (Hepburn) is a young royal visiting Rome whose life is a tightly scripted series of events and appearances. One day she impulsively blows it off—disappears out into the streets to live the way the normal people do. Disguising herself as a tourist, she falls in with Joe Brady (Peck), an impoverished reporter who can't believe the scoop that has landed in his lap. As he escorts the princess around the glories of Rome, he finds himself feeling both protective (he's Gregory Peck, after all) and smitten (she's Audrey Hepburn, after all). Which will carry the day—duty or love?

Why it's here: Princesses come cheap if you're a little girl in our culture. They're everywhere you turn: the Disney royal line of Ariel, Cinderella, Jasmine, Sleeping Beauty, Pocahontas, Snow White; the Anne Hathaway heroines of *The Princess Diaries* and *Ella Enchanted*; teen queens like Hilary Duff in modern dress; fallen parodies like Paris Hilton; faithful film versions of Frances Hodgson Burnett, princess dolls, princess books, princess costumes—all dedicated to the proposition that our wonderful daughters are princesses as well, the stars of their lives and heirs to all the charmed things that will happen to them. There are more royal houses in a single American elementary school than in all of pre–World War I Europe.

But. There are princesses and there are princesses. Some are born to it by bloodline, others by entitlement, and still others by grace. Audrey Hepburn is of the latter—the cinema's very own young and ardent royal.

True, Greg Peck is about as believable a cynical reporter as I am a lobsterman, and you can mourn Cary Grant's refusal to take the role eight ways to Sunday (he didn't want to be upstaged by the new girl). Grant might have put the film into the pantheon, but it has to be said that as a chaperone for Hepburn's coming-out party, Peck may be just right: He's gentle, admitting to his own enchantment at the same pace we are. He's the slightest bit dull so that she might glimmer that much brighter.

The film parses themes of duty and rebelliousness in a manner any young kid can understand; maybe their parents, too, if they can remember back to when they were taking orders instead of giving them. But it does so in a nonthreatening way: Audrey Hepburn is not about to go wear black and read Kerouac—that will come in *Funny Face*—let alone throw on a belly shirt, get a tattoo, and score some Oxycontin. Rather, she finds pleasure in simply walking down the *strada* without having to be anywhere at all, the same way kids unbend into any day they're not being hustled from one activity to the next. In fact, Princess Ann is very like a modern American child of privilege: She's the center of activity, yet she's powerless to move in any meaningful way.

My daughters recognized the rightness of the ending, in which the princess returns to her post, broadened and empowered by her adventures, but they mourned it too—mourned the loss of the independence they felt both Ann and they deserved. It would, and will, be coming.

Home video notes: Look for the 2004 Special Edition disc from Paramount: a restored print and decent extras.

What next: Dig out more Audrey. *Funny Face* (1957), with Fred Astaire, is tremendous, and *Sabrina* (1954) is fine too. *My Fair Lady* (1964) is very entertaining for a warhorse. When they're older, hit 'em with the fake Hitchcockisms of *Charade* (1963)— in which Hepburn finally got to play opposite Cary Grant—and the heartbreaking *Breakfast at Tiffany's* (1961).

SHANGHAI EXPRESS [B&W, 1932]

Directed by: Josef von Sternberg

Starring: Marlene Dietrich, Anna May Wong, Clive Brook, Warner Oland

Ages: 13 and up

The sell: No one believes you're good when they're sure you're bad.

The plot: A train leaves Peking for Shanghai, crossing a China torn by civil war. On board are a snooty missionary, an American roughneck, a British army doctor (Brook), a mysterious

Chinese businessman (Oland), and two women of ill repute, Hui Fei (Wong) and Shanghai Lily (Dietrich). Lily knew the doctor from before the days when she was a notorious "coaster," and when the war intrudes and he is taken hostage, she sacrifices what's left of her reputation to save him.

Why it's here: Marlene Dietrich movies—particularly the seven she made with her discoverer and greatest director, Josef von Sternberg—are rich, rich cake, and not really recommended to the average kid. I tried *Blonde Venus* on the girls one rainy afternoon, and even with a young Cary Grant in the cast and Dietrich singing "Hot Voodoo" in a gorilla suit, they came away more bummed out than anything. But that movie ends in a prolonged child custody battle—not much fun there—while *Shanghai Express* is an example of a particularly exotic Hollywood genre, the international train movie. Von Sternberg was also one of the great visualists of early Hollywood, and his movies are a pleasure to watch, with much of the drama seeming to take place on the surface of the baroque images.

Anyway, if the men here are stiffs, Dietrich seems so alive and so dazed with the wondrous absurdity of living that she burns through the plot conventions. *Express* is longer on atmosphere and style than on plot, but there are older kids who do nothing *but* seek a style to match their doubt, and this movie really deserves to go on their inner compost heap. "Every train carries its cargo of sin," says one character here, and ain't that the truth, baby.

Home video notes: Not on DVD as of this writing, but look for VHS copies.

Pause-button explanations: China, civil war, European colonialism—you might want to do a little homework beforehand.

What next: The other films in the Dietrich/von Sternberg collaboration, especially *The Scarlet Empress* (1934), with the star playing Catherine the Great. If you have younger kids, try the comic Western *Destry Rides Again* (1939) on them.

SPLENDOR IN THE GRASS (COLOR, 1961)

Directed by: Elia Kazan

Starring: Natalie Wood, Warren Beatty, Pat Hingle

Ages: 14 and up

The sell: "Don't they realize I'm me?"

The plot: 1928 Kansas: The oil boom has turned wildcatters into millionaires, and Mom and Pop are making a killing on the stock market. Wilma Dean "Deanie" Loomis (Wood) and high school football star Bud Stamper (Beatty, in his first role) are insanely in love and teetering on the precipice of going all the way. "Is it so terrible to have those feelings about a boy?" Deanie asks her mother (Audrey Christie). "No nice girl does," comes the prim reply. So what does that make Deanie? A basket case after Bud dumps her on the urging of his boorish new-money father (Hingle), who tells the boy, "There's nothing I wouldn't do for you son, if you do right." Deanie has a nervous break-down and comes out of the mental hospital to find the stock market crashed, the Stampers ruined, and Bud married to a sweet-natured immigrant's daughter (Zohra Lampert). How odd that Deanie's now the strongest person she knows.

Why it's here: I haven't shown this to Eliza and Natalie yet; at nine and eleven, there'd just be too many questions and anxieties. Anyway, when they're old enough, they probably won't want to watch it with me—maybe with their mom, or by themselves late at night, with a big bowl of ice cream and a box of Kleenex.

Splendor in the Grass is ostensibly about teenage love, teenage sex, and the societal and parental hypocrisies surrounding both of those things. Really, it's about how adolescence can be a period of almost unimaginably vibrant cruelty; how you can feel more alive than you ever have while simultaneously wishing you were dead.

Here's the female *Rebel Without a Cause*, in other words, and, as such, rather more dangerous. And Natalie Wood owns it. Elia Kazan directed *Splendor*, and he creates an intensely sympathetic hothouse atmosphere—the very first thing we see is two teenagers making out with reckless abandon while the world appears to swoon in the background—but Wood's Deanie is simply alive and falling apart before our eyes in a way anyone buffeted by youth recognizes.

Poor Warren Beatty: It's his first movie and he's playing a stick, the big man on campus who can't get a word in with his blowhard father (Hingle, turning in a rowdy and intentionally overacted performance as a Throbbing-Vein Dad). Bud's every high school hero who hits the wall after graduation. Deanie is just every girl whose internal operating system is crashing from conflicting data. The scene where she rises up out of the bathtub and shrieks at Christie, "I'm a *good* girl, Mama!" over and over with a terrifying smile on her face is enough to batter a viewer into tears. But, really, the whole movie sobs.

Pause-button explanations: You'll have to establish the historical context: the Roaring '20s leading to the precipice of the stock-market crash and the Great Depression. The parallels to any go-go economic era or bear-market slump we're passing through will be readily apparent even to teenagers.

What next: *Rebel Without a Cause* (1955), *West Side Story* (1961), *Love with the Proper Stranger* (1963)—all good Woods. *A Summer Place* (1959) is a hugely popular but much soapier treatment of similar themes.

SUNSET BLVD. (B&W, 1950)

Directed by: Billy Wilder

Starring: Gloria Swanson, William Holden, Erich von Stroheim

Ages: 12 and up

The sell: Stardom is madness.

The plot: Joe Gillis (Holden), a failed screenwriter with creditors on his tail, ducks into the Beverly Hills driveway of Norma Desmond (Swanson), onetime megastar of the silent screen and still rich enough to hire her former director/husband (von Stroheim) as a butler while living in opulent delusion. Between having Buster Keaton over for cards and burying her pet chimp in the backyard, Norma entertains fantasies of a comeback written by Joe. She's ready for her close-up, Mr. DeMille.

Why it's here: Because it's the cruelly empathetic freak-show flip side of *Singin' in the Rain*. That movie said that with pluck and kindheartedness, your career can survive even the talkie revolution. But it can't survive age. Not then, not now.

In *Sunset Blvd.*, Billy Wilder dared to admit that the film industry puts its elders out on the ice the moment the crowds look away. There are countless Norma Desmonds in L.A. and in the rest of our media culture, names that are ten or twenty or thirty years old and tarnished from disuse. These people are not ancient—Norma is as old as the actress playing her, which was a mere fifty-three—but, like retired baseball players, they're embarrassing reminders that suppleness does not last. Some of them may be ecstatic to finally be ignored. Others seethe.

Sunset Blvd. can take an innocent's breath away: It opens with the narrator's body being dredged from an algae-clogged swimming pool and then it dives into the muck. In flashback, the dead Joe Gillis tells of getting pulled into a rococo dementia peopled by fellow has-beens like Keaton and von Stroheim and Anna Q. Nilsson. And there's the chimp burial by night, the kind of thing that might roil Michael Jackson's nightmares. Norma treats it as her latest production: "I'd like a white coffin, and I'd like it specially lined with satin. White. Or maybe pink . . . or red! Let's make it gay!"

Wilder was savaged for bringing the subject up, of course. Old-guard Hollywood reacted to *Sunset* like a fart in a cathedral, and the best picture Oscar that year went to *All about Eve*, a movie whose show-business cynicism is much more conciliatory. *Sunset* is still shocking to anyone who accepts the wholesome traditions of classic movies even as they distrust them for being too shallow for the twenty-first century.

The audience I'm talking about is children, especially that rare breed that has already committed to old movies. This film is exactly as jaded as they've never dared to admit to themselves, and it offers a kind of freedom. *Sunset Blvd.* is for true believers at the exact moment they're ready to lose their faith.

Home video notes: Look for Paramount's 2004 Collector's Edition DVD, with extras that fill in the backstory and point out a lot of rich Hollywood trivia.

Useless trivia: The part of Norma Desmond was offered to Mae West, Mary Pickford, and Pola Negri before Swanson accepted it. Von Stroheim, Norma's butler/ex-husband/ex-director, really was a great silent film director who directed Swanson in *Queen Kelly*, the film that is screened one evening in Norma's mansion. The cardplaying "waxworks" are Buster Keaton, Anna Q. Nilsson, and H. B. Warner, all major stars of silent cinema and largely forgotten at the time of the film's release.

What next: It's hard to recommend other movies after *Sunset Blvd.* This is kind of the end of the line.

THE TEN COMMANDMENTS (COLOR, 1956)

Directed by: Cecil B. DeMille

Starring: Charlton Heston, Yul Brynner, Anne Baxter, Edward G. Robinson

Ages: 6 and up

The sell: The Old Testament's ready for its close-up, Mr. DeMille.

The plot: The story of Moses (Heston), from bobbing in the bulrushes to burning bushes, ten plagues, exodus, the Golden Calf, and beyond.

Why it's here: Maybe your kids have seen *The Prince of Egypt* and are ready for the ripsnorting three-hour-and-forty-minute high-calorie version. Or maybe they've been covering some of this in Sunday school, of whatever persuasion, and they want to see what the parting of the Red Sea looks like. Or maybe they're little Charlton Heston fanatics. Whatever, this movie is a great weekend Bible-story special: Divide it up into a two-day affair or wait for a rainy Saturday and hunker down with a tub of popcorn the size of the Sinai.

No one's going to say *The Ten Commandments* is great art—no one accused DeMille of art in his entire life. His rep was as Hollywood's master showman, from 1914's *The Squaw Man* to this, his final blowout (he was dead at seventy-seven two years later). No, this is the Classics Illustrated version of Exodus, with fourteen thousand extras—seriously—and Oscar-winning special effects that look like something a modern kid could do on a Mac.

Anyway, who wants a subtle *Ten Commandments*? The performances here are two-dimensional and bigger than life, with a great, goofy roster of Hollywood stars coloring outside the lines of their parts: Yul Brynner as a butch and gleaming Rameses, Anne Baxter purring through what was for her a production of

All about Nefretiri, Edward G. Robinson—*nyahh, see?*—selling out his own people as the fish-faced Dathan.

Heston? He's magnificently humorless, and he gives a performance of no nuance whatsoever, precisely what's required. He doesn't provide Moses with depth, but he brings him fully to life, and that's why *The Ten Commandments* is a fine epic for children of all ages, leagues better than *Prince of Egypt* but not particularly *greater.* If it's deeper Bible reading you're seeking, you should probably find a good rabbi.

Home video notes: The 50th Anniversary Collection DVD from Paramount includes DeMille's 1923 silent version of *The Ten Commandments* in addition to the 1956 remake. Makes for a very cool historical double bill if your tribe's up for it.

Pause-button explanations: You might go over the basics of the story if your kids are unfamiliar with it. Also, the plagues and the first Passover are fairly harrowing; look to the younger ones to make sure they're not flipping out.

Useless trivia: That's DeMille narrating and Heston providing the voice of God.

What next: Now's the time to break out the epics: *Ben-Hur* (1959) should be next, and older kids might be able to handle the intensity of *Spartacus* (1960).

TO KILL A MOCKINGBIRD (B&W, 1962)

Directed by: Robert Mulligan

Starring: Gregory Peck, Mary Badham, Robert Duvall

Ages: 9 and up

The sell: Father knows best.

The plot: The Depression in a small southern town. Scout (Badham) and Jem (Phillip Alford) are the two children of local lawyer Atticus Finch (Peck), who takes the unpopular case of a black man (Brock Peters) accused of rape. Atticus proves his client's innocence but isn't able to save him from the racist townspeople. Scout and Jem befriend oddball visiting kid Dill (John Megna) and worry about spooky unseen neighbor Boo Radley (Duvall), who appears when least expected and most necessary.

Why it's here: When we were little, you and I, *To Kill a Mockingbird* served as insistence that the world is a serious place—that to partake in it is a responsibility, a right, and a privilege. The plot imparts this message to its young characters just as the movie imparts it to young viewers, and watching it work on my daughters was something of a marvel. Eliza cried and cried when Atticus learns that Tom Robinson has been killed and Natalie sat there stunned, as if someone had dropped an anvil on her heart. The conversation we had afterward, about injustices and one's duty in addressing and fighting them, was the sort you always hope to have with your children but never seem to have time or an excuse for.

For obvious reasons, this is a sobering film for a father to watch with his kids. I'll never be as good as Atticus Finch, and neither will you. Gregory Peck probably felt the same way. The movie encourages a child to deify a parent while pointing out those less worthy—Boo's father or the horrible Mr. Ewell. Atticus is a god, perhaps (and no more so than when he shoots the rabid dog without his glasses), but he earns the distinction through diligence and thought and careful moral choice. *This* is the realization Scout and Jem come to during the course of the story, and that children watching the film arrive at as well: It's a choice. It's *your* choice.

Home video notes: Universal has put this out on DVD in a nice two-disc "Legacy Series" package, one of the few for which PR superlatives seem appropriate. The movie looks great; the extras are worth it.

Pause-button explanations: Oh, you'll have a *lot* to talk about with this one: racial injustice, crazy locked-up neighbors, rape trials. It plays very well with tweeners but isn't for small fry.

Useless trivia: The character of Dill was based on Harper Lee's childhood friend, writer Truman Capote.

What next: The following film.

12 ANGRY MEN (B&W, 1957)

Directed by: Sidney Lumet

Starring: Henry Fonda and eleven other guys

Ages: 7 and up

The sell: Stick to your guns.

The plot: Twelve jurors enter the jury room on a sweltering New York summer day. They have to decide whether a Puerto Rican teenager stabbed his father to death, and it looks like an open-and-shut case. Eleven of the men immediately rule the accused guilty. Juror no. 8 (Fonda) votes to acquit, and, over the ensuing hour and a half, convinces the others that the evidence just isn't there to convict.

Why it's here: This will be one of the very few times this book descends into pedagogy, because *12 Angry Men* isn't just a good movie, it's good *for* you. Or, rather, it's good for the children.

Don't be scared. It's just that there are so few movies that explain how the adult world—our adult world—works in such clear, easy-to-grok fashion. This movie is one of the very best civics lessons for small people out there, one that prompts thoughts and discussions about social responsibility that even a seven-year-old can grasp.

That's how old Eliza was when I was called for jury duty one spring. Some people resist the obligation, but I rather enjoy it, so I took the requisite days off from work, sat on a hard criminal courthouse bench, read a book, got called for a couple of voir dires, was summarily rejected from a couple of juries, got dismissed, and went home. "What did you do today, Daddy?" my daughter wanted to know. I explained as best I could—selection of peers, presumption of innocence, judges, evidence. Eliza's eyes began to cross.

Then I noticed that, in one of those synchronicities that suggest the Lord is a revival-house film programmer, Turner Classics was showing *12 Angry Men*. Starting in twenty minutes. So we cleared the deck of homework and watched, and, how about that, the movie's a hit with the kid. She gets it, both the drama and the point of it, and afterward asks such probing questions about the U.S. judicial system that I have to send her to her mother the lawyer for answers. But she *gets* it. I, in my fumbling daddy way, didn't do that. Henry Fonda did. And that's fine; he can leave the daddying to me (and from what Peter and Jane have said, that's just as well), and I'll leave the personification of all that is noble and true in our democracy to him and Jimmy Stewart.

The film isn't a nuanced work of art. It relies on rather too broadly drawn human types, and its insistence that justice will prevail if gentle, white, educated progressives lead the way is the proper shade of late-'50s naïveté. But all that's exactly what makes the movie great American agitprop and a wonderful experience for kids. As directed by Sidney Lumet, fresh from the earnest fields of early TV, *12 Angry Men* is a gimmick film: twelve men, one court case, one room, real time. And it's the gimmick that sucks young viewers in—that and the bare-bones demonstration of group dynamics. Once you get the setup, everything else is character: All other things being equal, personality decrees whether a juror is able to think his way past his own received wisdom or just hide behind it.

This makes sense to a child. My daughters come back from school with daily tales of who has played fair and who hasn't, of little moral dilemmas that offer countless responses. Every day is a multiple-choice test, for us as for them, but for them each choice is wholly new. *Men* not only validates their perception that this is so, it flatters them into believing that with care, thought, selflessness, and diligence they can make a difference. And if they don't believe *that,* they certainly aren't going to act accordingly. I'm not saying this movie can make you a better American citizen—although I'm open to the argument—but I am saying it can make you a more thoughtful human.

Okay. End of lecture. Onward.

Useless trivia: There's a 1997 made-for-cable version that integrates the jury, as it should (sorry, the title precludes any women, although there is a lady judge), with an aging Jack Lemmon as juror no. 8. It's not bad, but Fonda's the guy you want to sequester.

What next: Other good Hollywood civics lessons include *The Grapes of Wrath*, *The Ox-Bow Incident* (1943), and, of course, *To Kill a Mockingbird.*

MELODRAMA

Here's a secret: Some of the very best movies Hollywood ever turned out—paragons of craft, wit, and ripely throbbing feeling—were the melodramas. By which I'm referring to the women's weepies, those soapy tales of domestic torment that never got any respect except from their unsophisticated target audiences and from film academics who love to semiotically deconstruct Joan Crawford's male gaze (no, that's not a paradox; the woman had balls of steel, on film as in life).

Melodramas get right to the heart of the matter: love, death, family, betrayal. Their narratives are as blunt as a shovel but their visual style can go beyond baroque—the camera swoons down stairwells, the music sobs a threnody for lost love or the perfidy of children, entire decades pass in an orgasmic rush of dissolves. These movies were made expressly to speak to the inarticulate hearts of American women, and they are bursting with emotions let loose in the dark.

No wonder men hated them. More precisely, middle-brow guardians of culture have always sneered at "women's films" (in exactly the way today's reviewers and intellectuals sneer at "chick flicks," many of which have the same concerns and occasionally the skill of their golden age forebears). Much of art is about sublimating emotions, forcing them to behave according to the rules of various media: the paint on the canvas, the notes on the page, the steps of the dance, all those lovely, lovely words. Movie melodramas crank emotions as high as opera but without the face-saving graces of fat ladies and arias. Emotion *is* their medium. If you're not comfortable with that, it can seem vulgar, shameless, uncomfortable—*embarrassing*. Yet who says all art—or even meaningful entertainment—has to be pitched in the key of subtlety?

Children get embarrassed by emotions, too, but there's something about the grand gestures of melodrama that prompts respect. It may be that these films play as slightly more realistic fairy tales, with all the blood and thunder the Grimms put in and that our culture has gradually bleached out. At the very least, kids seem to be able to tell the honest heart-tuggers from the arrant corn, and they appreciate a film whose catastrophes and decisions mirror their own. A movie like *Bringing Up Baby* may tickle them silly, but it was *Now, Voyager*, with Bette Davis as the unloved daughter who becomes beautiful and (better) serenely wise, that had Eliza turn from the screen as the end credits rolled to inform me, "That (*sob*) was the best (*sob*) movie I've ever (*sob*) seen."

Okay, well, right, we've got girls. More to the point, we've got girls the right age, because it's only a matter of time before the window of their uninhibited enjoyment slams shut and melodrama becomes yet another thing to be giggled at and scorned. Or maybe not: Any teenage girl who doesn't respond to the aching mother-daughter dynamics of *Imitation of Life* needs to have her iPod revoked. (As for boys, plenty of them may love these films, and—trust me on this—not all of them will turn out to be gay.) Melodrama deals with what's on the plate in front of us; it just piles on the spices and invites us to pig out.

IMITATION OF LIFE (COLOR, 1959)

Directed by: Douglas Sirk

Starring: Lana Turner, Juanita Moore, Susan Kohner, Sandra Dee

Ages: 12 and up

The sell: Oh, mother, you just don't understand.

The plot: A down-on-her-luck young mother (Turner) hoping to become an actress befriends and reluctantly hires as housekeeper a black woman (Moore) with a daughter of her own. The years pass, the actress becomes famous, the daughter grows up to be Sandra Dee and in love with Mom's boyfriend (John Gavin). The other daughter (Kohner) grows up to pass for white, causing untold heartache to her mother and, ultimately, herself.

Why it's here: Because it's an absolute *killer*—I have friends who speak of seeing this when they were young and crying for days afterward. I personally didn't get around to *Imitation* until I was in college and director Douglas Sirk was all the academic rage. The Technicolor melodramas he had fashioned in the 1950s, hugely popular and considered soap-opera trite at the time, were being reevaluated and found to support whichever trendy analytic theory the professor happened to favor.

Of course, we all laughed at the parts of the movie we considered hokey and dated—the depiction of race relations, the ease with which Moore's character becomes Turner's maid, Turner's acceptance (after a few mild protestations) of that relationship, the woodenness of John Gavin as the hunk Turner and Dee fight over. (Men are *always* interchangeable in melodrama.) We thought we were being smarter than the movie by laughing at it.

At a certain point, though, we started to notice we were only laughing at the parts Sirk wanted us to. Yes, the lopsided relationship between the two women *is* absurd, by yesterday's standards as well as today's. Turner's character is a twit, even if she's the nominal heroine of the movie, and the movie actually criticizes the materialism it appears to celebrate. Moore plays the motherly black martyr so well you begin to wonder if the character enjoys it too much—certainly it gives her smothered daughter nowhere to turn. The movie's so astute about mother-daughter dynamics that it may be painful for a mother and daughter to watch together.

And it's the daughters who put *Imitation of Life* over. Dee, in one of her better performances, transforms slowly from a miniature Lana into an almost-recognizable human being, while Kohner is so piercingly human as Sara Jane that she hijacks the movie, as Sirk intended. It's in this character's confusion, anger, love, and guilt that the director pulls out all the stops. He's so shameless he even brings out Mahalia Jackson—*the* Mahalia

Jackson—to sing at the climactic funeral and reduce you to a soggy pile of Kleenex. You won't have to tell your children who she is. They'll *know*.

Or to boil everything I've just written down to one quote from Sirk himself: "There is a very short distance between high art and trash, and trash that contains the element of craziness is by this very quality nearer to art." Parents spend tens of thousands of dollars in college tuition to knock that eminently sensible notion out of their children's heads.

Home video notes: It's available on Universal DVD both singly and in a two-pack with the earlier 1934 version starring Claudette Colbert and Louise Beavers.

Pause-button explanations: You'll probably have to stop and sketch in the racial landscape of the pre–civil rights era, but bear in mind that the movie intends a viewer to be outraged at some of the supposedly casual injustices.

What next: More Sirk: The two best to start with are 1955's *All That Heaven Allows* (Jane Wyman shocks suburbia by falling in love with her gardener; the recent *Far From Heaven* is an homage to it) and 1956's *Written on the Wind* (screwed-up rich kids Robert Stack and Dorothy Malone use and are used by Rock Hudson and Lauren Bacall).

MILDRED PIERCE (B&W, 1945)

Directed by: Michael Curtiz

Starring: Joan Crawford, Ann Blyth, Eve Arden

Ages: 10 and up

The sell: Oh, daughter, you just don't understand.

The plot: Who killed Monte Beragon? In flashback, we meet Mildred Pierce (Crawford), a suburban housewife who is left with two young daughters after she kicks her cheating husband out. She gets a job waiting on tables but the desire for a better life sends her into the homemade pie business, then into restaurant entrepreneurship. Mildred's younger daughter dies and her older daughter (Blyth) grows into a money-hungry conniver who lures Mom's shady new husband into an affair. The shady new husband ends up dead, but whodunnit?

Why it's here: Stranded fascinatingly between film noir and women's weepie, *Mildred Pierce* has a number of excellent uses around the home. It's a good child's-first-Joan Crawford movie, since the star won her Oscar for it and her blunt, shoulder-padded intensity has rarely been better showcased. It also introduces a youngster to the pleasures of Eve Arden, sarcastic best friend extraordinaire and the first edition of a type the movies still regularly turn to (Heather Matarazzo in *The Princess Diaries*? *So* Eve Arden).

And it has the magnificent Ann Blyth as Veda, Mildred's daughter, a pert little thing who so believes the world owes her for the bust-up of her parents' marriage that she's willing to fake a pregnancy, bribe a fiancé, dance the hoochie-koochie in a cheap nightclub, and *schtup* her own stepfather to get what she wants, especially if it involves raking her mother's poor heart over the coals.

Do you really want to watch this with your kids? Well, yeah, provided they're not total naïfs. For one thing, *Mildred*'s a '40s movie so it's comparatively discreet; the most upsetting scene from a young person's point of view may be the death of daughter Kay from pneumonia (while Mildred is off having a well-deserved weekend with Monte—the nerve of the woman). That's easy enough to cushion; as the movie started, I told Eliza and Natalie not to get too attached to the character, and as soon as Kay let out a cough in one scene, they knew the jig was up.

But it's a toss-up as to whose jaw will hit the floor first—yours or your spawn's—as the selfishness, the manipulativeness, the sheer ornery *meanness* of sweet-faced Veda becomes apparent. Let me simply quote from the daughter's climactic speech to the dazed mother who has done everything, oh, everything for her: "You think just because you made a little money you can get a new hairdo and some expensive clothes and turn yourself into a lady. But you can't, because you'll never be anything but a common *frump* whose father lived over a grocery store and whose mother took in washing!"

Jesus. That quote all by itself defines Crawford's career-long persona and appeal, but, really, this is a movie to demonstrate how much spite can be stored in the small, self-absorbed bones of a daughter and to scare a young viewer into contemplating the evil a pretty girl can do. You don't admire Veda for it, either. You hate the little bitch.

Think about the many movies and TV shows your kids see in which kids rule triumphant and parents are the boobs. Now think of this as a minor but particularly intense course correction. They can groove on the camp aspects of *Mildred Pierce* later in life—as with any Joan Crawford movie, they're there by the tractorload—but for now Veda is the best Worst Case Scenario a child may come across. "Dad?" Eliza asked as she brushed her teeth after seeing the film. "I'm not like Veda, am I?" No, daughter, of course you're not. But thanks for asking.

Useless trivia: Guess who was considered for the part of Veda at one point? *Shirley Temple.*

What next: Crawford's best would have to include the tremendous *Humoresque* (1946)—a soap opera of total conviction and gorgeously shot, too—and the bizarrely entertaining *Johnny Guitar*

(1954), a Freudian Technicolor Western where the women wear the pants. Save films like *Torch Song* (1953) and *Queen Bee* (1955) until your kids are jaded, kitsch-seeking missiles of adolescence (and after that show them *Mommie Dearest*). Director Curtiz, of course, made *Casablanca*. Other movies based on James M. Cain books include *Double Indemnity* (1944) and *The Postman Always Rings Twice* (1946), suitable for twisted teenagers and up.

NOW, VOYAGER (B&W, 1942)

Directed by: Irving Rapper

Starring: Bette Davis, Paul Henreid (Zzzzz . . .), Claude Rains

Ages: 8 and up

The sell: Ugly duckling grows up, gets even, gets real.

The plot: Poor Charlotte Vale (Davis) of the Boston Vales, cursed with low self-esteem, a domineering mother (Gladys Cooper), and unplucked eyebrows. After a nervous breakdown sends her into the care of kindly psychiatrist Dr. Jaquith (Rains), Charlotte gets a psychological and physical makeover and emerges a beauty who falls in love with Jerry Durrance (Henreid) during a cruise. He's stuck in an unhappy marriage, and so their love cannot be, but Charlotte befriends his young daughter (Janis Wilson), who's suffering from the same psychological demons that once crippled the older woman. Don't ask for the moon, Jerry, when we have the stars.

Why it's here: Another emotional powerhouse—see Eliza's reaction in the introduction above—*Now, Voyager* allows a young viewer to identify with Charlotte as she grows out of her fears and learns confidence and the necessity of putting her dragon of a mother in her place (too bad it *kills* the old biddy, but what would a women's weepie be without an extra spoonful of guilt sprinkled on top?).

Which is to say that there are several thesis papers in this movie but that a kid will swallow the thing whole and digest it over time, and that's fine. The real lesson of *Now, Voyager* may be the performance of Bette Davis, the star who was not beautiful and therefore had to act. It's an assured, smart, feeling portrayal, but mostly it's incredibly sympathetic to all the Charlottes out there.

Useless trivia: You might want to point out to your kids that the bit where Henreid lights two cigarettes at once and passes one to Davis was a cultural touchstone back in the days when smoking wasn't a crime. You might also call their attention to Max Steiner's Oscar-winning score, still regularly imitated/parodied in commercials and other movies.

What next: *All About Eve* (1950), *Dark Victory* (1939), and *Jezebel* (1938) are all best Bettes. Davis, Henreid, and Rains reunited for *Deception* (1946), a love triangle about classical musicians that is crazy good fun if not actually good.

STELLA DALLAS (B&W, 1937)

Directed by: King Vidor

Starring: Barbara Stanwyck, Anne Shirley

Ages: 9 and up

The sell: Mother, you're embarrassing me!

The plot: Stella (Stanwyck) is an ambitious small-town factory worker's daughter who woos and marries WASPy up-and-coming executive Stephen Dallas (John Boles). They have a daughter, Laurel, but Stella's hard-partying ways alienate her husband, and the couple divorces. Stella brings up Laurel (Shirley), gradually realizing the girl would have a better life with the aristocrats. She ends up happily watching her own daughter's marriage to a rich young man from outside the window, in the rain.

Why it's here: A couple of reasons. It's an interesting relic of a time when class in America mattered more than it currently does (and it still matters): Stella simply is unable to rise above her status of uneducated prole, and even if she successfully passes her daughter up the social ladder, she has to forswear motherhood forever in the process. Ouch. She's glad to do it, though—she willingly pretends she's a drunken hoyden shacking up with horndog Ed Munn (Alan Hale) so Laurel will be properly horrified and go live with the rich stiffs. That, the movie implies, is about the best Stella can do for her kid.

Times have changed, thank you, enough so that the 1990 remake with Bette Midler retained the ending and made no sense at all. (She has to stay out of her daughter's life forever? *Why?* Who *cares?*) No, the reasons to watch this with your kid are (a) Barbara Stanwyck and (b) a little object lesson that says: No matter how mortifying your parents get—and they'll get more mortifying than you could ever believe possible—they love you beyond all boundaries and properness and what's fair or even sensible.

I watched this with Eliza (you may have noticed that I haven't watched many of the weepies with Natalie yet, mostly because she's been a little too young, but also because they simply don't seem her cup of chocolate milk right now), and her reaction was funny to see. Stella put her right off for all the reasons the character was supposed to make 1937 audiences cluck their tongues. She's loud and brassy, avaricious, marrying for social maneuverability rather than love; Eliza couldn't believe this was the heroine of the movie. "She's so *awful*," she said at one point, which really meant "she's so *tacky*," a word and a concept that, at nine, she hadn't yet come to grips with.

The only difference between grown-up women in a 1937 movie theater and Eliza was that the women doubtless knew someone like Stella or maybe had been a little like Stella—had lived long enough to have a broad understanding of human types and sympathy for their follies. Children, in their conviction that grown-ups are always as good as they urge kids to be, are less forgiving, and so Eliza's mouth went as thin as a parson's as she watched Stanwyck strut her stuff.

As the plot developed, though, and my kid began to understand the film's dilemma—Stella might never be able to transcend her social status but her daughter could, *if* Stella disappeared from the picture—I could hear the gears in Eliza's head whine with the strain of pulling in two opposing directions. Can a mother who's an embarrassment also be a mother who's good? Can you be a better mother by not being there at all? Is a life of wealth and opportunity worth trading a parent for? Is class better than crass?

You and I know the answers—at least I think I do—but a child could do worse than consider the questions. When the famous final sequence came, with Stanwyck watching her daughter's wedding through the rain-streaked window, as remote as a magazine spread, Eliza didn't cry. Her wires were too crossed. She did say, "That was *sad*," with a heartfelt, preoccupied frown, as if she were in the middle of solving an extremely difficult math problem. And then she went and lay down for a while.

What next: If you want to take in the glorious breadth of Stanwyck, try *The Lady Eve*, the hilarious *Ball of Fire*, and *Meet John Doe*—1941 comedies by, respectively, Preston Sturges, Howard Hawks, and Frank Capra—or noirs *Double Indemnity* (1944) and

The Strange Love of Martha Ivers (1946). Also a neat little romantic comedy called *Remember the Night* (1940), if you can find it.

TO EACH HIS OWN (B&W, 1946)

Directed by: Mitchell Leisen

Starring: Olivia de Havilland, John Lund, Roland Culver

Ages: 9 and up

The sell: Would you give up your child?

The plot: Jody Norris (de Havilland) is an older American woman in London during World War II. During a night of blackout duty with a British lord named Desham (Culver), she tells her story: As a young girl in heartland USA, she fell in love with a dashing World War I pilot (Lund) and bore his child after he was killed in combat. Ashamed of having a child out of wedlock, she arranged for close friends to raise the boy, who grew up thinking of Jody as a family pal. After becoming estranged from the parents, she moved to New York and found business success; she's now in London, where it turns out her pilot son (Lund) is posted. Will Lord Desham bring mother and son together at last?

Why it's here: All right, the plot is dated. Unwed mothers aren't shunned as lepers anymore, and their kids aren't tormented unless they've been asking for it. Actually, the plot is absurd: What woman gives her child to her best friends and then queers that friendship by hanging around too much?

That said, *To Each His Own* does what all good movies do: It gets you to buy into its terms as you're watching it. And on those terms, this delicate little four-hanky job—de Havilland's first Oscar—is incredibly effective. The ending alone is almost guaranteed to melt the entire household into happy, fulsome tears. Unlike *Stella Dallas*, this movie isn't about sacrifice. It's about sacrifice at long last rewarded and recognized. For a kid, the final scene is like dessert.

That's all I'm going to say, other than that de Havilland somehow gets you to believe she's both the innocent seventeen-year-old of the early scenes and the caustic fifty-something survivor of the finale. Good luck finding this movie—it's only on video, not on DVD—but have a snurfling good time when you do.

Pause-button explanations: The plot starts with World War II, flashes back to World War I, and gradually works its way back to World War II. You'll have to work the kinks out of the time line for younger viewers. Also, be prepared to discuss the social mores, then and now, surrounding unwed motherhood.

What next: *To Each His Own* was directed by Mitchell Leisen, who was something of a second-tier Ernst Lubitsch at swanky Paramount, and who remains an underrated director whose comedies and romances are almost ridiculously enjoyable. Not many of them are on video; ones that are include *Easy Living* (with a script by Preston Sturges), *Midnight, Remember the Night, Hands Across the Table* (1935), and *The Lady Is Willing* (1942). And if you ever come across *Arise My Love* (1940), or *Hold Back the Dawn* (1941) playing on Turner Classic Movies, *pounce*, as the old *New York Times* TV listings used to say.

SILENT DRAMAS

Under the theory that it's hard enough to show a kid a black-and-white movie, a black-and-white movie without sound should be an even tougher sell. So why are silent movies among my daughters' and their friends' favorites? Chaplin, Keaton, and Lloyd make sense—they're funny—and *Metropolis* carries a weird allure of its own (see chapter 1), but how do you explain that we threw on the original 1925 *Phantom of the Opera* one night at a friend's house and our kids and theirs happily huddled around the tube as though it were a campfire (it isn't even much of a horror movie; like the Broadway musical, it's mostly a ripping melodrama).

Here's an idea: Everything else in the tinsel culture they're inheriting from us shouts at them. Silent movies don't. Silent movies insist we look; they don't *happen* unless we look. We forget that the first twenty-five years of movies were silent and that by the end of that period the industry and the medium had achieved a remarkable degree of sophistication. Look at the complicated camera shots and epic sets in late-1920s silents; there was a whole field of vision that had to be reset to zero once sound came in. We like to think that everything before talkies was infancy. In fact it was the movies' first life, cut short.

I've included only a few silent dramas below; you can find others in the chapter on fantasy and horror. There's time for *Greed* and *Potemkin* and *The Last Laugh* later, when a child's attention span has matured. If you do want to go deeper, though, look up the online catalogs of both Kino Video and Image Entertainment, who between them are bringing much of the silent era into the DVD age.

EDISON: THE INVENTION OF THE MOVIES (B&W, 1891–1918)

Directed by: W. K. L. Dickson, Edwin S. Porter, many others

Ages: 7 and up

The sell: The first movies. *Ever.*

Why it's here: This is a real coffee-table package: four DVDs in a slick casing, with 140 short films made by the Edison company, two hours of scholarly interviews, and over two hundred additional photos and documents from the Museum of Modern Art's archives. And I'm telling you, some kids can't get enough of it. Eliza and Natalie watched the very first images on disc one—split-second blurs that *might* be human beings if you squint right—with a profound awe that was comical to see, and when their friends came over, they made them watch it, too.

And why not? How often do you get to see the actual beginnings of something? It's like being in the room when Alexander Graham Bell called out for Watson or having a home video of the *Titanic* going down. Sure, there's the movie *Titanic*, but to see the real thing? That's *proof*. And when you're little, you take all the proof you can get.

The movies in this set are proof of many, many things. Men with handlebar mustaches, for one thing—lots of *them*. But also Annie Oakley, the real Annie Oakley, shooting cards out of some guy's hand in a too-brief snippet. The Sioux Indians of Buffalo Bill's Traveling Wild West Show, brought across the Hudson to Edison's studio to shuffle stone-faced through a Ghost Dance, four years after Wounded Knee. Celebrities like boxer Gentleman Jim Corbett, and forgotten gloriosities like Fatima the Muscle Dancer (whose belly-writhing was such that a censored version was made available; both are on the disc). There's even a few movies of Edison himself, an instance of the staff turning the cameras on the boss.

Eventually there's news footage and little scenes with a semblance of plot. There's even one eerie experimental sound film—an Edison employee playing violin while two other male staffers waltz around him—that feels like lightning imported from Mars. And by the end of the first disc, there's 1903's twelve-minute *The Great Train Robbery*, the first blockbuster narrative film. By today's standards, of course, it's hopelessly crude, but the girls were enraptured by it. The only one I had to keep skipping over was 1903's *Electrocuting an Elephant*, which is exactly what the title says and upsetting enough that *I* can't watch it, let alone let my daughters near it.

Home video notes: This is a joint production of Kino Video and MOMA. If you can find an adventurous video store in your neighborhood willing to rent it to you, you're in luck. As of this writing, it's available for online rental at Netflix. Or you can buy the set for around $100.

Useless trivia: Edison didn't direct any of the movies; in fact, he didn't concern himself very much with the movie unit at all. Inventing things and figuring out how to make money off them were his specialties.

What next: Kino's *The Movies Begin: A Treasury of Early Cinema, 1894–1913* is the next logical step, since it includes the work of such other pioneers as the Lumière brothers and George Méliès and leads the viewer up to D. W. Griffith.

ORPHANS OF THE STORM (B&W, 1921)

Directed by: D. W. Griffith

Starring: Lillian Gish, Dorothy Gish

Ages: 8 and up

The sell: It's you and your blind sister, your parents are gone, and the French Revolution just hit the fan. Now what?

The plot: The Girard sisters, Henriette and Louise (played by the Gish sisters, Lillian and Dorothy), come to Paris in hopes of finding a doctor to cure Louise's blindness. The two are separated, with Henriette lusted after and romanced by various members of the French aristocracy while Louise lives in the streets with cruel beggar woman Mother Frochard (Lucille LaVerne). Come the Revolution, the Bastille falls, Robespierre rises, and the sisters are still seeking each other. Will Louise find Henrietta before the guillotine does?

Why it's here: D. W. Griffith was the first important director in the history of movies, and the guy who hammered out much of the cinematic language—close-ups and such—that we still live with. That said, there are more important Griffith movies than *Orphans*, and if you were taking a college course, I'd recommend them. But you're watching a movie with your children, and *The Birth of a Nation* (1915) is crippled by its racism—*Broken Blossoms* (1919), too, to a lesser degree—and the epic *Intolerance* (1916) is like asking them to juggle all three pyramids plus the Sphinx. *Way Down East* (1920), while a fine second choice, is too easy for the unsympathetic or the restless to pigeonhole as cornball moralizing (it's that but quite a bit more as well).

Orphans, Griffith's French Revolution epic, is never held up as one of the great director's best films, but it *is* one of his most enjoyable—a sort of sideways fusing of *A Tale of Two Cities* with a silent-era women's picture. Which means you get the storming of the Bastille *and* both Gish sisters, incandescent Lillian and down-to-earth Dorothy. It's typical Griffith for all that: a mixture of melodramatic but irresistible storytelling, sharp characterizations, and preachments that are from somewhere beyond the Victorian moon. Who but Griffith would use the French Revolution to warn the audience about Bolshevism? Who else would raise Danton to heroic stature while reviling Robespierre as a villain? (Both men had blood on their hands and eventually on their necks.)

Still, it's as an enjoyably pell-mell epic that *Orphans* works—that and a chance to see a rare sister act on-screen. Ironically, one of the heroines is a foundling, so you have an exceedingly rare case of genetic sisters playing adopted sisters. But . . . whatever.

Pause-button explanations: Lay the French Revolution groundwork.

What next: If they take to Lillian Gish, try *Way Down East* or, even better, *The Wind*, an incredible silent film from 1928, just before sound swept everything away, about a young woman going up against the elements in Texas and losing her marbles. It's probably Gish's single finest performance and a hell of a movie until the tacked-on studio ending.

SUNRISE (B&W, 1927)

Directed by: F. W. Murnau

Starring: Janet Gaynor, George O'Brien

Ages: 10 and up

The sell: Love hurts. And heals.

The plot: A farmer (O'Brien) is tempted away from his wife (Gaynor) by a vamp from the city (Margaret Livingston), who almost gets him to drown his meek spouse. Instead, husband and wife travel to the city for a day and slowly renew their love, only to face a potentially lethal storm on the sail back to the farm.

Why it's here: The story line is absurdly basic, the characters simple to the point of idiocy, and yet this is one of the most poetic and emotionally pure movies ever made, silent or sound.

You may have to get your kids past the opening scenes of the farmer in his temptation, which are witchy and kind of neat but also intense in a way that can be mistaken for the merely melodramatic. Once the wife flees to the trolley and we start that long ride into the heart of the city, it's hard not to be hooked, so exacting and universal are the emotions playing on the faces of O'Brien and Gaynor. The midsection of *Sunrise*, as the couple have small, wonderful adventures throughout the metropolis, is like watching two children fall in love before your eyes.

The star of the movie (although your kids won't appreciate this) is director F. W. Murnau, the German Expressionist wunderkind who made his Hollywood debut here. The camerawork, editing, set design, sound track (Murnau strategically deployed sound effects throughout the film), and performances are all of a dreamlike piece, and the effect is almost unbearably tender.

So, obviously, it's not a movie for cynical children; showing it to them is like giving a Matisse to a goat. It's for the quiet ones who recognize the sublime when it's placed in front of them. The vast majority in the middle won't be better or worse off for seeing it. Eliza and Natalie fall into that category; they gave it a polite, not unpleased *meh* when we watched it one rainy Sunday, and their father the fool movie freak had to keep his mouth clamped shut. But there are the rare films that ask to be watched again every long once in a while, to see if they'll finally detonate in one's sensibilities, and this is one of them.

Home video notes: For reasons best known to the Fox Home Entertainment marketing department, *Sunrise* is as of this writing available on DVD only as part of a boxed set with three other Fox best picture winners: *All about Eve*, *Gentleman's Agreement*, and *How Green Was My Valley*. It comes with an excellent commentary track by cinematographer John Bailey, though. With any luck it'll be available as a stand-alone DVD soon.

Useless trivia: The first film to win the best picture Oscar. Actually, the 1929 Academy Award for "Best Picture, Production" was won by the World War I dogfight movie *Wings*, while Murnau's film won "Best Picture, Unique and Artistic Production."

It won the art-house prize, basically. Gaynor won best actress and Charles Rosher and Karl Strauss won for cinematography.

What next: If they respond to Gaynor, try to find Frank Borzage's *Seventh Heaven*, also from 1927 and a great melodrama from an underrated master. It's not on video but occasionally pops up on TV. Gaynor also stars in the first version of *A Star Is Born* (1937).

5

· · · ·

MUSICALS

CLASSIC HOLLYWOOD MUSICALS aren't so much a genre as a religion: You believe in them or you don't. Even if you do uphold the faith, individual films don't vary wildly. *Singin' in the Rain* is much closer to *Top Hat* than any two films from the drama chapter—say, *Mildred Pierce* and *How Green Was My Valley*—because the governing impulse in musicals is always the same: to give melody and movement to joy. All of real life says "You can't do that," but everything in musicals says "Yes, you can," and *that's* the secret behind Gene Kelly's milewide grin, Astaire's cool certainty, Ann Miller's pizzazz. Only Judy Garland brought herself to doubt, and the tremor in her voice was the distance she constantly measured between Oz and reality. She was the exception. The pleasure of Hollywood musicals lies in the creativity with which they simultaneously deny and amplify the workaday world. They hint at so many possibilities.

So, yes, they're wonderful for kids to watch, because they offer hope of grace and they make it look easy. At a certain point, however, a child watches a movie musical and decides that it's too easy, calls it corny, and is on the way to adolescence. To such prototeens, musicals become childhood toys to be put away, along with Barney and *Little House on the Prairie* and other celebrations of the unironic. They'll come back when they're adults, if they understand that musicals are the rare world in which everything goes right, even when it goes wrong, and therefore deserve to be treasured. You may even have that exceptional, abnormal child who loves musicals and never lets them go, and who transfers that love to the school stage or to the big, gassy affairs that pass for musicals on Broadway. (In which case, one word of advice: Sondheim.)

In any event, start 'em young and start 'em with *Singin' in the Rain* (see chapter 1). If you steep your kids in musicals before anything else—beginning with color, slowly folding in black and white—the context is set for all the riches old Hollywood has to offer.

But there are so *many* of the things—happy people all bursting into song—and they look so similar. Is there a difference in quality between, say, *On the Town* and *Easter Parade*? For the purposes of this book, not really. The best way to understand where a musical's coming from is to see which studio made it. With no other genre does house style matter so much.

Warner Bros. specialized in hyperactive urban backstage musicals: Dick Powell and Ruby Keeler providing the sugar, Jimmy Cagney and Joan Blondell the sass, and Busby Berkeley the demented pinwheel choreography. Twentieth Century Fox did backstagers too, but wholesome middle-American ones— cornfed as well as corny—starring Alice Faye and then Betty Grable, with Carmen Miranda thrown in occasionally like salsa at a New England boiled dinner.

Universal had teenage singing sensation Deanna Durbin, who might be worth rediscovery with your children; her films are on video (*One Hundred Men and a Girl* is probably the best) and they're sappy but honest, and musically rather smart. RKO had Astaire and Rogers and that was enough. Columbia had Rita Hayworth and that was almost enough; they had to borrow

Gene Kelly from MGM for *Cover Girl*. Paramount had zilch: a crafter of sophisticated dramas and elegant comedies, Adolph Zukor's outfit never quite "got" the musical.

But MGM: sweet Jesus. Not only did Louis B. Mayer's dream factory boast "as many stars as there are in heaven," it specialized in more *types* of movie musical than its rivals. There were the Mickey Rooney/Judy Garland let's-put-on-a-show pep rallies (*Babes in Arms, Strike Up the Band, Babes on Broadway, Girl Crazy*). There were the swank song-and-dance revues featuring that oddly bewitching human metronome Eleanor Powell (*Broadway Melody of 1936*, and later, *1938* and *1940*). There were the Nelson Eddy–Jeanette MacDonald operettas, prim and sawdust-dull exercises unworthy of nostalgia. (If you want to see what MacDonald could do, dig up the sexy little comedies she and Maurice Chevalier appeared in for director Ernst Lubitsch, the sole exception to the Paramount-couldn't-make-musicals rule.)

Most important for your little homeschooling experiment, there were the films put out by MGM's musicals unit from the mid-1940s through the late 1950s, overseen by a Tin Pan Alley lyricist-turned-producer named Arthur Freed. These include most of the classics people associate with the genre, including the jewel in the crown, *Singin' in the Rain*. Astaire had come over to MGM by then; Garland was still there; Gene Kelly had arrived. Betty Comden and Adolph Green were writing the scripts and the lyrics (at least for the new songs; Freed was a master at recycling old hits and transmuting them into gold standards). Vincente Minnelli and Stanley Donen were directing; upstarts like Michael Kidd handled the choreography along with Donen and the dancers; associate producer Roger Edens did whatever everyone else was too busy to do. Rent the series of *That's Entertainment* clip shows if you want to sample the musical numbers piecemeal, but by all means move on to the individual movies themselves. The Freed unit musicals represent the final transformation from the "backstage musical" (in which

song-and-dance numbers are "performed" by the characters in
theatrical settings) to the "story musical" (where characters sing
and dance because they have to, not because they're professional
entertainers).

In other words, the MGM musicals became the kind we
carry around in our own heads, the ones by which we give private rhythm and meaning to our lives. You know what I mean:
You find yourself walking down a sidewalk and suddenly click
into a pulse of steps as surely as Fred Astaire, or feel some bit of
scat singing burst out of your soul and hover just behind your
lips. Haven't you? Maybe not. Maybe this is what Walkmans
have replaced, and iPods, and all the rest—the human need for
a secret sound track, an inner organizing principle. Movie
musicals prompt a less solitary form of the endeavor, one that
requires us to invent our own lyrics and to make our own steps,
and these, unquestionably, carry over to our outer lives. They
encourage us to let the dreaming do the work rather than the
technology.

Unlike in other chapters, I've treated musicals in groups—
starting with MGM—or dealt with an individual musical as
emblematic of its type. There are variations between the ten
Astaire-Rogers films, but for the purposes of this book it suf-
fices to highlight two or three and warn about the weakest,
rather than keep saying, "And in this one Fred and Ginger
dance the Piccolino, and in this one he sings 'Never Gonna
Dance,' and in this one they fall in love while bickering pleas-
antly, no, wait, that's all of them." If a child likes one of the
films, he or she will like most of them, and they'll enjoy "collecting" them as well.

MGM MUSICALS

Arranged in order of must-see status, from essential to merely enjoyable:

Singin' in the Rain *(color, 1952)* See chapter 1.

Meet Me in St. Louis *(color, 1944)* See chapter 1.

On the Town *(color, 1949)* Kelly, Sinatra, and gooney bird Jules Munshin as sailors on leave in "New York New York, it's a wonderful town / The Bronx is up and the Battery's down." Delightful, silly, charmed; the first musical to film on location, and it has a sense of place few others in the genre do. Half the songs are by Leonard Bernstein, the others by Roger Edens. Not to be confused with the longer and lesser *Anchors Aweigh* (1945), with Kelly and Sinatra in the navy again.

Easter Parade *(color, 1948)* Gene Kelly broke his ankle playing touch football, so Astaire came out of early retirement to join Garland as two hoofers thrown together when his longtime partner (Ann Miller) goes her own way. It's a fascinating pairing of the most neurotic musical star in Hollywood history and the least, with Miller in the middle stealing the film by singing "Shakin' My Blues Away." Songs by Irving Berlin.

The Band Wagon *(color, 1953)* Adorably fake-cynical bit of backstage frippery that pokes fun at the pretensions of postwar Broadway. Kids love the "Triplets" number, with Fred Astaire, Nanette Fabray, and Jack Buchanan dressed up as whiny babies, but the highlight is Fred and Cyd Charisse "Dancing in the Dark."

The Pirate *(color, 1948)* Ripsnorting, enjoyably hammy musical comedy about a woman (Garland) in the Caribbean engaged to a local politico but obsessing over dashing pirate Macoco. Enter

Kelly as a traveling actor who pretends to be the pirate to win her over. Directed by Vincente Minnelli, it's a good one for boys, and it has some surprisingly tart things to say about who we are versus who we pretend to be, if you can hear them through the ruckus.

The Harvey Girls *(color, 1946)* Mail-order bride Garland ends up working for a "Harvey House," a hotel/restaurant meant to provide wholesome comforts to cowboys in the Old West. Angela Lansbury is the sultry saloon singer—go ahead, read that sentence again—who opposes her. I'm missing the magic on this one, but the girls loved it and ran around singing "The Atchison, Topeka, and the Santa Fe" until we had to duct-tape their mouths closed.

Kiss Me Kate *(color, 1953)* Wacky update of/homage to *The Taming of the Shrew* is good fun especially if your kids know who Shakespeare is. Howard Keel and Kathryn Grayson play divorced actors called back together for a musical version of *Shrew* with songs by Cole Porter—the very musical we're watching, I guess. How meta. Ann Miller dances on a tabletop to "Too Darn Hot," and Keenan Wynn and James Whitmore play Damon Runyon–style goons singing "Brush Up Your Shakespeare." Shot in 3-D, so why haven't they put it on DVD in that format?

An American in Paris *(color, 1951)* Kelly and Minnelli get a little big for their britches in this gorgeously shot best picture winner that now looks more dated than some of the era's slighter stuff. Of course it's still worth seeing, seventeen-minute climactic ballet, Gene dressed as a Harlequin, and all. Great Gershwin score.

Seven Brides for Seven Brothers *(color, 1954)* Hale and hearty bit of Broadway Americana, with Keel and his six all-dancing frontier brothers coming down from the mountain to claim their brides and getting set on their collective ear by Jane Powell and company. There's a barn-raising dance that turns into a free-for-all dance-fight and Keel sings, "Bless Your Beautiful Hide" so lustily your kids will imitate him whether they want to or not. It's another good starter musical for boys, and much wittier than it appears on the surface.

It's Always Fair Weather (color, 1955) This one's here because it's the author's favorite MGM musical, and *finally* a DVD version has been released that sets the film's wide-screen dance routines in the proper letterboxed frame. Grab it: It's a peak experience to see Gene Kelly, Dan Dailey, and Michael Kidd do a dance routine with trash-can lids on their feet—the men arranged three across, in perfect sync—or Kelly tap-dance on rollerskates while singing "I Like Myself." Added bonus: Cyd Charisse in a boxing gym with the pugs all singing "Baby, You Knock Me Out."

For Further Study: Yolanda and the Thief (color, 1945, truly bizarre), *Royal Wedding* (B&W, 1951, Astaire dancing on the ceiling, and ask your kids how he did *that*), *Show Boat* (color, 1951), *Good News* (color, 1947, fun college pep). Avoid: *Gigi* (color, 1958) unless you really want your kids going to school singing "Thank Heaven for Little Girls."

NON-MGM MUSICALS

FOOTLIGHT PARADE (B&W, 1933)

Directed by: Lloyd Bacon, dance numbers directed by Busby Berkeley

Starring: James Cagney, Joan Blondell, Ruby Keeler, Dick Powell

Ages: 7 and up

The sell: Introducing Busby Berkeley, with an assist by Mr. James Cagney

The plot: Chester Kent (Cagney) is a Broadway producer whose livelihood is threatened by talking pictures until he gets the bright idea to stage musical "prologues" before the movies (not a bad idea; even today, they'd beat the ads and trivia-for-morons slides they show in multiplexes). Soon he has a number of prologues out on the road, but one of the dancers is spying for a rival company. Can Chester create and stage three prologues in one night?

Why it's here: For the Busby Berkeley mind-melt and for Jimmy Cagney in outrageous overdrive. Two years after *The Public Enemy* (see chapter 6), *Parade* proved Cagney could play something other than gangsters, and his Chester Kent is a scream: aggressively browbeating his adoring casts and crews to push harder, faster, further. It's a performance of immense charm, and quintessentially New York—that adrenaline pulse still beats in the city's corners.

Footlight Parade also introduces a first-time viewer to the Warner musical stock company: Ruby Keeler as the good girl who's just gotta dance (the movie starts her out as a bespectacled nerd before allowing her to assume her rightful colors); blowsy Joan Blondell as the shy (!) secretary with a crush on Chester; Dick Powell, the grinning singing juvenile of whom a little goes a very long way (to his credit, he seemed increasingly in on the joke throughout his career); Frank McHugh as the besieged director. The movie's pretty up front about who's sleeping with whom—this was one of the last movies to slip under the radar before the censorship code changed the rules, and you may be surprised at how sophisticated, even risqué, it is.

But if Cagney and the rocketing pace keep your kids watching, the payoff is in the film's grand finale, which consists of three progressively bonkers Busby Berkeley production numbers: "Honeymoon Hotel," "By a Waterfall," and "Shanghai Lil." Each could no more take place in a real theater than *Lawrence of Arabia* could unfold in my hat, but audiences of the day understood that and rolled with it and, after a brief bark of surprise, so will your children. This is the magic of movies, after all: that they can turn themselves inside out like some kind of cosmic sock and leave planet Earth entirely.

I don't know if I could describe the "By a Waterfall" sequence any better than that, other than to say that its endless wedding-cake tiers of dancing girls, now backlit, now swimming in exploding kaleidoscopic shapes, always smiling, suggest that Berkeley somehow invented fractal geometry by studying an artichoke. They are literally like nothing your kids will have ever seen before—unless they've come across a watered-down reference in *The Simpsons* or something—and they will be gaga in disbelief. And how often does that happen?

Pause-button explanations: The movie zips along so quickly you'll probably have to pause just to explain what's going on.

What next: Berkeley served as dance director (rarely a full-fledged director) for Warners from 1931 to 1937, and films bearing his gonzo touch include *42nd Street, Gold Diggers of 1933* and *1935* (whose "Lullabye of Broadway" finale is a lulu and possibly the man's peak), and *Dames.* Then he moved to MGM and worked with Garland (*Babes in Arms, Babes on Broadway*), directed Gene Kelly's debut (*For Me and My Gal,* 1942) and dropped into the Fox lot to make *The Gang's All Here* (1943). Carmen Miranda as "The Lady in the Tutti Frutti Hat," expanding into an infinite horizon of citrus fruits? That's Berkeley in a clamshell: precise, Rabelaisian, uncontainable.

FUNNY FACE (COLOR, 1957)

Directed by: Stanley Donen

Starring: Fred Astaire, Audrey Hepburn, Kay Thompson

Ages: 6 and up

The sell: The last classic musical—and, yes, that's Eloise's mother.

The plot: Dick Avery (Astaire) is a fashion photographer seeking a new face for a magazine (think *Vogue*) run by powerhouse editor Maggie Prescott (Thompson; think Diana Vreeland or Anna Wintour). During a shoot in a Greenwich Village bookshop, he meets mousy intellectual Jo Stockton (Hepburn) and determines to turn her into a supermodel. Jo is willing to go with him to Paris, but mostly to meet Flostre, the star philosopher of "empathicalism." Where do her allegiances land—uptown or downtown?

Why it's here: Not for realism. The plot is a rehash of things Fred was doing with Ginger Rogers twenty-five years earlier (see *Top Hat* below), the goof on Jean-Paul Sartre and existentialism is heavy-handed, and Astaire has three full decades on his costar. Yet the movie has a gossamer charm; it *works*. The colors are as seductive as a magazine spread and the Gershwin songs— "S'Wonderful," "He Loves and She Loves," the title tune— shimmer with the aching, careworn loveliness of things that have stood the test of time. It feels like the last exhalation of the MGM musical, and in fact it was; Paramount imported all the major players of the Freed unit for this one-shot.

And it has Astaire and Audrey, two of the most naturally elegant life-forms in this or any other universe. The least sexual of the major stars, Fred has no interest in Hepburn *that way*, at least on-screen—he's about appreciating her as an aesthetic object, then as a dance partner, and only then as a friend and lover.

Hepburn, for her part, exuded ardor more than lust, and she seems to respond to his touch. They're surprisingly well matched, and at its best the movie is a ballet between two people delicately but truly comfortable with each other. Among its other assets, the movie's a neat object lesson in the many things love can be besides heavy breathing. My daughters, attuned to a movie's *ewww* factor, loved it.

Pause-button explanations: The crazy, bossy magazine editor who sings "Think Pink" at the beginning and accompanies Fred and Jo to Paris? That's Kay Thompson, author of the *Eloise* books, and, indeed, she acts much like that belle of the Plaza all grown up.

Useless trivia: Astaire's character is based on real-life photographer Richard Avedon. The dresses are by Givenchy.

What next: See the MGM musicals section above.

A HARD DAY'S NIGHT (B&W, 1964) AND HELP! (COLOR, 1965)

Directed by: Richard Lester

Starring: The Beatles

Ages: 4 and up

The sell: Meet the Beatles.

The plot: *Hard Day's Night*: The Fab Four play songs and flee their fans. *Help!*: The Fab Four play songs and flee a crazed Indian cult that wants to kill Ringo.

Why it's here: Despite the plot synopses above, you probably want to start your kids with *Help!* (Actually, you probably want to start them with 1968's *Yellow Submarine*, but that's animated and not germane to this book.) *Help!* is in color, it has a plot, it's more conventionally silly. The songs are arguably better—Lennon and McCartney were nearing the early peak of their craft, and the Dylan-influenced guitar jangle on songs like "You've Got to Hide Your Love Away" is sublime. The hugger-mugger with the cult of the ring is dated—racist, sure, but also just lame—but it's not so scary that small children won't be able to have a good time.

I was eight when *Help!* came out and remember seeing it from the way-back seat of our old Rambler station wagon at a Boston-area drive-in; in my mind's eye, the silhouette of my father's head still takes up half the screen. But I recall being delighted at the camaraderie of the boys—the ski vacations they took together, the apartment block they shared (four doors, one big room), as though my gang from school had grown up and still lived together. Above all, *Help!* furthered the playful myth of togetherness that was the Beatles' secret weapon; as has been pointed out elsewhere, they were the first rock group in which each member was as important as the others and yet the sum was infinitely greater than the parts.

A Hard Day's Night, the Beatles' first, should be saved for when your kids start asking questions about the group. Not *if* they ask, but *when*, because the Fabs still retain the cultural clout to be everywhere. (Seriously: As I type these words, Natalie has just had an argument with her sister, stormed into her bedroom, and put on "Revolution"—the fast single version—REALLY LOUD.) By the time a child is five, he or she already knows a ton of Beatles songs. Even if you've never played them, the music is omnipresent.

A Hard Day's Night is a fictionalized version of the madness that surrounded the Moptops when they first appeared, and it codifies the four into the personalities by which we came to know them. John was the anarchist prankster, Paul the cheeky doll, George the shy one with soul, and Ringo was Harpo and Curly and Chaplin rolled into one: the sweet, funny-looking clown.

Did this have anything to do with who they were in reality? Only tangentially; starting with John, the individual group members would come to push and pull at their public personas with varying degrees of success. In this movie, though, it seems so fresh, so newly discovered, that you could cry.

The music, too, is staged to come out of the Beatles' lives. In a way, *Hard Day's Night* is a throwback to the old Hollywood musicals in which characters sang because they were show people and that's what show people did. The Beatles don't play songs to further the plot; they play because they're rockers steeped in years of working the dives of Liverpool and Hamburg. The movie isn't propelled forward by the songs; rather, it stops in its tracks to admire and groove with them. In 1964, this is what we paid to see: the Beatles actually playing (it was lip-synching, but close enough). Today, your kids get the same charge from the movie: the Beatles, actually alive and young. The movie's plot is filler. It's the songs we're here for.

This would become the model of the new rock musical, with *Help!* providing a more conventional alternative; between those two poles sailed the rock movies of the next twenty years. Even the music videos that took off in the mid-'80s owe their grammar to the first two Beatles films. Watching these movies with your kids is like showing them the DNA of the culture in which they swim.

Home video notes: The *Hard Day's* DVD released by Miramax in 2002 has audiovisual purists in a rage because the original mono sound track has been rechanneled into fake home-theater stereo. It's perfectly acceptable for the small layperson, but look for the 1997 MPI DVD release of the film if this bothers you.

Pause-button explanations: You'll probably have to help your children separate fact from fiction a bit: That's not Paul's real grandfather, those people aren't really trying to kill Ringo, and so on.

What next: *Yellow Submarine* (1968), *Let It Be* (1970), and, if you must, *Magical Mystery Tour* (1967).

A STAR IS BORN (COLOR, 1954)

Directed by: George Cukor

Starring: Judy Garland, James Mason

Ages: 12 and up

The sell: A star is defined and destroyed. Or: Judy Garland, the graduate course.

The plot: Norman Maine (Mason) is an established Hollywood star filled with self-loathing and self-administered scotch. He discovers a struggling singer named Esther Blodgett (Garland) and, with his help, she becomes Vicki Lester, newly minted movie star. They marry and are briefly happy, but the studio buys out Norman's contract after his on-set misbehavior makes him a liability. Vicki wins an Oscar; Norman shows up at the broadcast and accidentally backhands her onstage. Deciding that he's weighing his wife down, Norman drowns himself; Vicki introduces herself at a memorial as "Mrs. Norman Maine."

Why it's here: Because it's the flip side to *The Wizard of Oz*—the end of the Yellow Brick Road—and because any child old enough to understand that fame can go wrong and to wonder how it affected one particular talent will find all sorts of troubling answers here.

In the film, that talent is Mason's Norman Maine, boozy and

coasting on acrid fumes of celebrity. In reality—and, again, any reasonably sentient older child will pick up on this—the distressed star is Judy Garland, whose character is the young and naive Esther/Vicki but who looks beyond youth and age (she was thirty-two) and who at times seems physically buffeted by her demons. The movie was Garland's comeback after four years offscreen—a black hole of pills, suicide attempts, divorce, remarriage, and career salvaging. It was a triumph and her last major film; the concert hall would be the site of her best work from here until her suicide in 1967.

Star's a long film, especially if you're watching the restored version, and the first half ends with a huge production number called "Born in a Trunk" that rivals the "Broadway Rhythm" number from *Singin' in the Rain*. But where that film is a rowdy vision of the film industry weathering a crisis of the past, *Star* is set in 1950s Hollywood, during a crisis of the present. Everyone's staying home to watch TV, and drunk washout stars like Norman Maine (and, by implication, Garland) are a drag on the bottom line—perhaps that's why she sings like the ceiling's about to come crashing down. The movie has the glooms. Why watch it with a kid?

Because the central relationship is so disarmingingly tender, for one thing. When I watched the movie with Eliza, my little Miss Priss was initially put off by Norman Maine. Such an awful man, and *drunk*. Tch. And the Garland here, puffy and a little crazy-eyed, is not the one she knew and loved from *Meet Me in St. Louis* and *The Harvey Girls*.

The way the movie bares the clockwork cruelty of the studio system hooked her, though. Eliza couldn't believe it when Esther is handed a new name and identity with her paycheck, just like that, and she nearly rose from her seat in outrage over what the makeup department does to the poor girl. More important, *Star* lets its two characters grow toward each other at a pace and in a fashion that feels honest and privileged. Probably

Garland knew how hard it is to maintain a sane relationship in Hollywood; possibly she knew how hard it is to live with a star who's an emotional train wreck. And so Norman and Esther's marriage feels like an island of calm before the storm hits. By the film's midpoint, Eliza loved these two as much as they loved each other.

A Star Is Born is an odd movie: much of it filmed against patently unreal rear projections, it contains emotional and biographical truths harsher than anything modern movies dare grapple with. It's not for every child, but for some I think it deepens things a little. In a culture that insists all our children are stars waiting to be born, this movie whispers *It might hurt more than you think.*

Home video notes: One of the first movies shot in wide-screen CinemaScope, *A Star Is Born* has been available in cropped prints that are reasonably useless; if you're still using VHS, look for the wide-screen edition or skip it. The film was also cut down from 181 minutes to 154 after its premiere, and various "restored" versions exist, including one that uses still photos with the sound track to piece together a missing segment early on. The 2001 DVD version is wide-screen, has the most extensive restorations (it's 176 minutes), and offers nice extras.

Pause-button explanations: You'll definitely have to stop and explain what's going on when the still photos kick in (see above).

What next: If they're up for it, show your kids the 1937 original, starring Fredric March and Janet Gaynor (again, Esther played by an actress at the very end of her career—funny, huh?). It's in early Technicolor and is quite good, but it's a straight drama rather than a musical. There's an even earlier version called *What Price Hollywood?* (1932), also directed by Cukor and also worth seeing. The Barbra Streisand/Kris Kristofferson 1976 rock remake does not fall in the purview of this book, he wrote diplomatically.

TOP HAT (B&W, 1935)

Directed by: Mark Sandrich

Starring: Fred Astaire, Ginger Rogers

Ages: 5 and up

The sell: Just watch.

The plot: Plot is not the point in Astaire-Rogers, but here goes: Dancer Jerry Travers (Astaire) meets and annoys Dale Tremont (Rogers) when he tap-dances above her hotel room one night. He pursues her most ardently, but she mistakenly thinks Jerry is his friend Horace (Edward Everett Horton), who is married to her friend (Helen Broderick), so she's appalled at his cheating ways. Jerry follows her to Venice, where Dale is engaged to vain fop Alberto (Eric Rhodes) but wins her back with voice and feet.

Why it's here: 1936's *Swing Time* is generally thought the best of the ten Astaire-Rogers films—its climactic routine, "Never Gonna Dance," is the most complex and dramatic thing they ever did—but Fred's a bit of a cad in that one and the movie's blackface tribute to Bill "Bojangles" Robinson provides a cultural dissonance you may not feel like discussing right out of the gate. Save it for later, after your kids have their sea legs in this black-and-white RKO wonderworld.

Top Hat—everybody's second choice and many people's first—is a simpler affair, so simple it's almost a toy. When the movie heads to Venice in the second half of the film, we don't get the real city but a joyfully ridiculous Art Deco approximation, with the cast floating around in gondolas the size of shoe boxes. It's like a party on a kiddie ride.

Astaire doesn't look like much when you first encounter him, but a child soon figures out what makes him tick: He makes a virtue of lightness—of voice, of feet, of bearing. Ginger is Fred's fussy real-world opposite, insisting on gravity until she catches his rhythms and gets pulled into the dance. Their first number together, "Isn't It a Lovely Day (to Be Caught in the Rain)," sets the pattern: unpleasant situation, Fred breezes through it, Ginger joins in on his tailwind, the whole dance becomes greater than the sum of its limbs and steps.

Top Hat has a fine supporting cast as well: Horton as the fuddy-duddy friend (if you recognize his voice, baby boomers, that's because he provided narration for the "Fractured Fairy Tales" on the old *Rocky and Bullwinkle Show*), Broderick as his unpretty but sophisticated wife, Eric Blore as a snooty little butler, and Rhodes as the Continental twit who must be removed for the course of true love to run smooth (Mussolini was so offended he banned the film, but, really, Rhodes is about as Italian as Chico Marx). Together, they provide the blueprint from which all subsequent Astaire/Rogers films followed.

And, yes, there are the Irving Berlin songs, including "Cheek to Cheek," which all kids should know if they're to participate in a culture beyond Disney and Nickelodeon and Xbox. (Yes, even in the twenty-first century. They don't want to know now, but they will later, and hopefully you want them to.)

Home video notes: Available alone or as part of a boxed DVD set with four other A/Rs—good ones, too.

Useless trivia: Rogers's dress in the "Cheek to Cheek" sequence kept shedding feathers, to Astaire's utter exasperation—he caustically nicknamed her "Feathers" as a result. Kids always want to know if they were really in love, and the answer, of course, is no. They were two thoroughgoing professionals who respected each other, were friendly on the set, and didn't socialize much off it. Each worried about their career being limited by the public demand for more Astaire-Rogers movies; in both cases the fears were groundless.

What next: The best: *Swing Time* (1936), *The Gay Divorcee* (1934), *Roberta* (1935), *Follow the Fleet* (1936), *Shall We Dance* (1937). The rest: *Flying Down to Rio* (1933; their first together, and they're not the stars), *Carefree* (1938), *The Story of Vernon and Irene Castle* (1939), and—made in 1949, long after the heyday— *The Barkleys of Broadway*.

WEST SIDE STORY (COLOR, 1961)

Directed by: Robert Wise and Jerome Robbins

Starring: Natalie Wood, Richard Beymer, Rita Moreno, Russ Tamblyn

Ages: 6 and up

The sell: Shakespeare in the streets

The plot: Two teenage gangs, the Puerto Rican Sharks and the white Jets, clash over the same piece of New York's Hell's Kitchen. Tony (Beymer) is a good kid who grew up best friends with Jets leader Riff (Tamblyn); Maria (Wood) is the sister of Sharks leader Bernardo (George Chakiris). Tony and Maria spot each other across a high school dance floor and suddenly there's no one else in the world. This is not good for intergang relations. True to the source, almost everybody ends up dead.

Why it's here: For the songs, for Natalie Wood, and to introduce the thought that Shakespeare is portable—that great story lines can apply to different times and places and thus to your child's time and place. Natalie and Eliza saw *West Side Story* right around the time they clicked on who Shakespeare was. A local park staging of *Romeo and Juliet* had piqued the girls' interest; even with the dense hedges of prose, they got a little weepy at the end.

Then one night Lori and I went out to dinner while her parents babysat, and when we returned we discovered they had rented *West Side Story* and watched it with the girls. Really? All that stabbing and rumbling and unjust death? Our youngest must have been four or five. (Here, incidentally, is one of the paradoxes of parenting: It's acceptable for you to show your kids *Freddy Meets Jason XXVI*, but it's not okay for your parents or in-laws to show them a *Rugrats* episode if it hasn't been submitted for approval in triplicate.)

Well, they were fine, obviously. Eliza cried buckets, which we were coming to understand was her stamp of approval, and Natalie demanded that I sing "Officer Krupke" every night for the next six months, which I did, nervously dancing around the line "with all their marijuana / they won't give me a puff." By the way, if *West Side Story* seals the deal on Shakespeare, it also opens the door to Stephen Sondheim, who wrote the lyrics to Leonard Bernstein's music. The girls have since stumbled onto brilliant Sondheim musicals like *Into the Woods* and *Pacific Overtures* while stalling *Sweeney Todd* for the time being. In general, kids quickly figure out that his work goes deeper, with deeper melodies, than almost any other modern musicals they'll hear.

If *Romeo and Juliet* is the backbone of *Story*, the song-and-dance numbers are its flesh and blood. "The Jet Song," "America," "Maria," "Officer Krupke," "Tonight," "Somewhere," "I Feel Pretty"—is there another musical with this high a batting average? The cast is a mixed bag of acting and ethnicities: You can't fault Tamblyn as Riff and Rita Moreno as Maria's friend Anita, but Beymer's a bit of a board and as Bernardo, Chakiris is a magnificent two-dimensional bull.

Then there's Wood as Maria. She's about as Puerto Rican as

my aunt Ethel and her singing was dubbed by Marni Nixon, and you don't care a whit because she makes Maria so immediate and ardent and alive. I think Natalie Wood put across the dangerous thrill of young love better than any actress of her time—perhaps in all of movies. Maria is the most tragically innocent of her key roles; Judy in *Rebel Without a Cause* the angriest; Deanie in *Splendor in the Grass* the most unforgettable, lit up and destroyed by her emotions. Some of these movies will talk to Eliza and Natalie more clearly when the girls are older. For now, Maria hints at glories and losses and still feels pretty enough to dance.

Home video notes: Trust me, you want to watch this Super Panavision production wide-screen, since cropped TV prints give you half the visuals at a time—ruination for a carefully choreographed dance routine. Luckily, the current DVD from MGM offers the letterboxed version.

Pause-button explanations: Do your Shakespeare spadework before the movie begins, if you feel you need to.

Useless trivia: Shot on location in Manhattan on the future site of Lincoln Center—the start of construction was held up so shooting could finish.

What next: Back to the Bard with *Kiss Me Kate* (1953) or forward into the future with Baz Luhrmann's 1996 *Romeo + Juliet*, starring Leo DiCaprio and Claire Danes.

1960s MUSICALS: THE RED GIANT PHASE

By the late 1950s, the classic Hollywood musical was on its way out. The stars were aging—as were producers, choreographers, and everyone else involved—and the culture was slowly turning away from Tin Pan Alley and toward rock 'n' roll. There *were* successful musicals in the decade from 1955 to 1965—in terms of box office, critical acclaim, and awards—but today many of them seem bloated with prestige, lumbering and self-important, and as a group they lack the vastly pleasurable zing of the earlier stuff. They're the last dinosaurs before the meteor hit: amazing to look at but fatally slow of step.

That includes the entire run of Rodgers & Hammerstein musicals filmed by Fox: *Oklahoma!* (1955), *Carousel* (1956), *The King and I* (1956), *South Pacific* (1958), and the mother of them all, *The Sound of Music* (1965). *King* is the best, *Sound of Music* the best suited for kids—E. and N. watched it for half a year before retiring it from the rotation—and all seem to weigh a ton. Still, if you like one of them, you'll probably like them all. Except for *South Pacific*, which is just bad.

The same, sadly, goes for *My Fair Lady* (1964), whose producers gave Audrey Hepburn her most famous role by stealing it away from Julie Andrews, who had originated Eliza Doolittle on Broadway. (Don't worry, Andrews evened the score with *The Sound of Music* and *Mary Poppins*.) To add insult to injury, the producers dubbed Hepburn's voice with that of Marni Nixon while letting costar Rex Harrison croak his way through the movie like a grackle. At 170 minutes, *Lady* is a stagy haul, but it's become such an institution that most people assume it's a four-star classic. It isn't, but the songs are cute and you won't be able to avoid it.

The Music Man (1962) has a pulse, at least, and that oompah-licious title tune gets kids marching around the living room. This may be the best of the Red Giant musicals because Robert Preston throws every last ounce of his energy into the role of mountebank music teacher Harold Hill, and the supporting cast does what they can to keep up with him. *Music Man* was one of the first films I ever saw in a theater, and I still recall the "Pick-a-Lot/Good Night Ladies" medley and Hermione Gingold bellowing "BAL-zac!"—I didn't know what it meant, but I knew it was dirty—and the cast magically popping into uniform at the end. Still, with a song that was covered by the Beatles ("Till There Was You") and a leading lady who would be playing the mother of the Partridge Family on TV before the decade was out, this was the Hollywood musical perched on the verge of extinction.

First, though, came the 1968 best picture winner, *Oliver!*: an upbeat, toe-tapping musical about starving orphans and whores getting beaten to death. This one has great songs by Lionel Bart—"Consider Yourself," "Where Is Love," "I'd Do Anything," and the deathless "Food, Glorious Food"—and a gaping cognitive dissonance between subject matter and genre.

All these latter-day musicals came straight from Broadway— Hollywood was no longer making originals for the screen—and they weren't so much adapted for the movies as simply taken outside and shot. *Mary Poppins* (1964) was one of the last originals, but since it's part of the Disney library—and is thus sold to your kids at every video store into which they wander—it doesn't need my help here. (That said, damn good songs and damn strange story line.) *Fiddler on the Roof* (1971) was the end of the line: Three hours long (and you feel every second), it plays as if your nana and a full minyan attended its transference from Broadway to screen. Still, if you're Jewish, you *will* be seeing this movie, so you might as well learn to love it.

Other musicals from the End Times? There are Elvis movies, a genre unto themselves, and unless you have a healthy sense of humor or a hunka hunka burning idolatry, *Jailhouse Rock* (1957) and *King Creole* (1958) are all you need to see. I won't get into early rock movies here, but *Bye Bye Birdie* (1963) is worth noting, as it represents the Broadway reaction to Elvis and '50s teen culture: high-spirited, fearful ridicule. But, *man*, is Ann-Margret hot in it—I'm sorry, she just is—and Paul Lynde is hilarious, and the movie offers a window into a time when *The Ed Sullivan*

Show was the center around which American culture spun. Really.

Birdie is my wife's secret favorite movie musical, by the way, because she saw it when she was little and memorized every song; it doesn't take much to get her warbling "What's the story? Morning Glory?" By contrast, I didn't see *Birdie* until I was a fully grown adult and then had to confess I found it pretty terrible, with none of the natural graces of the previous decade's musicals. But that just points out how movies seen when we're young—seen before we *wise up*—can matter most. Our daughters have watched *Bye Bye Birdie*, too, and after initial perplexity, they love it almost as much as their mother. And I envy them for it.

6

. . . .

ACTION, ADVENTURE, AND WESTERNS

THIS CHAPTER BUNDLES a number of genres together for your shopping efficiency: action movies, adventure epics, gangster flicks, Westerns, mystery thrillers, war films, and swashbucklers.

The underlying connection, I suppose, is that these are mostly boy movies, in principle and in inherent hormonal propulsion. What does *that* mean? Just that the casts are primarily male, that the focus is on their actions, and that women offer either support or danger but are rarely part of the core team. These are androgen-fueled films, but I'm hardly suggesting they're only for boys to watch. On the contrary, Eliza and especially Natalie have seen many of them, enjoyed many of them, and—who knows?—have gleaned something that may stand them in good stead, in the same way a boy might be a larger person for watching *Camille*. If you have a small home audience that's resisting the more interior dramas in other chapters, slap one of these puppies on and see if anything happens.

CAPTAIN BLOOD (B&W, 1935)

Directed by: Michael Curtiz

Starring: Errol Flynn, Olivia de Havilland, Basil Rathbone

Ages: 6 and up

The sell: Hang Johnny Depp—*this* is a pirate.

The plot: Dr. Peter Blood (Flynn) saves the life of a wounded rebel and for his treason is condemned to a life of slavery in Port Royal, Jamaica. There the governor (Lionel Atwill) mistreats the prisoners, but Blood eventually befriends and falls in love with the governor's niece, Lady Arabella (de Havilland). With his fellow slaves, he escapes and takes over a Spanish ship, becoming the notorious (but honorable!) Captain Blood and maintaining an uneasy alliance with the French pirate Levasseur (Rathbone). Rapiers are taken out for a duel on the beach when the sneering Levasseur threatens Arabella.

Why it's here: All Errol Flynn movies are in color, even the ones that aren't. *Captain Blood* made him a star and de Havilland, too—he was the silent-movie action hero at last reborn for the talkies, and she showed more grace, intelligence, and fire (and plain gob-smacking prettiness) than anyone expected. With this film, Michael Curtiz became Warner Bros.' top house director, Basil Rathbone consolidated his standing as the best S.O.B. in the business, and composer Erich Wolfgang Korngold invented the modern film score. And they all got back together for *The Adventures of Robin Hood* (see chapter 1), a film that plays like a live-action illuminated manuscript.

Not that *Captain Blood* is a test run. Ernest Haller's black-and-white photography is excellent and atmospheric, and the spark between the two stars gives the movie real heat. (They never got together, despite having sizable crushes on each other. For one thing, Flynn was married. For another, that mattered to de Havilland.) There's a different sort of spark between Rathbone and Flynn; at times you feel Basil wants to disembowel the star simply because *nobody* deserves to be that effortless on-screen. There aren't that many sword fights in this movie, but the one at the end makes up for the lack—it's like lethal male dancing.

Captain Blood is notable, too, because the hero's a *good* pirate—maybe he sails against the Crown but he saves Port Royal in the end and even becomes its new governor. And he never really does anything that would trouble a censor's sleep (or de Havilland's). True, the dread pirate Blood robs from the rich and gives to the poor, but that was always fair game in Hollywood, that town built by arrivistes. Besides, Blood lets others do the nasty work before coming in for the glory and the girl. If that isn't a management training seminar, I don't know what is.

Pause-button explanations: Why is that nice doctor being punished for helping someone who's hurt? The movie lays out the basic history but you may have to provide historical and geographical backup.

Useless trivia: The unknown Flynn got the role only after Robert Donat dropped out and Brian Aherne turned it down.

What next: Flynn and Curtiz's other great pirate movie, *The Sea Hawk* (1940), and Burt Lancaster's ridiculously enjoyable *The Crimson Pirate* (1952), with the Technicolor for once to back the title up. Tyrone Power's swashbucklers *The Mark of Zorro* (1940) and *The Black Swan* (1942) are also worth their weight in doubloons. And of course there's the 1950 *Treasure Island*, with Robert Newton *arrr*-ing up a storm. Interesting factoid: *Treasure* was Walt Disney's very first foray into live-action movies, and its success probably influenced the decision to add a ride called "Pirates of the Caribbean" to Disneyland in 1967.

DESTRY RIDES AGAIN (B&W, 1939)

Directed by: George Marshall

Starring: James Stewart, Marlene Dietrich, Brian Donlevy

Ages: 6 and up

The sell: J-J-Jimmy Stewart as a gunfighter? That's right, a funny Western.

The plot: Times are tough in the town of Bottleneck. Gambling hall owner Kent (Donlevy) runs the place and has appointed the town drunk as sheriff. Luckily, the sheriff was once a deputy under the famous gunfighter Tom Destry and calls upon his son, Tom Destry Jr. (Stewart) to help clean up Bottleneck. Tom turns out to be a gentle soul but manages to do as asked, both despite and because of saloon singer Frenchy (Dietrich).

Why it's here: From the moment they get their first look at "brutal killer" Stewart—standing on a train platform holding a canary cage in one hand and an umbrella in the other—your kids will be hooked. This is a rollicking, ingratiating comic Western with nothing on its mind except a good time. It delivers. The movie saved Dietrich's career, and you can see why: Always little more than the most special special effect in her previous movies, she's clearly having a grand time here (she and Jimmy were an item off-camera, which didn't hurt). This is the movie where she sings "See What the Boys in the Back Room Will Have," has a catfight with Una Merkel in the saloon, and creates the archetype that Mel Brooks and Madeline Kahn would spoof so drolly as Lili Von Schtupp in *Blazing Saddles*.

Useless trivia: The legend goes that Dietrich set her cap on Stewart but that he was interested in little more than reading *Flash*

Gordon comics—until the actress had the costume department make up a life-sized Gordon doll and that was that.

What next: *Johnny Guitar* (1954) is a wonderfully demented variant on some of the same characters and themes; great for older kids who'll get the joke.

GUNGA DIN (B&W, 1939)

Directed by: George Stevens

Starring: Cary Grant, Douglas Fairbanks Jr., Victor McLaglen, Sam Jaffe

Ages: 8 and up

The sell: Three big boys at play, at war. Hold your questions until the end, please.

The plot: The Rudyard Kipling poem turned into high Hollywood adventure. Sergeants Cutter (Grant), MacChesney (McLaglen), and Ballantine (Fairbanks) are British soldiers in India during the Thuggee uprising. Cutter's in it for the glory and adventure, McChesney loves his elephant, and Ballantine loves Emaline (Joan Fontaine), who wants him to marry her and stop all this nonsense. The men and their native bearer Gunga Din (Jaffe) are trapped by the murderous cult of Kali and are almost witness to the massacre of their entire platoon, but Din's sacrifice saves the day.

Why it's here: The PC police are all over this one and, really, there's no way to defend it. It's a Hollywood movie about British soldiers with California extras in East Indian brownface. It's based on a poem by Rudyard Kipling, the most gifted apologist for the imperialist Raj. And it casts Sam Jaffe—a forty-seven-year-old onetime math teacher from the Bronx last seen playing the High Lama in *Lost Horizon*—as the groveling but ultimately brave Hindu water boy of the title.

It's just a *terrible* film, full of wrong things, so how do you come to grips with how insanely good it is? Along with *The Adventures of Robin Hood*, *Gunga Din* is probably the best action adventure to come out of the entire studio era—a rumbustious playdate of a movie with the three stars rolling around on the rug giving each other pinkbellies.

There are parts of *Gunga Din* that are exquisitely funny—anything to do with McLaglen and the elephant, for instance. Other parts are rather terrifying, and once a kid sees the scene where the guru (played by, um, the Italian-born Eduardo Ciannelli) exhorts his murderous followers to "Kill for the love of killing! Kill for the love of Kali!" that line will be in his or her repertoire for life. The action scenes are plentiful and intensely staged, Cary Grant is at his breeziest (it's not one of his more intelligent roles, and that's how he plays it), there's heroism and sacrifice, and it's all as involving and even, within its limited context, as fair-minded as George Stevens can make it. What's not to like?

Two things, neither of which meant much in 1939 and both of which are unavoidable today (and here is the curse of old media that hangs around beyond its freshness date: that it forces us to confront our parents' blind spots and therefore our own). First, looking at the people of a differently colored country as a mass of uncivilized potential maniacs is dangerous business nowadays. In *Gunga Din*, there are the British (us) and there are the wogs (them), and barring the occasional noble savage like Din, the wogs are not to be trusted. If this sounds like a root attitude behind some of our current geopolitical situations, well—it is.

Second, *Gunga Din* asks a child to cheer for the conquering army against the freedom fighters, which is true to Kipling and the Raj but sits uneasily with our usual way of doing business. Hollywood likes rebels because rebellion is key to America's sense of self—the little guys against George III or the Death Star. In *Gunga Din*, the imperial storm troopers *are* the heroes, and the rebels are the crazed assassins who must be stopped. Interesting. And, to a small viewer, discombobulating in not necessarily bad ways.

Immediately after I wrote the above paragraphs, my wife and I went out to dinner with Kim and Jack. Nice couple, two boys, the older of whom is *Star Wars*–besotted to the point of bringing his own bag of lightsabers everywhere he goes because you never know when you might run into Darth Vader at the supermarket. I mentioned *Gunga Din* to Jack, and he immediately said it had been his father's favorite movie, period, full stop. The old man, German-Irish with a crush on English pomp, saw the film when he was seven and never got over it, and he made sure his son saw it when the time came. Jack, too, was emotionally KO-ed by the film and by the same aspect his father had been: "The black guy was the *hero*. The character they dumped on and treated as a child turned out to save the day. You never took him seriously and in the end he was the bravest of them all. I wept about that."

So. What to do? Show your kids the film. Let them enjoy it and listen to what they say. Sometimes kids see through to the things that matter.

Pause-button explanations: See above. A simple description of British colonial expansion (which would by necessity have to include America) would probably open doors to some interesting conversations.

Useless trivia: Surprise: India banned the film on its initial release.

What next: *The Four Feathers* (1939) is a British-made adventure epic covering some of the same ground and with some of the same problems. *The Charge of the Light Brigade* (1936) casts Tasmanian Errol Flynn as a British lancer; it's more grand Hollywood hokum from the *Captain Blood/Robin Hood* team. *Beau Geste* (1939) has Gary Cooper, Ray Milland, and a young Robert Preston in the French Foreign Legion. Then there's *Lawrence of Arabia* (1962), too violent and morally complex for younger audiences but excellent—even essential—meat for thoughtful teenagers.

HIGH NOON (B&W, 1952)

Directed by: Fred Zinneman

Starring: Gary Cooper, Grace Kelly

Ages: 7 and up

The sell: Do what's right, even when everyone else is wrong.

The plot: Hadleyville, New Mexico. Marshall Will Kane (Cooper) is getting married to pretty Quaker Amy Fowler (Kelly) and retiring that very day, but news comes that Frank Miller (Ian MacDonald) is out of prison and heading back to town to kill Will. It's 10:35, the train arrives at noon, and Miller's boys are waiting at the station. Kane asks the citizens of Hadleyville for help and, one by one, they turn him down. In the end, he turns in his badge and faces the bad guys on his own.

Why it's here: I could say that *High Noon* is important for its political message. (It was intentionally crafted as an allegory for the moral cowardice of the McCarthy era, in particular those who turned their backs on the Hollywood Ten after they defied the House Un-American Activities Committee.) I could say that it imparts an immensely important lesson to young viewers about the importance of sticking to your guns. But, really, what's cool about the movie—what captures a kid's interest before anything else—is that it plays out in real time.

Or as close to real time as Zinneman could get away with. The movie's eighty-five minutes long and takes place from 10:35 to about 12:15—a hundred minutes, close enough—with clocks visible throughout town. It's an unsubtle way of ratcheting up suspense, and it works as advertised. Then there's the shock of the townsfolk leaving Will Kane in the lurch. Not just the townsfolk: His wife's a pacifist Quaker and, besides, she's been married for ten minutes and wouldn't mind seeing her husband live through the day. His deputy (Lloyd Bridges) secretly covets Will's job himself. Everyone has their reasons and everyone is inherently selfish; only Will is acting selflessly. (He could run; why doesn't he run? Because a man's gotta do what a man's gotta do.)

One of the most amusing activities for a parent is watching their child become poleaxed with moral outrage over this film. *High Noon* makes kids splenetic, so unfair, so *wrong* are the citizens of Hadleyville, and this of course makes them examine their own internal code of honor, which was precisely Zinneman's and writer Carl Foreman's pedagogical intent. They just wanted it to work on grown-ups, when there's a case to be made that *Noon*'s moral lesson is most effective with viewers who are still adjusting their ethical factory settings. It's a very good movie with the lingering taste of spinach, but there are more than enough sweeteners to put it over—and at eighty-five minutes, it's the movie equivalent of fast food.

Pause-button explanations: You can sketch the historical background of the blacklist era if your kids are old enough and you can make it interesting.

Home video notes: The 2002 Collector's Edition from Republic has all the making-of documentaries, commentaries, and random appearances by Leonard Maltin a young movie freak could ask for.

Useless trivia: Cooper was suffering from a bleeding ulcer throughout filming—no wonder he looks pained.

What next: *Rio Bravo* (see below), John Wayne's answer to *High Noon*. Also, Gregory Peck's *The Gunfighter* (1950), which has similar concerns, minus the political backdrop.

THE MALTESE FALCON (B&W, 1941)

Directed by: John Huston

Starring: Humphrey Bogart, Mary Astor, Peter Lorre

Ages: 8 and up

The sell: Never show your cards.

The plot: Sam Spade (Bogart) and his partner Miles Archer are hired by the ladylike Brigid O'Shaughnessy (Astor) to look for her brother. After Archer is killed and Spade crosses wits and fists with dapper killer Joel Cairo (Lorre), sinister Kaspar Gutman (Sidney Greenstreet), and lethal little gunsel Wilmer (Elisha Cook Jr.), it turns out everyone's after a rare, jewel-encrusted medieval statue of a falcon.

Why it's here: The classic gumshoe flick, from the burnout hero to the secondary characters cluttering the plot like a touring company of the Seven Deadly Sins. Based on the Dashiell Hammett novel, *Falcon* was John Huston's directorial debut, and it made Bogart an A-list star after a decade of scrabbling for the gold ring. At last he was Bogey, and the gallery of types that surround him was consolidated here too: the shady dame, the effete killer, Mr. Big. Bogart needs them to function, to throw up the roadblocks he cuts through with a snarl or a punch, and in fact Lorre and Greenstreet followed the star to both *Casablanca* (1942) and *Passage to Marseilles* (1944), like a Pug and a St. Bernard tailing after their master.

The plot barely makes sense to an adult, and it'll probably

cause children's heads to spin like Linda Blair's. You might even want to hold off on murder mysteries in general until you feel sure your home audience is at the right stage of brain development. Kids need to be able to keep a movie like this in the front drawer of their short-term memory so they can riffle the index cards when a clue comes along. They have to be able to listen to dialogue and understand what the character *isn't* saying, or what he's *really* saying.

My daughters, then aged seven and nine, watched *Falcon* with mounting incomprehension and increasing satisfaction. They finally gave up even trying to understand what was going on, but the movie somehow makes a virtue of this. Lorre is such a delightful creep and Greenstreet such a hearty villain and Elisha Cook such a rabid ferret that you settle for the pungent character studies. Astor's Brigid is a woman who wears many personalities, and that was a new one on Eliza and Natalie: The ending made them gasp in shock for the first and maybe the last time while watching a classic whodunnit.

And there is Bogart, who seems like the only movie hero capable of dealing with this crew without getting a toe shot off. The girls watched *Falcon* for him and came away sated; if they had no idea what was going on, they also had no idea what Bogey would do next, and that was the greater and more addictive mystery.

Pause-button explanations: If you want to keep your kids up to speed with the plot, you'll be pausing a lot. Expect a lot of "What's going on?" and decide beforehand whether you'll be a pedant or let the little buggers dog-paddle for themselves.

What next: Hit Bogart's private-eye classics first. Hawks's *The Big Sleep* (1946) is the best bet: Based on a Raymond Chandler novel with a script cowritten by William Faulkner, it's even more confusing than *Falcon*. Better, too. *To Have and Have Not* (1944) and *Key Largo* (1948) are two more crime dramas Bogart made with

Lauren Bacall; in the first one, made when the two were falling in love, it's like watching a mating dance between tigers. If your children haven't seen *Casablanca* (1942), now's the time. And if they want other gumshoes, there are plenty to choose from: Dick Powell shedding his crooner image as Philip Marlowe in *Murder My Sweet* (1944), William Powell and Myrna Loy in the *Thin Man* series (see below), Alan Ladd in *The Blue Dahlia* (1946).

THE PUBLIC ENEMY (B&W, 1931) AND WHITE HEAT (B&W, 1949)

Directed by: William Wellman/Raoul Walsh

Starring: James Cagney

Ages: 9 and up

The sell: The best bad boy

The plots: In *The Public Enemy*, Tom Powers (Cagney) rises from street urchin to small-time hood to the muscle for a Prohibition bootlegger. On the side of the angels are his brother (Donald Cook) and sainted mother (Beryl Mercer); on the other side are Tom's slightly more cautious pal Matt (Edward Woods), various gangsters, and a couple of tootsies (played by Mae Clarke, who gets a grapefruit in the face, and Jean Harlow, who launched a career). Tom dreams big, plays mean, dies badly. *White Heat* imagines how Tom Powers might have turned out had he lived—and had his mother (Margaret Wycherly) been a criminal old buzzard herself.

Why they're here: For no other reason than Cagney, really, and to see two explorations of the thug hero that are brutal, critical, charismatic, and not at all sympathetic. Eliza and Natalie loved *Public Enemy*, loved Cagney, and were thoroughly appalled at the character he plays. "He's just *evil*," Eliza said in summary judgment after Tom shoots the horse that has thrown and killed his gangster boss (she might also have added that Tom's stupid—who kills a horse for revenge?). This was a new one on both of them: an irredeemable central figure. They knew he deserved whatever he got, but the ending, Tom mummified on his mother's doorstep and falling inward with a sickening thud, shocked them into silence.

And yet they, and I, couldn't take our eyes off the guy. Cagney came from the streets of Manhattan, a song-and-dance man who turned into one of the nicest fellas in Hollywood, but he grew up with kids like Tom Powers and *White Heat*'s Cody Jarrett, and he knew how sadistically attractive they could be—and how, at the end of the day, they were just sons of bitches.

The Warner Bros. gangster classics Cagney appeared in were unrepentantly violent and macho for their time, cobbled to-gether from tabloid headlines and gangland lore—the celebrated bit where Cagney smacks girlfriend Mae Clarke in the face with a grapefruit came from a real-life Chicago mobster who had actually used an omelette. Audiences loved these films while keepers of the public morals whimpered and wrote editorials about copycat violence. Eventually Hollywood caved—between Cagney and Mae West, something had to give—and in 1933 instituted the Motion Picture Code of happy endings and twin beds that lasted until the 1960s. If you want Cagney unleashed, look for his pre-Code films: *Picture Snatcher, Taxi!, Ladykiller, Blonde Crazy*. They're all unbelievably frank for "old movies" and will blow the socks off any teenagers in your house (as will Edward G. Robinson's *Two Seconds* from 1932).

White Heat, made eighteen years after *Public Enemy*, is a differ-ent animal. Cagney had tired of gangster roles by the late '30s and successfully remade himself as a hoofer, light comedian, crusading hero. This film marked his return to mayhem, and it's a more mature response to the classic Warner Bros. gangster films, closer in ways to the ambiguities of film noir. And Cody Jarrett is a thug of almost Shakespearean proportions. Egged on by unseen demons that occasionally reduce him to moaning psychosis, he's both killer and mama's boy, with a gang that includes a hatchet-faced mother (Margaret Wycherly) who's been telling him it's Cody versus the world since he was a child. The early scene in which he sits in her lap was the star's idea and Wycherly plays along beautifully.

Yet this isn't a psychological portrait, as became fashionable when the Method boys showed up (Cagney had only contempt for the new breed of actors who "did it only for themselves and not the audience"). It *is* a richer performance because the star freights Cody with a sort of hysterical sadness. Tom Powers was a bastard because it made him feel good. With Cody, everything else just makes him feel much, much worse.

There are two scenes your kids will remember for all eternity. One is the jailhouse sequence when Cody learns his mother has died; the news is passed from con to con like an awful game of telephone, and then the demons strike. My daughters watched this with growing disbelief; the movie seemed to be buckling at the edges. The other scene is the top-of-the-world finale, one of the most ecstatic, even orgasmic, climaxes of any Hollywood movie. In it, Cagney finally strips the remaining veneer of civilization from his tough guys and reveals the screaming big-baby id beneath.

Pause-button explanations: You'll need to give some context about Prohibition for *Public Enemy*. Also: Let's just say it's not a milestone in film feminism.

Home video notes: The Warner Bros. "Gangsters Collection" puts these two, plus *Angels with Dirty Faces*, *Little Caesar*, *The Roaring Twenties*, and *The Petrified Forest* in one excellent box. The standalone discs have nice extras as well.

Useless trivia: In *Public Enemy*'s machine-gun scene, real bullets were used, with Cagney dancing very nervously ahead of the spray. Also, James Cagney never, ever said "You dirty rat, you killed my brother." But you can, if you want to.

What next: *Scarface: Shame of the Nation* (1932), Howard Hawks's Al Capone movie with Paul Muni laying the groundwork for Pacino fifty years later; *Little Caesar* (1931), Edward G. Robinson's breakthrough; *High Sierra* (1941), which served the same function for Bogart (not 1936's *Petrified Forest*, which is based on a stage play and it creaks); *Angels with Dirty Faces* (1938); and *The Roaring Twenties* (1939).

RIO BRAVO (COLOR, 1959)

Directed by: Howard Hawks

Starring: John Wayne, Dean Martin, Ricky Nelson, Angie Dickinson

Ages: 6 and up

The sell: The block party of classic Westerns

The plot: Sheriff John T. Chance (Wayne) and his deputy Dude (Martin), a former sharpshooter and current drunk, bring in badman Joe Burdette (Claude Akins) to the town jail. Joe's corrupt rancher brother Nathan Burdette (John Russell) aims to break him out by any means necessary before the U.S. marshals get to town, and if that means bringing in his gang to kill the sheriff, so be it. Chance ends up defending the jail with Dude, the untested teenager Colorado (Nelson), and toothless old Stumpy (Walter Brennan), with a little help from shady Feathers (Dickinson).

Why it's here: Because it's tremendous old-school fun and probably the most relaxed Western ever made, even with all those guns going off at the end. And, as advertised, it's the answer film to *High Noon*, made because Wayne and Hawks were offended by the idea of a lawman who has to beg for help. (It should be noted that the Duke once admitted *Noon*'s Will Kane was a hell of a part and that he wouldn't have turned it down himself—but he was handing Gary Cooper a best actor Oscar at the time, so a little jealousy is understandable.)

Rio Bravo says it's a man's world, and men don't ask—this applies to mortal danger as well as directions. Self-sufficiency is the main order of business. One onlooker gauges Chance's backup and snorts, "A bum-legged old man and a drunk—that's all you've got?" "That's *what* I've got," snaps the sheriff, and the message is clear: Make do and don't fuss. "Sorry don't get it done," he tells Dude, whose drinking is only a symptom; his greater crime is regret.

This all sounds terribly serious, but *Rio Bravo* is one of the great Western picaresques, approaching late-inning Shakespeare in its wisdom and humor and ease. The movie is long (two hours and twenty minutes) and at times it seems like nothing much is happening except people jawing wonderfully at each other, and there are certain kids and adults for whom it will be a baffling and deadening experience. The villains are almost secondary. The romantic subplot between Chance and Feathers (Angie Dickinson, delightful) is more a running commentary on the ways men and women drive each other crazy, and, once again, the woman is the chaos factor and happy to be so. If this *is* Shakespeare, a *Tempest* in a Western teapot, then Feathers is Ariel.

And there's the sublime moment in the jail, just before the storm breaks, where everyone just sits down and sings. Until then, you've almost forgotten you've got both a Rat Pack member *and* one of the better early rock 'n' rollers in the cast. If the scene is a contractual obligation for Dino and Ricky Nelson, it works in context as an unforced statement of calm and solidarity. Even Walter Brennan joins in, quavery and enthusiastic. (But Wayne doesn't, since singing is what the troops do when the general's waiting for action and, anyway, there's a chance his singing voice would spook the horses. He smiles, though, and that's something to see.) One of the songs in this sudden hootenanny is called "My Rifle, My Pony, and Me," and we are invited to compare these sentiments with the Oscar-winning tune from *High Noon*, "Do Not Forsake Me, Oh My Darling." Even a kid can't miss what's going on here. Community rises from individual responsibility, not the other way around.

Useless trivia: Dmitri Tiomkin wrote the music for both songs; the tune for "My Rifle" was actually used, with different words, in the earlier Hawks/Wayne Western *Red River*. If you've got a young formalist in the house, call attention to that long opening scene, which plays out entirely without dialogue. *Rio Bravo* is also the source for John Carpenter's urban actioner *Assault on Precinct 13* (1976) as well as one of Quentin Tarantino's favorite movies. Seriously—Bruce Willis quotes a bit of Wayne's dialogue here in *Pulp Fiction*.

What next: Hawks's *Red River* (1948), a more serious cattle-drive drama starring Wayne (in one of his career-best performances) and Montgomery Clift. The director's final two films, *El Dorado* (1966) and *Rio Lobo* (1970), both starring Wayne, are basically remakes of *Rio Bravo*, and even more loosey-goosey.

THE SEARCHERS (COLOR, 1956)

Directed by: John Ford

Starring: John Wayne, Jeffrey Hunter, Natalie Wood

Ages: 12 and up

The sell: What happens when being a hero turns you into a villain?

The plot: Ethan Edwards (Wayne) returns to Texas from the Civil War to live with his brother and sister-in-law (whom Ethan clearly loves) and their children. A Comanche raid wipes out the entire family except for young Debbie Edwards, who is taken captive. Ethan and his half-breed nephew Martin (Hunter) follow the trail for five years, Ethan's hatred of Indians growing and growing until it becomes clear that he intends to kill Debbie, who has by now grown up to be part of the tribe (and played by Wood).

Why it's here: Because it riddles the Western with doubts and complexities. *The Searchers* is for when you want to move a kid beyond entertainments like *Stagecoach* and *Destry Rides Again* and be gripped by a harder drama, one with moral as well as physical dimensions.

At what point does someone watching this for the first time understand that Ethan Edwards is not a nice man? At what point do they understand the movie's greater point: that men like Ethan are necessary for civilization but will always remain outside it? The first is a child's realization, probably coming when Ethan stampedes the buffalo so the Indians will starve. The second is a revelation, underscored by the film's final, effortlessly eloquent image of the door closing on its hero. We stay inside. He doesn't.

It's not a Western for young children. There's that sequence where Ethan returns from burying the body of Lucy Edwards (Pippa Scott) in a gully; he's visibly shaken by what has been done to her, and when one of the search party pushes for details, he cracks—John Wayne *loses it*—and furiously tells the man never to ask him again. More upsetting, in a sense, is the earlier scene just before the Comanches attack the family, when Lucy suddenly understands the full import of the situation and lets out one of the most unsettling screams I've ever heard. There are movie screams and there are movie screams, some operatic (Fay Wray meeting King Kong), some comic (Una Merkel in *Frankenstein*), some purely functional (whoever has to scream when the lights go out in a murder mystery). Lucy's is the scream of someone who knows she is going to die very badly and very soon, and it offers not a shred of hope.

For older kids, though, there's a lot to chew on here and also a lot to enjoy, particularly Ward Bond as the high-spirited military commander/preacher whose motives occasionally dovetail with Ethan's. Hunter, young and handsome and troubled in a modish way, lets us hang our sympathies on someone while we sort out our feelings about Ethan. But that sorting out is the true drama of *The Searchers*, and the searching mostly goes on in our hearts and heads. Would Ethan be more effective if he were less of a racist creep? Or do we know and just not want to admit that a kinder man would have given up after one year or three, that hatred is a greater spur than love, that the graveyards of American settlement are filled with the bones of vicious men? And do we call them heroes now because we've forgotten what it took, or because we still carry their DNA?

Pause-button explanations: A grown-up Western in the mid-1950s, *Searchers* has to get some of its points across obliquely. You may need to help spell some things out. For instance, just before the raid, there's a throwaway shot of a tombstone for Ethan's mother, killed by the Comanche, that partly explains his hatred of Native Americans. There's also the possibility that Debbie might even be Ethan's daughter; Ford was circumspect about the matter on the set.

Useless trivia: Ethan's catchphrase "*That'*ll be the day" was the source of Buddy Holly's first hit song.

What next: More grown-up Westerns? Go straight to Ford's *The Man Who Shot Liberty Valance* (1962), with Wayne and James Stewart working out a more thoughtful variant of *Searchers's* concerns. Then head to the cycle of tough, small masterpieces Stewart made with director Anthony Mann, five in all, with *The Naked Spur* (1953) the best of the bunch; like *Searchers*, it looks at classic Western conventions through a lens darkened by the losses and lessons of World War II. If your kids are old enough and can handle the violence, move on to Sam Peckinpah (*Ride the High Country*, *The Wild Bunch*), Sergio Leone (*The Good, the Bad, and the Ugly* and the transcendent *Once Upon a Time in the West*), and Clint Eastwood.

SHANE (COLOR, 1953)

Directed by: George Stevens

Starring: Alan Ladd, Jack Palance, Brandon De Wilde, Jean Arthur

Ages: 6 and up. No teens, though.

The sell: Black hat. White hat. Little boy watching.

The plot: A world-weary gunfighter without a name—all right, with one name, Shane (Ladd)—rides into the Wyoming Valley and tries to settle down with the homesteading Starrett family, Joe (Van Heflin), Marian (Arthur, in her final film), and little Joey (De Wilde). The powerful Ryker clan aims to take over the settlers' land for ranching and sends in a hired killer named Wilson (Palance). Between long, langorous looks at Marian, Shane comes to grips with his own gift for killing.

Why it's here: Every so often, Hollywood puts out a Western that tries to renew the old clichés by pumping them up with simplicity. *Stagecoach* (see chapter 1) is one; so is Clint Eastwood's *Unforgiven*. (Sergio Leone's spaghetti Westerns, on the other hand, are grandly serious pop art parodies.)

Shane is perhaps the best and weightiest of the bunch. It boils the genre elements down to their most iconic—Evil Rancher, Reluctant Marksman, Shoot-out on Main Street—and lets them play out on a colorful but elegiac canvas. It's not a movie for itchy children; too solemn, a little slow. With a good print and as big a screen as you can manage, though, *Shane* is a life experience. Along with *Stagecoach*, it's also an excellent introductory Western.

And not because of the kid, either. Young audiences often grab on to a young actor in a movie; they see the grown-up action through his or her eyes, as the filmmakers intend them to. Brandon De Wilde does serve the same purpose here as, say, Mary Badham and Philip Alford in *To Kill a Mockingbird*, but the difference is that De Wilde's Joey Starrett is annoying—whiny and seemingly not all that bright. I always thought so, at least; your mileage may vary. He gets off the famous closing line— *Shane! Come back, Shane!*—and he has some funny facial reactions when Shane gets busy with fist and gun, but you sense that cutting to a cat would have got a similar laugh.

Still, having Joey as a filter makes the story less simplistic and more "important," because it preserves a sense of mystery. What's the real relationship between Shane and Marian? We never truly know, because we only see as much as the kid does. What's the real nature of Shane's past? It's immaterial, to the movie and to the boy and therefore to us. Looking through Joey's tiny eyes makes Palance's Wilson all the more terrifying and Alan Ladd all the taller.

Add Loyal Griggs's Oscar-winning color cinematography, intensely beautiful locations in Jackson Hole, Wyoming, and a quiet farewell performance from Arthur—as if she had somehow escaped Frank Capra's loving grip by traveling back in time—and you have a keeper.

Useless trivia: Montgomery Clift and William Holden were slated to star as, respectively, Shane and Joe, but dropped out for other projects. In desperation, director Stevens looked at a list of available actors and cast Ladd, Heflin, and Arthur within minutes. The film was nominated for six Oscars, including best picture, director, and two supporting actors (Palance and De Wilde, so what do I know?). Ladd wasn't even nominated.

What next: Proceed to the films above and slowly fan out into complexity. Make sure your kids are interested in Westerns, though.

THEY WERE EXPENDABLE (B&W, 1945)

Directed by: John Ford

Starring: John Wayne, Robert Montgomery

Ages: 9 and up

The sell: War is Hell.

The plot: The early days of World War II. Following the Japanese attack on Pearl Harbor, the crews of U.S. PT boats in the Philippines try to slow the enemy assault while protecting the locals. It's a losing battle, for the time being.

Why it's here: Because it's arguably the best movie about World War II until *Saving Private Ryan* and because it's one of the best war movies, period. Certainly it's the one your child should see if he (or she) is into playing battleground in the backyard.

Here's the dilemma with this genre: It's not in a kid's long-term interest to watch propaganda that sugarcoats what war is and does, but it's also probably not the best idea to show them *Platoon* or *Ryan* until they're equipped to handle carnage and inglorious death. Not all classic Hollywood war movies lie, though. *They Were Expendable*—the title reflects the attitude of the U.S. Navy toward the crews of the PT boats—was based on a book by men who were there and made by a director who served in the navy, and it stars Montgomery, who was a Pacific PT boat captain with a Bronze Star to show for it. (And then there's Wayne, whose iconic patriotism has always been qualified by the fact that the actor not only didn't serve but seemed to spend much of the war looking for ways *not* to serve, something that has never really been fully explored or explained.)

Filmed in 1945, when it was clear the Allies were going to win, *Expendable* honors those who died before the outcome was a sure thing, when the Japanese were sweeping across the Pacific and forcing Gen. MacArthur to flee the Philippines. Audiences late in the war didn't fancy being talked down to—they could handle the bad news—and so there's a burned-in cynicism about upper-echelon navy motivations that's the exact opposite of propaganda and rather startling to find in a black-and-white Hollywood war movie. There's also a lingering sadness and awareness of loss—a knowledge of the preciousness of every moment, especially in the scenes that involve Donna Reed—that few war movies even contemplate. Defeat and death hang over everyone in *Expendable* and no one feels particularly heroic about it.

There are enough action sequences to keep a small explosives junkie happy, but the thrust of the movie is elegiac, absurdist, even angry. These are necessary qualities to any child's view of armed conflict.

Useless trivia: Montgomery was the father of *Bewitched*'s Elizabeth Montgomery.

What next: *Battleground* (1949) is the other great studio-era World War II film, this one focusing on the struggle in Europe during the Battle of the Bulge. It's even more no-nonsense than *Expendable*. *All Quiet on the Western Front* (1930) is undeniably creaky but still makes a potent antiwar statement. Other good World War II films about the Pacific theater include *Wake Island* (1942) and *Guadalcanal Diary* (1943), while *The Best Years of Our Lives* (1946) is a powerful multi-Oscar winner about postwar readjustment. Stanley Kubrick's World War I drama *Paths of Glory* (1957) is a brilliant statement about the folly of war (as is the nuclear comedy *Dr. Strangelove*—see chapter 3—for entirely different reasons).

THE THIN MAN (B&W, 1934)

Directed by: W. S. Van Dyke

Starring: William Powell, Myrna Loy

Ages: 8 and up

The sell: Believe it: Marriage can be fun.

The plot: Nick Charles (Powell) is a West Coast private eye recently married to heiress Nora (Loy). With their terrier Asta, they arrive in Manhattan only to be embroiled in a mystery surrounding the disappearance of the title character (Edward Ellis), an inventor who has apparently murdered his scheming secretary/girlfriend (Natalie Moorhead), among others. But who's really the culprit? The inventor's daughter (Maureen

O'Sullivan), his estranged ex-wife (Minna Gombell), her gigolo husband (Cesar Romero)? Or is it someone else? Between industrial-strength martinis, Nick and Nora get their man.

Why it's here: The *Thin Man* series, six films in all, purveyed Murder-Mystery Lite: in them, the comedy is equal to the sleuthing. These are breezy, often hysterically funny entertainments that lay out the basics of the detective genre for an audience of first-timers—the crime, the gallery of suspects, the offhanded but keen deduction, and the climactic gathering of the potentially guilty for the revelation of sticky-fingered guilt (followed by frenzied shrieks of "All right, it was me! I did it! And I'm *glad*!").

But this isn't why Natalie and Eliza saw the first film in the series and immediately clamored to see them all. There's Asta, obviously; smart and yappy and given to chewing clues, he makes up for all the shopworn dog close-ups in other movies. Much better, though, *The Thin Man* offers up a seductive portrait of modern marriage as endless, loving play.

Nick and Nora never argue, even when they disagree—even after they have a son in the third entry, 1939's *Another Thin Man*. In them the glow of honeymoon never fades: They're as delighted to see each other in the morning as they were the first morning. Refreshingly, they still drive each other crazy in all the ways men and women do, and that's somehow part of the game. Nora catches Nick doing a nearly invisible gander at another woman:

> *Nora:* Pretty girl.
> *Nick:* Yes, she's a very nice type. (Powell bites off that last word pleasantly, as if to say "I wasn't looking at *her*, I was looking at her *type*.")
> *Nora:* You've got types?
> *Nick:* Only you, darling. Lanky brunettes with wicked jaws.

This is what our own parents called class, and it is a quality so near extinction that anything you do to get your children to see it, understand it, value it, is energy well spent.

Now: Is the Charles joie de vivre a direct product of the couple's herculean intake of liquor? Nick especially partakes of scotch, gin, and bourbon in massive quantities, at all hours of the day, and Powell is a smart enough actor to play the character as always slightly sozzled. Nick wobbles a little, slurs a bit, and yet perceives clues, connections, and motivations the others—all lesser mortals except for Nora, who's not a pro, and Asta, who's a dog—never catch. Would he be a better detective sober, or a worse one? It's immaterial. Booze and cigarettes, the rudiments of cinematic sin, are defined and redeemed in him.

And, look, people drank in those days. As a child of the '60s and '70s, I grew up with parents who had been children of the '30s and '40s, and they *drank*. As did their friends, as did everyone they knew. Not the beer-pounding and candy martinis of today, but serious cocktails and rye straight up. My childhood summer memories are of deck chairs and ice clinking in tumblers, other kids' fathers' pale knees in Bermuda shorts, heavy glass ashtrays with lipstick cigarettes mysteriously smoldering, the laughter outside growing bolder as we dropped off to sleep. Did the drug culture of the late '60s take our cultural and physical tolerance for all this away? People drink still, obviously, in some ways more than ever, but they also seem to get stupidly drunk more easily. We are a generation that cannot hold its liquor. I've visited an old law partner of my father's, a man in his seventies, only to have him put me under the coffee table within half an hour of my first martini while he sips his third and talks about his tennis game.

That is the world Nick Charles lives in.

What did the girls think? They watched *The Thin Man* and cackled at Nick's dipsomania, recognizing it for the absurdity it is. *Nobody* could drink that much and be upright, let alone solve a murder; this they knew. It added to the fun this couple had, to the fun this movie was, but it didn't glamorize drinking so much as spoof it. There's time enough for discussions after the movie, not to mention screenings of *The Lost Weekend* and *Days of Wine and Roses*. For now, the *Thin Man* movies give them something entirely different: a series of enchanting hints that living with a person you love can be the best sort of playdate. The lesson to parents is even more pressing: Be like this, if you can.

Pause-button explanations: You'll have to work out who's who and who done what, especially after the ending, which feels rushed.

Home video notes: You can rent the six films individually, but the 2005 Warner DVD box really is great fun: Each disc also includes short subjects and cartoons, since audiences of the day would have seen these before any of the features.

Useless trivia: The "Thin Man" isn't Nick, as newcomers to the films assume. He's the inventor who's the focus of the mystery in the first movie; the studio brass, no dummies they, worked variations on the title for the next fifteen years.

What next: The first sequel, 1936's *After the Thin Man*, may actually be the best of the batch. It costars a young Jimmy Stewart and gives him a lulu of a scene toward the end. The next are: *Another Thin Man* (1939), *Shadow of the Thin Man* (1941), *The Thin Man Goes Home* (1945), and *Song of the Thin Man* (1947), by which point Powell and Loy look very, very tired. In general, the quality gradually diminishes along with Powell's alcohol intake, but if your kids are fans they won't notice.

THE DARK PLEASURES OF FILM NOIR

There are children who suspect things, and for them, film noir offers confirmation: The good are condemned to screw up and die, the wicked prosper (until they, too, screw up and die), and greed and self-interest work their way into the cracks of everything we do. It may be that all children suspect these things after a certain age, when the fairy tales we tell them (or, more properly, ourselves) no longer jibe with what they see and understand.

The term was coined by French critic Frank Nino in 1946 and was meant to describe the inky, paranoid look of certain Hollywood movies: suspense films and private eye mysteries, tales of lust gone criminal like *Double Indemnity*. The auteurist critics of postwar France—future directors with names like Truffaut and Godard—expanded on the term while embracing the movies as the source of certain human truths, relayed with gutter artistry and honesty.

In America, of course, film noirs got no respect at all. They just made money, and not even much of that. A movie like *Narrow Margin* with pop-eyed Marie Windsor as a slut under government protection? It was a B movie barely allowed to unspool during daylight hours, flying beneath the radar and flattering only audiences astute enough to read the fine print of fate and behavior. If the mainstream culture of the Eisenhower era shone sunlight everywhere, film noir is where the shadows went. Literally—these movies are visually stunning dances in the dark, their heroes stumbling because they can't see the woman in their arms or even their own two feet. No one's to be trusted except the bad girl, like the tootsie Gloria Grahame plays in *The Big Heat* (1953), after gangster Lee Marvin has thrown a pot of boiling coffee in her face and turned her into an avenging angel wrapped in gauze.

These films are for the hard-core old-movie kid: teenagers looking for a style to dress their cynicism in, those who don't trust the governing culture of their own time. In their refusal to be soothed, noirs were the punk, the screamo, the death-metal of their day. They still refuse to play nice.

Following is a chronological cook's tour through fifteen high points of the genre. Any one will do for a start, although *The Big Heat* may be the film at the center of the Venn diagram, containing all the elements others share only in parts. Private eye movies—especially the ones with Bogart—are dealt with above and excluded here. Also, many of these movies have been remade in the last two decades, almost always to painful effect. The hard-boiled attitude—the cold, attractive laughing at fate these remakes want to trade on—dies the moment you take it out of its time period. Read the DVD case carefully and accept no substitutes.

Laura *(B&W, 1944)* Detective Dana Andrews falls for the dead woman whose murder he's investigating (played by the bewitching Gene Tierney, so you don't really blame him for necrophilia). A protonoir: photographed in dazzling black and white but with one foot in drawing room mysteries of an earlier era.

Double Indemnity *(B&W, 1944)* Gloriously mean tabloid true-crime saga, with Fred MacMurray as a morally bankrupt insurance salesman hoodooed by hot-to-trot Barbara Stanwyck into killing her husband. They're like rats lost in their own maze, and Edward G. Robinson as MacMurray's boss keeps moving the cheese. (Remade, more or less, as 1981's *Body Heat*.)

Gilda *(B&W, 1946)* Rita Hayworth lays the groundwork for film noir femme fatales to come while laying all the men in the movie. Although Glenn Ford and George Macready seem to have eyes for each other as well. Not so much true noir (whatever that may be) as a startling aberration of Hollywood kink.

The Killers *(B&W, 1946)* Director Robert Siodmak takes a Hemingway short story and uses it as a springboard to create arguably the first no-nonsense noir classic. Burt Lancaster and Ava Gardner got their breakthroughs as, respectively, the honorable sap and the two-timing shady lady; incredibly photographed by Woody Bredell, as if anyone noticed at the time. (Remade in 1964 with Ronald Reagan in the bad guy role.)

Kiss of Death *(B&W, 1947)* Richard Widmark made his film debut as Tommy Udo, a giggling little hoodlum who pushes an old lady in a wheelchair down the stairs to her death. *That'll* make the kids pay attention. (Remade in 1995 with David Caruso.)

Out of the Past *(B&W, 1947)* Film noir for postgraduates. We defy your film junkies to keep the scoreboard of crosses and double-crosses straight, but Robert Mitchum at his Mitchumiest and the fine-boned, plenty tough Jane Greer make it worthwhile. Plus: Kirk Douglas as a heel. Greer: "Is there a way to win?" Mitchum: "There's a way to lose more slowly." (Remade as *Against All Odds* in 1984.)

The Third Man *(B&W, 1949)* Moral postwar European noir, so maybe it doesn't count, but Robert Krasker's photography is sharp enough to draw blood, and Orson Welles is remarkably lovable as the hateful Harry Lime. Oh, and it's one of the best and most atmospheric movies ever made. Really. (Remade in 1997. In Croatia.)

D.O.A. *(B&W, 1950)* Edmond O'Brien is slipped some poison and has twenty-four hours to find his own murderer. Nifty little twister set in San Francisco, with O'Brien sweating bullets. Wouldn't you? (Remade in 1988 with Dennis Quaid.)

The Asphalt Jungle *(B&W, 1950)* The first heist movie? Certainly the one that drew the blueprint: the crew of criminal specialists, the safe that can't be cracked, and all the ways everything can go wrong. Great cast, too, from Sterling Hayden to an unknown named Marilyn Monroe. (Remade by every heist movie since.)

Night and the City *(B&W, 1950)* British film noir, with Widmark as a hustler playing both ends of gangland London against each other. Brilliantly seedy; love that pro wrestler subplot. (Remade in 1992 with Robert De Niro.)

The Narrow Margin *(B&W, 1952)* Trampy Marie Windsor is a mobster's widow on a cross-country train trip to testify before a grand jury. Charles McGraw is the detective trying to protect her from an onslaught of hoods. It's a good lesson in how to squeeze the maximum in suspense out of the minimum in location. (Remade in 1990 with Gene Hackman and Anne Archer.)

The Big Heat *(B&W, 1953)* Fritz Lang's inquisition into how a nice, clean-cut cop (Glenn Ford) might go up against the mob and turn into a heartless instrument of vengeance. Essential viewing, for the young Lee Marvin as a creep, for Gloria Grahame as a party girl deepened by trauma, and for the way Lang slowly lowers the doom on his hero.

Pickup on South Street *(B&W, 1953)* Kids, meet Sam Fuller. Now duck. Nervy little B thriller about a pickpocket (Widmark again) who accidentally dips into a purse containing some top-secret Commie microfilm, with Jean Peters as the unwitting owner of the purse and the great Thelma Ritter as a street merchant at the end of the line.

The Sweet Smell of Success *(B&W, 1957)* One for the older kids who can appreciate dialogue and characters steeped in the Manhattan nihilism of the cool jazz era. Burt Lancaster is an all-powerful gossip columnist and Tony Curtis the spineless press agent of whom Lancaster's character says, "I'd hate to take a bite out of you. You're a cookie full of arsenic." Your teenagers think they're cool with their little indie movies? They're going to flip when they see this. (Remade in 2002 as, appropriately, a flop Broadway musical.)

Touch of Evil *(B&W, 1958)* Made long after Hollywood had stopped returning his calls, Orson Welles's Mexican-border thriller has a legendary opening shot, the director playing a crooked cop the size of Shamu, and enough sleaze to make you forget it's a masterpiece of the fallen world.

7

. . .

HORROR, SCIENCE FICTION, AND FANTASY

DO CHILDREN *WANT* to be scared?

I wonder this whenever I go to a horror movie and the most terrifying thing about it is that a parent is sitting a few aisles over with a couple of little kids. Could be a PG-13 thrill ride like, I don't know, *War of the Worlds* or the most recent *King Kong*—CGI adrenaline boosters that push the buttons of fourteen-year-old boys but are overpowering to a toddler. Or it could be balls-out R: teen dice-'n'-slice, the characters slipping in gore on the floor, *boo* scenes coming at you every thirty seconds.

And of course you have to ask: What's wrong with the parents? Do they look forward to the night terrors, the bed-wetting, the unexplained crying jags? Or, alternately, do they want their children to have rhino skin, to be unmoved when it comes to depictions of human suffering and death? I think—I hope—this book has established that kids aren't the innocents we often like to take them for, but they still can be warped if you really work at it. More than anything else, what makes such parents think their kids are having fun? How are *they* having fun? Where do we send the social services van?

But then I talk to my friend and coworker Renee, who *was* one of those kids. When she was five—*five!*—her mother took her to see the original *Night of the Living Dead*, with its limb-chomping zombies and that scene where the lovely little dead girl stabs her mother to death with a masonry spade. And eats her. Was Renee scared? Are you kidding? She *freaked*. Was she scarred for life? Renee laughs the laugh of the most sensible, even-keeled person I know and says, "Of course not. *It was a movie.* Even at five," she says, "I understood that, and I knew my mother liked the scary ones and that she liked to take me along." The upshot is that you can talk trash cinema with Renee like no one else, and she gets the joke as well as the part that's deadly serious.

Maybe you have a Renee at home. Probably not, but maybe. Is it worth finding out? I guess you have to ask yourself whether *you* like being scared. The movies below offer various ways into the fear/pleasure conundrum: the slow, cautious on-ramps of fantasy (*The 5,000 Fingers of Dr. T*, *The Thief of Bagdad*), the surprise left turn of '50s science fiction (*Mysterious Island*, *The Day the Earth Stood Still* back in chapter 1), the sudden trapdoor of silent horror and the great Universal monster movies. As you navigate between the films, always treat a kid's response as the correct one—when he or she says, "I don't want to watch it anymore," that's when the movie comes off.

That insistence, by the way, is different from the momentary shriek. As mentioned earlier, Natalie gabbled in blind panic when the robot Gort moves in on Patricia Neal in *The Day the Earth Stood Still*, and I briefly considered stopping the show. But we hung on, and the sequence quickly sorted itself out as Neal remembers the secret words that give her mastery over the massive tin man. Her mastery became Natalie's mastery; my daughter actually came out of that minute of film a braver soul. The movie remains one of her all-time favorites. Do children want to be scared? When they sense they'll be saved in time, they do.

SILENT HORROR

NOSFERATU THE VAMPIRE (B&W WITH COLOR TINTING, 1922)

Directed by: F. W. Murnau

Starring: Max Schreck

Ages: 12 and up

The sell: The original Dracula, and the ugliest sucker of them all

The plot: Jonathan Hutter goes to Transylvania to close a real estate deal with the sepulchral Count Orlok (Schreck). The count travels back to his new digs by coffin, bringing the plague with him. Jonathan discovers Orlok's gruesome secret but only his wife, Nina, has the power to vanquish the vampire.

Why it's here: There isn't any gore in this movie, obviously, but, good Christ, is it unnerving: a visual poem of decay. This is due to the portrayal of Count Orlok as a gargoyle from hell: crinkly bald head, staring eyes, little ratlike teeth, fingernails the late-period Howard Hughes would have admired. It's a silent movie and yet you can almost hear Max Schreck's slurping intakes of breath. (The actor's name translates as "maximum terror," which sounds like a brilliant publicity move on somebody's part, but in fact it was the actor's given name and he had a solid stage and screen career in Germany before his death at fifty-seven in 1936.)

Count Orlok is a monster, yet, oddly, no one comments on it. Bela Lugosi isn't much of a sex god in the 1931 Hollywood *Dracula*, but at least he can pass for human. Orlok can't, but he still has the same seductive power over Nina. More than any other screen vampire, he exudes the allure of death—of pestilence and defeat, of all the negatives the sun tries to crowd out.

You're glad to see him go, but you also can't get him out of your head. He may speak most clearly to the mordant teenager in your house—and maybe the one in your own heart.

The film, directed by the great F. W. Murnau (see *Sunrise* over in the drama chapter), has the intentional quality of a dream. The filmmaker used every trick in the 1922 special-effects playbook: stop-motion animation, negative images, even a process shot when the dawn hits the vampire at the end. These may seem hokey today, but they also contribute to the unceasing sense of waking nightmare. *Nosferatu* keeps popping up in the culture—Werner Herzog made a near shot-for-shot remake starring Klaus Kinski in 1979, 2000's *Shadow of the Vampire* intimated that Schreck (played by Willem Dafoe) was a real vampire, and a brief snippet of *Nosferatu* has even appeared in a 2002 *SpongeBob SquarePants* episode. None of these have been able to dilute the film's nagging dread.

Home video notes: Two choices here. The 2001 Special Edition from Image Entertainment features a great pipe organ score and runs eighty-one minutes. The 2002 version from Kino runs ninety-three minutes at a slower, more normal speed, and has two lesser electronic music tracks, one a pretty ungodly experimental noise bath and the other a fake pipe organ. Both DVDs tint the nighttime scenes (shot in daylight, as was common practice) the appropriate blue.

Useless trivia: You may notice that this is basically *Dracula* with the names changed. Bram Stoker's widow noticed, too, and she successfully sued the pants off Murnau's producers with the result that prints of the film were confiscated and destroyed. We still have *Nosferatu* only because she couldn't get them all, but there nevertheless remains no definitive version of this masterpiece.

What next: Time for more German Expressionist horror: *The Cabinet of Dr. Caligari* (Robert Wiene, 1920), *The Golem* (Paul

Wegener and Carl Boese, 1920), and *Waxworks* (Paul Leni, 1924) all join *Nosferatu* as part of Kino's "German Horror Classics" DVD box. And if you haven't caught Fritz Lang's *Metropolis* yet (see chapter 1), stop there first.

THE PHANTOM OF THE OPERA (B&W WITH COLOR TINTING, 1925)

Directed by: Rupert Julian

Starring: Lon Chaney, Mary Philbin

Ages: 8 and up

The sell: No songs. Much creepier.

The plot: The Paris Opera is haunted by a mysterious Phantom (Chaney) who lives in the catacombs and pines for his protégée, bubbleheaded singer Christine (Philbin). Once she gets a look at his hideous mug, she runs to handsome Raoul (Norman Kerry), but the Phantom has unpleasant tricks up his flounced sleeve.

Why it's here: We had seen this once already on video, but I took the girls along when I had to cover a screening of the 1925 Lon Chaney classic with a live performance of an original new score by the Boston-based Alloy Orchestra. Not much of an orchestra, really: just three talented gentlemen who stood at the back of the college auditorium and fiddled with gongs and bells and keyboards, prickling our scalps with pleasurable fear throughout the film. For a moviewise grown-up accustomed to amputated and sped-up versions of the original *Phantom*, seeing it on a big screen with a clean print—including the experimental color techniques that boggled audiences in 1925—was a revelation. To my kids, it was more than that: It was a peak movie experience.

The movie's not art, never has been. It's a Grand Guignol potboiler, equal parts epic and freak show (this goes for all of the versions of the story, from the original novel to the Andrew Lloyd Webber musical). Chaney's performance is the reason to see it; that and all the lady-and-the-tiger trapdoor suspense once Raoul follows Christine down to the depths. There are rising moats, secret entrances, halls of mirrors that turn into deadly ovens. The Phantom turns out to be an adept snorkeler—who knew?

Christine, for her part, turns out to be a ninny of the first order. She's happy to suck up to the mysterious Phantom for career advice until she gets a look at him, and she rips off his mask after having been given precise instructions to *not* do just that thing. The Phantom, like many love-besotted men, has chosen wrongly.

The unmasking scene, of course, is the famous one, Chaney's hollow-skull visage gasping right out at us. It's among the greatest *"boo"* shots of all, so if you've got tenderhearted tweeners, prepare them. For my money, though, the mask the Phantom wears before and after this scene is more nightmarish: a bland plaster false face with mannequin eyes and a ribbon of gauze hovering below the nose that hints at the wrecked mouth behind it.

Chaney was a master of sympathetic menace—you fear the Phantom and fear *for* him—but he also knew how to terrorize an audience with suggestion. In general, though, *Phantom* is more ripping yarn than horror, and so a good introduction to the genre and to classic monsters.

Home video notes: The print the girls and I saw is available on DVD from Image in a two-disc spectacular that packages the original 1925 release and the 1929 rerelease; the latter features one of the most eerily beautiful sequences in all of silent film, in which Christine and Raoul tryst on the Opera House roof in black and white while on the dome above them, listening to their trite endearments, is the Phantom, red hand-tinted cape billowing behind him in the midnight wind. The girls and I talked about that one all the way home.

Pause-button explanations: If they're fans of the Andrew Lloyd Webber *Phantom*, adjust expectations accordingly, and warn them that the chandelier falls early. Natalie wanted to know if Lon Chaney was any relation to Dick Cheney; after mulling over the infinite possible responses, I had to admit that, sadly, he wasn't.

Useless trivia: Chaney used fish skin to pull his nose back into the proper dessicated tilt.

What next: If the star rocks their little boats, proceed to *The Hunchback of Notre Dame* (1923), which is to the Disney cartoon what this *Phantom* is to Lloyd Webber. Much of Chaney's later filmography is available, made at the height of the silent era before he died in 1930 at forty-seven of throat cancer. *Man of a Thousand Faces* (1957), starring Jimmy Cagney, is a good biopic of the actor.

UNIVERSAL HORROR

The Frankenstein monster, Dracula, the Mummy, the Werewolf—these are the common ogres of our imagination. All arose from a handful of films that Universal Pictures cranked out between 1931 and 1935, with a few fresh recruits arriving at the turn of the 1940s. And they will not go away: Rereleased to theaters, popping up on TV, the subjects of adoring profiles in Forrest Ackermann's mid-'60s *Famous Monsters of Filmland* magazine (as essential to young boys of the era as the latest issue of *Mad*), made into plastic glow-in-the-dark snap-together models, looming from the studio tour, available in costume shops, remade with modern state-of-the-art CGI grue, arriving now on DVD in special editions from whose holographic covers the creatures lurch into your lap—the Universal monsters are omnipresent. Without seeing the movie, your three-year-old could tell you that's Frankenstein (or, if he or she is an unusually precise three-year-old, the Frankenstein *monster*, since Frankenstein is of course the name of the insane young doctor who creates the thing). Every tyke knows what a vampire is, but where does this knowledge fly in from? Do they see these characters parodied in ads and understand that they're a laughable variant of something too scary to contemplate?

That's possible: The first Universal horror movie my daughters saw wasn't a Universal horror movie at all but rather Mel Brooks's *Young Frankenstein*, made in 1974 for 20th Century Fox but a pitch-perfect comic distillation of that black-and-white world of moors and madness. So they came to *Frankenstein* through the back door—and they still haven't opened it. They both loved the Brooks film but have steadfastly refused to watch the original, and aside from waving the DVD case in their direction every six months or so—or pinning their little eyes open *Clockwork Orange*–style—there's not much I can or want to do about it.

On the contrary, I understand this. The year I was eight, a local Boston TV station showed the Universal horror classics in the week leading up to Halloween. One film per day, conveniently scheduled during the two hours between school and dinner, when I should have been doing homework. Who could do homework? I watched them all, growing more uneasy with each film. By the time they got to *The Mummy*—the least monstery of the bunch, ironically—I had to turn off the TV in a panic during the opening scene, when idiot Bramwell Fletcher opens the tomb and the moldering *thing* in the corner starts moving. (I was then terribly confused when I came back a

minute later and the creature had somehow turned into a with-
ered but human villain played by Boris Karloff.)

Around the same time, I labored mightily over those foot-
high "Famous Monsters" plastic models, getting strings of
Duco cement all over the kitchen and cursing the way eight-
year-old boys do. These models sat on the top shelf of my bedroom bookcase, along with their smaller plastic figurine cousins,
and when the Great Blackout of November 9, 1965, hit, and I
had to go to sleep with a candle and a small AM radio broadcast-
ing the news of the pall of darkness spreading from Canada to
Pennsylvania, I piled all my beloved monsters into my arms and
took them out to the back porch, where they wouldn't be able
to get in when they came to life, as I knew they would.

So there's precedent, in my life at least, for not force-feeding
children these movies. I do know I enjoyed them all very much,
at that age and later, and I still come back to some of them. The
best of them—*Bride of Frankenstein* is probably *the* best—have
wit and style, a remarkable playfulness to offset the dread. The
worst of them have turned to interesting dust.

Still, they're of a piece, and they saved Universal's bacon during the Depression. "Uncle" Carl Laemmle was the least psychotic and in some ways the most innovative of the early movie
moguls—he created the whole notion of movie stars when he
billed Florence Lawrence by name in 1910, the first producer to
do so—but he had run out of tricks by the early '30s and the
studio came close to going under. Then came **Dracula** (B&W,
1931) and Bela Lugosi, as good an audience diversion from the
sound of Depression America going down the toilet as any, and
the studio started ransacking the beasts of literature.

Dracula has not aged well. It's as if someone left the coffin
open and let in the air. The dialogue is stagebound and the lim-
itations of talkie technology mean that everyone stands around
near the microphone. And—I hate to say this—Lugosi just isn't
very menacing. In 1931, the whole Eastern European–nobility

business may have still fluttered women's hearts and warmed their pants, but today the count is a stocky, grimacing figure out of our collective drawing-room past. There's a frisson of weary happiness when he says things like "Cheeldren of da night . . . Vot muzeek dey make," but the best scenes come early, in Dracula's castle, with his wives skittering in the background like multiple Morticias and poor Renfrew going around the bend with madness. In fact, Dwight Frye's Renfrew is much the best part of the film, once he goes bonkers and starts in on the insects— "Flies? Poor puny things! Who wants to eat flies? Not when I can get nice fat *spiders*." The count, by contrast, is too languid to stir real fear in anyone but the stick figures with whom he shares the screen.

Frankenstein (B&W, 1931), by contrast, remains the real deal, as manic and expressionistic as *Dracula* is moribund. Part of the improvement came from the studio bringing in a stylist: James Whale had directorial chops and a subversive sense of humor that *Dracula*'s Tod Browning, a workhorse of the late silents and early talkies, never possessed. And of course there's Boris Karloff—billed simply as KARLOFF and even "?" in the publicity, no matter that he was a well-spoken British gent by the name of William Henry Pratt.

Frankenstein is a madhouse of a movie, with Colin Clive as the title character barking like a gentleman's club lunatic—"It's alive, it's alive, it's *alive!*"—and Dwight Frye slavering away as Igor (except that he's called Fritz), and all those Tesla coils zapzapzapping. Marvelous, and Karloff is the icing on a moldy cake, moaning and growling like the biggest, most dangerous baby alive.

And that's it, really—the monster is a child, confused and always doing the wrong thing, like throwing the little girl in the water after he runs out of flowers. Oops. If your children are tough enough to see the movie, they can't help but identify with Frankie baby, tottering on his too big feet, getting the adults so riled up that they send him to his room (and then burn it down with torches). Credit goes to Jack Pierce's makeup, of course—who thought up the neck bolts?—but the humanity, the puzzlement, the glimmers of joy, and the infantile temper tantrums come from Karloff.

Even better is **Bride of Frankenstein** (B&W, 1935), although a little of Una O'Connor's comic-relief shrieking goes a long way. The monster is almost the side story here, as Whale brings in Dr. Pretorius (played by the cadaverously droll Ernest Thesiger) to show off his miniature people and offer Dr. F. assistance in making a mate. She, of course, is Elsa Lanchester with a proto–B-52s fright wig, jabbing her neck like a bird and hissing like a cat—if anything, she's scarier than Karloff. It's a surprisingly modern film, less moving than the original but funnier, with a sly sense of camp that pops out in the oddest places. Of the two *Frankenstein*s, it's probably the easier to take for younger viewers.

Between those two, Whale made **The Old Dark House** (B&W, 1932) and **The Invisible Man** (B&W, 1933), both worth seeing. *House*, as the name implies, is one of those travelers-stranded-in-a-storm stories, but Whale manages both to spoof what was already an old ragbag of clichés and play it straight. The result is a little-known and eccentrically chilling delight, with rising young actors like Charles Laughton, Melvyn Douglas, and Raymond Massey among the travelers, and Gloria Stuart, the old lady from 1997's *Titanic*, back when she was a silly young thing. Karloff plays the grunting alcoholic butler—this, friends, is where Lurch in *The Addams Family* came from—while Thesiger reappears as the twitty Horace Femm and the fifty-something actress Elspeth Dudgeon is made up to play the 102-year-old bedridden patriarch Sir Roderick Femm. Oh, and there's Brember Wills as a crazy little firebug cackling on the stairwell. I'm telling you, this is one wild movie.

The Invisible Man is comparatively straight-up horror and more unnerving for it, with Claude Rains achieving fame as— well, as an invisible man. How about that? You give an acclaimed, star-making performance and nobody knows what you look like. There *is* that final sequence, though, after the insane killer invisible scientist has at last been brought to bay and is carried into the house to die in peace, and his body comes back to visibility in steps, as though he were an anatomical model: muscle, bone, skin. The startling thing about this film (and it's true to the H. G. Wells original) is what a nasty megalomaniac Dr. John Griffin becomes, and how thoroughly he revels in the spookier aspects of his condition. Again with Una O'Connor screaming and Gloria Stuart emoting, but the grabber here is Whale's puckish exploration of invisibility and the power that goes with it. Like everyone else, kids wonder what it would be like to not be seen, and this movie indulges that curiosity and goggles at it in happy terror.

The Mummy (B&W, 1932) is pretty discreet, though, and your kids will probably translate that as *boring*, especially if they've seen the rock-'em-sock-'em modern *Mummy*s with Brendan Fraser and several million dollars' worth of CGI grandstanding. Those are action movies, whereas the original cultivates an eldritch sense of romantic doom. It *pines*, in a horrible way. After the freaky-deaky opening scene in the tomb, *Mummy* turns into the tale of the resurrected Im-Ho-Tep/Ardath Bey, who is played by Karloff with classy wardrobe, papery skin, and the weariness of a man who has been waiting three thousand years. All he wants is his princess Anckesen-Amon, who he's convinced has been reincarnated as plummy Helen Grosvenor (Zita Johann); also on board are good guys/deadweight Edward Van Sloan and David Manners from *Dracula*. But *The Mummy* isn't *Dracula*, even if it was directed by *Dracula*'s cameraman Karl Freund, getting a welcome promotion here. The movie's slow but it's rarely dull, and it's carried by Freund's knack for spooky atmosphere. It will probably find a warmer home among Goth teens than little kids.

The Werewolf of London (B&W, 1935) gets the nod for the first movie to deal with lycanthropy, and I remember being terrified by it as a child. Henry Hull's transformation from proper British scientist into hirsute werebeast is both well done for its day and intriguing: Each lap dissolve is like another curtain whisked away from something you're not supposed to see. Aside from providing Warren Zevon with a great song title, though, *Werewolf* hasn't aged particularly well; the visual trappings are rich but Hull's a cold fish with or without hair. The movie that truly kick-started the franchise was **The Wolf Man** (B&W, 1941), made after Universal had rereleased *Dracula* and *Frankenstein* in the late 1930s to great box office success. There's some sentiment involved here, since hero Larry Talbot is played by Lon Chaney Jr., a sweet hulk of a man who never showed the craft or wit—or even talent—of his famous father but whose very haplessness wins you over. Abetted by makeup man Jack Pierce again, Talbot morphs into a beast after getting bitten by a crazed fortune teller (Bela Lugosi!), and then the movie just lets the fog machine rip. Forgoing the subtlety of the '30s movies, *Wolf* is as bluntly effective as that silver-headed cane Claude Rains carries around.

After that it's sequels and parodies all the way. **Son of Frankenstein** (B&W, 1939) keeps Karloff as the monster but casts sneering Basil Rathbone as Baron von Frankenstein and posits Bela Lugosi as Ygor; a lot of the energy of the original film is still there, remarkably, and Lugosi rocks. **Ghost of Frankenstein** (B&W, 1942) puts Lon Chaney Jr. in those size 20s and we're off on a downhill slope; in **Frankenstein Meets the Wolf Man** (B&W, 1943), Chaney has to play the Wolf Man, of course, so *Lugosi* has to play the Frankenstein monster—the only time he did so. There's also **House of Frankenstein** (B&W, 1944), but only if you must.

On the *Dracula* front, the first sequel was **Dracula's Daughter** (B&W, 1936), with Gloria Holden having a kinky personality crisis in the title role. In many ways it's better than the first film but it's still no *Bride of Frankenstein*. **Son of Dracula** (B&W, 1943) miscasts Chaney as the caped Count Alucard (tell your kids to spell it backward), and he remains the only actor to have played the Frankenstein monster, the Wolf Man, *and* Dracula. **House of Dracula** (B&W, 1945) was the last of the serious remakes, and it's a fun Saturday afternoon mess.

Then came the Abbott and Costello parodies, starting with **Abbott and Costello Meet Frankenstein** (B&W, 1948), and you can stop right there; no need to bother with *Abbott and Costello Meet the Killer Boris Karloff, Meet the Invisible Man, Meet Dr. Jekyll and Mr. Hyde,* and *Meet the Mummy*. Because these are all silly and nonthreatening, they're useful for introducing very young kids to the Universal monsters. But *Meet Frankenstein* is the only one that's remotely funny, and I do mean remotely.

OTHER HORROR, FANTASY, AND SCI-FI

CAT PEOPLE (B&W, 1942)

Directed by: Jacques Tourneur

Starring: Simone Simon, Kent Smith

Ages: 8 and up

The sell: C'mon, look at the title. People who turn into cats.

The plot: Nice, healthy, dull Oliver Reed (Smith) marries a Serbian-born beauty he meets in New York. Irena (Simon) is a shy and elegant woman, glad to be embraced by her husband's bluff normality but somehow waiting for the other shoe to drop. She explains that a man's kiss will turn her into a crazed beast; the marriage suffers and Oliver sends her to psychiatrist Dr. Judd (Jeff Conway). Irena, meanwhile, becomes jealous of her husband's coworker (Jane Randolph) and starts stalking her. . . .

Why it's here: *Cat People* was remade in the 1980s as a trendy gorefest, but the original is known and beloved by old movie freaks because it's scary as hell while showing you *nothing*. It's a good first horror movie for little kids, but only on the face of it; *Cat People* whispers things more powerfully than most movies say out loud.

In large part this was a budgetary restriction. The studio, RKO, was in dire financial straits and decided to borrow the Universal horror formula; the head office gave producer Val Lewton a title that had tested well—*Cat People*—and told him to make a movie out of it. No money for fancy lap dissolves or costumes; just enough to pay the cast and crew and put up a few sets. So Lewton, director Jacques Tourneur, and writer DeWitt Bodeen decided to spend the movie hinting at awful things.

Thus *Cat People* gets under your skin and stays there, because it never actually comes out and *says* whether Irena is a cursed panther-woman or just seriously bipolar. The whole notion of a marriage thrown off by the wife's sexual frigidity was dicey in 1942 and would have been commented on if this hadn't been a B movie. It flies over kids' heads, too; they get caught up in the central mystery while falling in love with Simon's Irena, a woman attracted to our earnest, unironic American world while terrified she'll claw it to shreds. Simon even looks feline with her flat cheekbones and almond eyes, and far back in those eyes you sense the contempt with which a house cat watches its owner, waiting for the neck to be exposed.

The famous scene here is when the coworker is trapped in a nighttime swimming pool by *something* prowling and growling in the shadows, but you'll remember the pet store sequence, too—the animals screaming at Irena in a rage—and the odd-looking woman at a bar who stares at Irena and calls her "*my sister*" in a dark Slavic tongue. The movie as a whole has a Continental sadness to it. There are so many things Americans don't understand, it says—foreigners, screwed-up love, the beast in all of us.

Home video notes: Available on DVD as a stand-alone disc and as part of a Val Lewton boxed set (see below), both from Turner.

Pause-button explanations: Maybe not during the film, but you'll have a great conversation afterward about the "realness" of Irena's condition.

What next: *I Walked with a Zombie* (1943), Lewton and Tourneur's follow-up to *Cat People*—it sounds grade-Z but it's actually a startlingly poetic Jamaican remake of *Jane Eyre*, with Frances Dee as a nurse to a plantation owner's comatose (or voodoo-cursed) wife. Recommended for thoughtful tweeners, girls especially, and their parents—though that Jamaican zombie is a fright. The other Lewton-produced titles in the Warner Bros. boxed set include *The Leopard Man* (1943), *The Body Snatcher* (1945), *Isle of the Dead* (1945), *Bedlam* (1946), *The Ghost Ship* (1943), the terrific *The Seventh Victim* (1943), and *The Curse of the Cat People* (1944). There's not a dud among them, but it should be pointed out that *Curse* isn't really a sequel or a horror film so much as it is a strange and touching story about a little girl's fantasy life—directed by Robert (*Sound of Music*) Wise back when he was very young.

THE 5,000 FINGERS OF DR. T (COLOR, 1953)

Directed by: Roy Rowland

Starring: Hans Conreid, Tommy Rettig

Ages: 5 and up

The sell: Dr. Seuss made a movie?

The plot: Bartholomew Collins (Rettig) is a little boy who hates piano practice and Dr. Terwilliker (Conreid), his chirpy martinet of a piano teacher. Bart dreams himself into a fantasy in which Dr. T oversees a gulag for piano-playing little boys. Mom (Mary Healy) has been hypnotized, but can Bart get the nice plumber Mr. Zabladowski (Peter Lind Hayes) to rescue her before the big recital, played by five hundred boys on the longest set of ivories you've ever seen?

Why it's here: Yeah, Dr. Seuss made a movie. A really weird movie. Actually, Roy Rowland directed this midsize studio film; the good doctor, real name Theodor Seuss Geisel, wrote the story, cowrote the script, and had input on the sets and costumes. The two rollerskating guys connected by one beard clearly sprang from the brainpan of the man who gave us Star-bellied Sneetches, North-Going Zaxes, and that poor, dumb woman who named all her kids Dave.

That said, this is pretty lugubrious business: slow going during some of the songs and oddly set-bound and cramped throughout. My daughters liked it without loving it (and they *love* Dr. Seuss). But Rettig, the future star of TV's *Lassie*, appealed to them, and we all wanted to know where we could get one of those beanies with the Happy Little Fingers on top. At best, this is a more than acceptable Hollywood approximation of the literary subversion Geisel was up to at the time, and it beats sold-out obscenities like the Jim Carrey *How the Grinch*

Stole Christmas and the Mike Myers *The Cat in the Hat*. Nothing in those two films approaches the rigorous Seussian philosophy Mr. Zabladowski offers toward the end of *Dr. T*: "We should always believe children. We should even believe their lies."

What next: A good book

FORBIDDEN PLANET (COLOR, 1956)

Directed by: Fred McLeod Wilcox

Starring: Walter Pidgeon, Anne Francis, Leslie Nielsen, Robbie the Robot

Ages: 6 and up

The sell: Monsters from the Id! And they're not your children!

The plot: An expedition led by Commander John Adams (Leslie Nielsen, in pre–*Naked Gun* serious-hero mode) lands on Altair-4 to learn the fate of a colony of earthlings. Only survivors are Dr. Morbius (Pidgeon) and his fetching daughter Altaira (Anne Francis), with whom Adams gets involved. There's also Robby the Robot, able to speak 187 languages and cook breakfast. The mystery of Altair-4 concerns a race of superbeings named the Krell that vanished overnight; Morbius has tapped into their technology as well as their Achilles' heel: an invisible beast made from his own psychological energy. Uh-oh, Daddy's Monster from the Id doesn't like men flirting with his baby.

Why it's here: Because it's the first big-budget, seriously intended science-fiction movie of its era—the story was modeled on Shakespeare's *Tempest*—and because it provides the root DNA for so much of today's sci-fi. Even Gene Roddenberry admits he stole from this movie for *Star Trek*, including the idea of "beaming down" to a planet, and from *Star Trek* to *Star Wars* is an easy leap. Robby the Robot popped up again on TV's *Lost in Space* and what are R2-D2 and C-3PO if not Robby split into two personalities? And Pidgeon's character, with his psychological demons and unresolved paternal issues? Go ahead, call him Darth Morbius. I'd even go so far as to consider the last act of Steven Spielberg and Stanley Kubrick's *AI: Artificial Intelligence* a remake of *Forbidden Planet* turned inside out, with the Krell come to Earth to puzzle over *our* bones and Robby turned into an electronic little boy.

Nielsen's a total stiff—there's a reason the actor elected to go into self-parody—but the rest of the movie's great fun in that earnest/cheesy/thrilling high-'50s way. Some of it's even quite terrifying: the approach of the Monster from the Id, an invisible behemoth tossing trees out of its way like twigs, is up there with the Gort/Patricia Neal face-off from *Day the Earth Stood Still* for primal heebie-jeebies.

In general, though, this is just as thought-provoking as a child wants out of science fiction. It leads to speculation about one's own id monsters, for instance. If Morbius's line, "My evil self is at the door and I am powerless to stop it!" doesn't resonate with your kid, then he or she isn't a kid. The movie also prompts one to consider the temporary nature of all great civilizations, like any good *Star Trek* episode should. Dad can settle for gawking at Anne Francis.

Home video notes: The Warner DVD comes with a great pulp poster cover—Robby holding the inert body of Altaira as though he were about to ravish her in some unspeakable hydraulic fashion—that has absolutely nothing to do with the film.

Pause-button explanations: You'll have to explain what the id is, although the movie makes it pretty plain. Also, the dialogue is pretty tight-lipped when it comes to explaining the future tech the characters take for granted; younger viewers may need some assistance.

Useless trivia: Really, based on *The Tempest*: Morbius is Prospero, Altaira is Miranda, Robby is Ariel, and—okay, this is a stretch—the Monster from the Id is Caliban. Which makes Leslie Nielsen Ferdinand. Just don't call him Shirley.

What next: This and *The Day the Earth Stood Still* (see chapter 1) are the entry gates for all the space operas and sci-fi monster movies of the '50s, which run from the sublime to *Mystery Science Theater 3000* fodder. George Pal's *The Time Machine* (1960) has great special effects, creepy future Morlocks, and a brainbender of a concept. The 1953 *War of the Worlds* is an excellent replacement for the Spielberg version until your kids are old enough for genuine terrors. *Them!* (1954): giant ants, and that's all you need to know. *The Thing from Another World* (1951): Ten little scientists at an Arctic research station menaced by a killer vegetable from outer space; it's scarier than it sounds (and make sure you don't rent the supergory 1982 John Carpenter version unless you have a teenage horror connoisseur at home). *When Worlds Collide* (1951), *This Island Earth* (1955), and *Earth vs. the Flying Saucers* (1956) all still provide Hollywood with genetic material for remakes (specifically, *Armageddon*, *Signs*, and *Independence Day*).

THE GHOST AND MRS. MUIR (B&W, 1947)

Directed by: Joseph L. Mankiewicz

Starring: Gene Tierney, Rex Harrison, Natalie Wood

Ages: 9 and up

The sell: Can you fall in love with a ghost?

The plot: England, 1900. Young widowed mother Lucy Muir (Tierney) moves into the isolated cliffside Gull Cottage to get away from her late husband's meddlesome family. She quickly

learns why no one wants to live there: It's haunted by the shade
of the late sea captain Daniel Gregg (Harrison), who scares
bothersome intruders out. He can't scare Lucy, however, and
after the two come to a wary understanding, he dictates his
memoirs for her to publish. A romance with a children's book
author (George Sanders) threatens the pair's odd relationship,
but that's as it should be, isn't it? You *can't* love a ghost, can you?

Why it's here: This is more love story than horror film, obviously—and while there are laughs, it's certainly not a comedy in
the manner of the 1970s TV sitcom of the same name. The
movie's a subtler and more rewarding thing, gently insisting on
the right of a woman to live her own life, and if that involves
getting involved with a person nobody else can see, so be it.
There's a hint—just a hint—that Captain Gregg may be the
shared figment of Lucy's and her daughter Anna's imaginations,
and nine-year-old Natalie Wood is so precocious as the latter
that you easily can imagine her thinking up phantasms. But
Tierney, that unparalleled screen beauty, doesn't give Mrs. Muir
similar depths. Instead, the character has grace and inquisitive-
ness and a lovely sense of trust in a given situation.

The Ghost and Mrs. Muir thus confounds a kid's expectations—
who isn't scared of ghosts? But of course this ghost isn't scary—
he's a blusterer, and he's played by that nice man from *My Fair
Lady*. The movie puts a young viewer in a privy position right
next to Tierney; by the time the other characters start running
from Gregg in terror, your child knows better.

Which makes the ending a little hard to take, as poetic as it is.
[Okay, spoiler: After seeing that Lucy is falling for Miles Fair-
ley—played by George Sanders, so you know he can't be
trusted—Captain Gregg retires from ectoplasm and disappears
from her life. Miles turns out to be a rat, she casts him over, and
in several sequences that unfold like brief, lovely afterthoughts
we see Lucy pass into solitary old age, occasionally attended by

her grown daughter. She dies—discreetly—and joins the good captain in eternity. End of spoiler.] The tragedy of *The Ghost and Mrs. Muir* is that these two can't get together in life, but *is* it a tragedy? Their chasteness, the impossible purity of their love, makes what they have unique. It's also nicely unsullied by the physical—what a kid would call the *ick* factor. Anyway, they'll have each other forever in the afterlife. For a child nervous around representations of lust in films and TV and the culture at large, this movie offers a charming if totally perverse sanctuary.

So Eliza was deeply touched by the film, and she watched it obsessively for a few weeks before moving on, but she never cried. That's because the ending is grave and correct. *Ghost* says the most precious things are those we keep to ourselves.

Useless trivia: Another beautiful score from Bernard Herrmann and Oscar-nominated black-and-white cinematography by Charles Lang Jr.

What next: An even eerier supernatural romance is 1935's *Peter Ibbetson*, with Gary Cooper and Ann Harding as lovers who meet in their dreams. Also try *The Uninvited* (1944), an atmospheric tale of a haunted house on the Cornwall coast; plenty spooky, but it focuses more on the mystery of what happened to the ghosts when they were alive (and on the lingering smell of mimosa). You might also want to look for *Blithe Spirit* (1945), in which Rex Harrison is alive and even married but haunted and taunted by the ghost of his first wife (Kay Hammond). Also: the ectoplasmic comedy of the *Topper* films and *I Married a Witch* (1942), the latter with Veronica Lake setting up the house that Elizabeth Montgomery and *Bewitched* would someday call home.

THE INCREDIBLE SHRINKING MAN (COLOR, 1957)

Directed by: Jack Arnold

Starring: Grant Williams, a giant spider

Ages: 10 and up

The sell: Let's get small.

The plot: Scott Carey (Williams) passes through a mysterious mist while out boating and several months later starts to shrink. His wife promises to stand by him, but that's kind of hard when your husband is living in a dollhouse in the living room. As he dwindles in size, Scott has to take on increasingly bizarre challenges: a cat, a spider in the basement, a drop of water. Eventually he accepts his fate and heads out into a subatomic future.

Why it's here: All you have to say to a kid is: Guy shrinks until he has to fight off the family cat. Cue it up, Mom. But, more unusually, *The Incredible Shrinking Man* has the chutzpah to follow through on its basic premise. Guy shrinks. Why? Doesn't matter. When's it going to stop? *It's not.*

The movie has been read as a statement of mid-'50s alienation, a naggingly doubtful negative to Eisenhower-era positivism. Okay, if you say so. To a child, *The Incredible Shrinking Man's* very real power comes from the way it exploits our curiosities about size and fears about proportion. Don't you think kids think the world is too big for them? (Remember being at your parents' parties, looking up through the thickets of lower limbs.) Don't you think they worry about how to grow into that world? (Eliza trying to hustle her height, chagrined she's the shortest in her class.) Isn't the idea of the process reversed—happening to an adult, no less—some combination of delicious revenge and worst-case scenario?

Anyway, who doesn't think it would be kind of cool to live in a dollhouse, or to battle a spider with a pin? And who doesn't feel they wander unseen sometimes through their own home, parents and siblings looking right through them? *Incredible Shrinking Man* asks us to adjust to changing perspectives, to use the things at hand, and to look among the molecules for our fellow travelers. It's Zen Buddhism through the back door of cheap '50s sci-fi: What if Scott Carey shrinks into nothing? What if he's already there?

Useless trivia: That's Orson Welles doing the narration. By 1957 he would have done the narration for a diaper ad.

What next: More '50s sci-fi. Random *Twilight Zone* episodes. The following film. Avoid *The Incredible Shrinking Woman* from 1981—it's a misfired satire—though *Honey, I Shrunk the Kids* (1989) and *Fantastic Voyage* (1966) are fun if you're into the whole tiny-people meme.

INVASION OF THE BODY SNATCHERS (B&W, 1956)

Directed by: Don Siegel

Starring: Kevin McCarthy, Dana Wynter, Carolyn Jones

Ages: 12 and up

The sell: Everyone you know is an alien, and *you're next.*

The plot: Dr. Miles Bennell (McCarthy) returns to his small town of Santa Mira, California, to find several of his patients terrified that their friends or relatives are no longer who they were. Initially skeptical, he discovers that aliens have landed and laid giant "seed pods," which turn into emotionless replicants of the townspeople. Can the good doctor and his sweetheart (Wynter) get out of Santa Mira before they too are taken over? Better not fall asleep.

Why it's here: What makes you an individual? Your emotions? The many little moments of uncertainty and improvisation with which you bumble through the day? Or are we just our eccentricities? Are we made from the sum of our deviations from the norm?

These are some of the themes addressed by *Invasion of the Body Snatchers*, the first, greatest, and scariest of the cinema's sci-fi paranoid fantasies. The movie has been interpreted as an allegory about Communist takeover, as an allegory about McCarthy-era groupthink, as an allegory about suburban conformism. All work just fine: *Invasion* was crafted by the gifted B-film director (and future Clint Eastwood mentor) Don Siegel as a straight-up alien invasion flick with open-ended resonances. The intentional lack of special effects throws us back onto the human element—to the horror of feeling like we're the only people in a world of complacent replicants.

See where I'm going here? Among all its other attributes, the movie is one of the most fertile and compelling metaphors for teenage estrangement going—for the sense a smart adolescent can have, upon waking up one fine day, that he or she is *different*. That everyone else is smug, uninteresting, uninterest*ed* in all the amazing and troubling things a kid sees. Maybe she or he has friends who see those things too, and they scorn their sold-out zombie parents and teachers, staying up late and fighting sleep just as Kevin McCarthy and Dana Wynter do. To doze off—to not be awake and aware—is to risk becoming one of Them.

This is not a movie for young kids. It's scary in ways that can't easily be soothed away, and the scene with little Jimmy Grimaldi, afraid to go home to the mother who no longer *is* his mother, is not someplace you want to take a toddler. But watching *Invasion* with a teenager, someone who's begun to suspect how unknowable other people really are and how alone we are in our skins—someone who is feeling alienated—is, perversely, a pretty effective bonding experience.

Home video notes: Republic Home Video still has yet to do right by *Invasion*. The one DVD out there lets you watch the film in wide-screen or pan-and-scan, but it includes the "happy" ending the studio insisted Siegel shoot after test screenings left audiences a little shaken by McCarthy looking into the camera and shrieking "You're next!" Now the hero alerts the authorities; presumably the marines will take care of the rest. Avoid the colorized videotape version.

Useless trivia: Remade twice, both times well but more explicitly: 1978's *Invasion of the Body Snatchers* and 1993's *Body Snatchers*. There's another remake in the works as of this writing, *The Visiting*, with Nicole Kidman and Daniel Craig, due out fall 2006.

What next: *Invaders from Mars* (1953) is a kitschier but in some ways even scarier movie, told from the point of view of a little boy (Jimmy Hunt) whose parents and their friends become Martian mind-slaves.

KING KONG (B&W, 1933)

Directed by: Merian C. Cooper and Ernest B. Schoedsack

Starring: Fay Wray, Bruce Cabot, Robert Armstrong . . . and *Kong*

Ages: 8 and up (see chapter 2 first, though)

The sell: Big monkey on the Empire State Building

The plot: Big monkey on the Empire State Building

Why it's here: Because it remains the primal primate movie experience, in spite of being remade by well-meaning filmmakers in 1976 and 2005. Terrifying, too; this is one of those cases where just because it's an old movie doesn't mean it can't boil your children's eyes in their sockets. Prepare for emotional engagement and extreme distress when Kong bounces off the skyscraper to his doom. Still, it'll be a lot less horrifying to tiny viewers than the 2005 version and is thus a preferred alternative.

Home video notes: *Kong* finally came to DVD in 2005—timed to the appearance of the Peter Jackson remake—in a "special edition" that contains more than you need to know unless you're a fanatic. All that should matter to you is that the print is good and that scenes long excised have been restored (though they're problematic scenes from a family-viewing standpoint: Kong flossing his teeth with an islander, plucking off Fay Wray's clothes, etc.).

Pause-button explanations: The natives on Kong Island don't pass the political correctness test, being members of the dreaded Ooga-Booga tribe. Also, you may want to stop and explain that there are no digital effects anywhere in this movie. Introduce the name of special effects wizard Willis O'Brien, who created all the Kong sequences, yet who isn't even credited.

What next: *Mighty Joe Young* (1949), a rather more kid-friendly reworking of the same material from directors Cooper and Schoedsack, featuring actor Armstrong back in iron-lunged Carl Denham mode and special effects by O'Brien and a new kid named Ray Harryhausen (see below). You may even want to start with *Joe* and work back to *Kong*.

MYSTERIOUS ISLAND (COLOR, 1961)

Directed by: Cy Endfield

Starring: Joan Greenwood, Herbert Lom

Ages: 6 and up

The sell: It's like TV's *Lost*, except with giant chickens.

The plot: A group of Union soldiers in the Civil War escape Confederate prison in a hot air balloon and land on the island of the title. They're joined by two shipwrecked Englishwomen and all attempt to set up a livable situation, stymied by the appearance of giant bees, birds, crabs, and squid. Turns out that Captain Nemo (Lom) is to thank for the hyperthyroid poultry.

Why it's here: I'll probably hear from the legion of Ray Harryhausen droolers on this one, and it's true that the master of stop-motion special effects did better work on better movies. If you want to start elsewhere, by all means rent *The Seventh Voyage of Sinbad* (1958), with its battles against the Cyclops, or *Jason and the Argonauts* (1963), with its sword-wielding skeletons. The fact remains that *Mysterious Island* was the first Harryhausen I came across, and I saw it multiple times on TV—it always seemed to be playing on holidays, in the afternoon, when the grown-ups were sleeping off the tryptophan. My sisters and I, itching in rumpled suits and dresses, lay in front of the big living room RCA and gorged on pumpkin pie and Harryhausen.

He was a kid of thirteen himself when he saw *King Kong* and immediately set out to become the heir of Willis O'Brien. Harryhausen did most of the character animation in *Mighty Joe Young*, earned his stripes on *The Beast from 20,000 Fathoms* (1953) and *It Came from Beneath the Sea* (1955)—both excellent creature features—and worked on a pair of pretty good flying-saucer films (*Earth vs. the Flying Saucers* and *20 Million Miles to Earth*, 1956 and '57, respectively). Then he moved into the meticulous frame-by-frame animation of mythology that came to take up his mature filmography. His last film as effects supervisor was 1981's *Clash of the Titans*—the one with Harry Hamlin as Perseus.

That brings up an interesting point: Aside from the special effects, Harryhausen's movies can be surprisingly lame. These aren't enduring classics of cinema. Rather, they're possibly the best Saturday matinee adventure movies ever made. The casts tend to be made up of bland pretty boys and fetching B-movie damsels, and the music—usually by Bernard Herrmann—is often more memorable than the dialogue. But when you're a kid, who cares? For years, all I remembered of the wonderful Joan Greenwood in this movie is when she fights off the giant chicken, and all I remembered about Michael Craig is when the monstrous bee walls him up inside a honeycomb.

Groundbreaking in its day, Harryhausen's work of course looks dated in the light of technological advances. Pixar can do more with a few cycles of CPU time than dear old Ray was able to do in months (that said, the company did name the nightclub in *Monsters, Inc.* Harryhausen's). But part of the allure of *Mysterious Island*—or *Seventh Voyage* or any of the old-guard classics—is the handmade funkiness of the effects. These movies are labors of love in a way that the miracles of, say, *The Lord of the Rings* could never be. A kid watching this may even get the sense that someone cared enough to fashion what they're seeing with slow, honest, patient craft. And that they could do it, too.

Home video notes: You can rent *Island* as a stand-alone DVD, but there are a few good Harryhausen boxed sets from Sony available, one that collects his three *Sinbad* films and one that boxes *Island* with four other sci-fi titles.

Useless trivia: *Mysterious Island* actually *is* based on a Jules Verne novel (*L'île mystérieuse*, 1875), although the arrival of Captain Nemo at the end of both book and film feels like little more than a special guest appearance.

What next: If you haven't already seen *The Seventh Voyage of Sinbad*, proceed immediately thereto.

THE THIEF OF BAGDAD (COLOR, 1940)

Directed by: Ludwig Berger, Michael Powell, Tim Whelan, and an uncredited Zoltan Korda, William Cameron Menzies, and Alexander Korda

Starring: Sabu, Conrad Veidt, Rex Ingram

Ages: 7 to 12

The sell: So *that*'s where Disney's *Aladdin* got all its ideas.

The plot: Prince Ahmad (John Justin, as absurdly white-bread an Arab as anyone else here) is tricked into imprisonment by his evil vizier Jaffar (Veidt), who takes control of Bagdad. Ahmad escapes from jail with the help of boy thief Abu (Sabu) but quickly falls in love with the princess of Basra (June Duprez), whom Jaffar also covets. Before the movie's done, Abu will have been turned into a dog, ridden a flying carpet *and* a mechanical horse, battled a giant spider, called up a rollicking genie (Ingram), looked into the All-Seeing Eye, and saved the day.

Why it's here: With the right kid, this opulent, overstuffed Technicolor fantasy can be grand fun: an illuminated storybook of marvels. With the wrong kid, it can be confusing and scary. I have one of each. Eliza and Natalie watched this once and only once, when they were quite young; E. got so creeped out by Veidt's vicious Jaffar, with his pale eyes the color of a desert snake, that she got the willies and asked never to see the movie again. N. dug it—because Sabu gets turned into a dog and because there are touches of the old-movie brutality she rather enjoys: an offscreen execution, the princess's fat fool of a father getting stabbed to death by a mechanical six-armed dancing toy. A right Roman at the Coliseum, my littler one. That said, the spider battle gave her pause. In fact, she left the room. But recently she asked to see the movie again, so we waited until big sister was elsewhere and gave it another go.

I understand where Eliza is coming from, though, for *Thief of Bagdad* is too much, really—that's what's fun about it, if you can catch the spirit. Too many story lines cribbed from *The Thousand and One Nights*, too many flashbacks, too many directors—including Michael Powell, the best England had to offer after Hitchcock left. A powerful producer, Alexander Korda, who wanted to do it all, and who wasn't above hiring his brothers to help him do it all (Vincent did the staggering production design and Zoltan chipped in with directing).

The result is a splurge of a movie, capering along the border between magic and kitsch, and at times so rich as to give you gas. Gotta love Sabu, though. Try the movie, then, in stages and with an eye to your audience. And try it when they're youngish—by the time they're teenagers, it'll be too corny for them to handle gracefully.

What next: The original *Jungle Book* (1941) is more Sabu and more Korda; it hasn't held up quite as well as *Thief* but is certainly worth a look. Also worth digging up is the 1924 *Thief of Bagdad*, with Douglas Fairbanks giving an incredibly fun, athletic performance in the lead; the Kino DVD is the one to find.

EXTRA CREDIT

FREAKS (B&W, 1932)

Directed by: Tod Browning

Starring: Olga Baclanova, Harry Earles, Johnny Eck, Violet and Daisy Hilton

Ages: 15 and up

The sell: We will make you one of us.

The plot: A traveling circus. Cleopatra (Baclanova) is a beautiful but vain trapeze artist beloved by midget Hans (Earles). When she learns he's to inherit money, she woos and marries him, but is distraught at the wedding banquet when his sideshow friends drink to her freak future. They discover that she's two-timing Hans with the circus strongman and wait for a dark and rainy night to take their revenge. . . .

Why it's here: Because it's politically incorrect, morally repugnant, and unforgettable. *Freaks* is, of course, the horror movie that stars actual sideshow attractions of the early 1930s and that takes pains to remind us they're human before insisting they're vengeful monsters not to be crossed. The banquet scene, with the freaks cavorting drunkenly, chanting "one of us, one of us" and offering a giant loving cup to the horrified Cleopatra, is half the stuff of nightmare, and the climactic sequence in which they crawl through a downpour bearing glinting tools of dismemberment is the other half. Once again, with feeling: *Do not show this movie to young children.*

Yet *Freaks* is a brainbuster for disaffected teenagers, not because it allows them to gawk at human deformity unimpeded by politeness or a parental smack on the back of the head, but because the movie says that however monstrous these characters may get if pushed far enough, normal people are worse. Greed is a "normal" attribute; using others for your own gain is what "normal" people do. The freaks are freaks not because they're joined at the waist, like the Hilton sisters, or missing everything *below* their waist, like Johnny Eck the hand-walking Half-Boy, or microcephalics like Zip and Pip the pinheads, but because they care for each other and protect each other from outsiders. In the end, the scariest part isn't that they come at Cleopatra and the strongman like extras out of a Bosch painting but that we're with them all the way.

Pause-button explanations: Aside from pausing every so often to assure yourself that you're seeing what you're seeing—say, the armless and legless Prince Randian somehow rolling a cigarette using only his mouth—there's a wealth of discussion in whether the movie exploits the freaks or is sympathetic to them. The correct answer is both, obviously, but how do you feel about that? And how does your teenager feel about that?

Useless trivia: Banned for thirty years in England. The film is sixty-four minutes now but premiered at ninety minutes, with an ending in which the strongman appears as a singing castrato. Studio brass, disgusted by the finished film, ordered the cuts; the lost footage has never been recovered.

What next: Nothing. This is the last stop on the classic horror express, the point at which the line between movie and reality begins to buckle. You can transfer to the David Lynch Limited if you want, but that's a whole other book.

8

· · · ·

FOREIGN-LANGUAGE CLASSICS

I'LL KEEP THIS chapter short, because it's really the doorway to a different subject altogether: not old culture but *other* culture. Still, learning to like foreign films is much like coming to terms with old movies—they're a different cinematic language that you need to start kids on early if you're going to start them at all.

Should you start them at all? Does early exposure to foreign movies spoil children for simpler American cuisine? Will it turn your kids French?

Look. Showing one or two or three movies that are from other places and in another language—folding it into the regular fare like the occasional dash of curry—isn't going to kill your children, as long as you share the experience with them. This is important: No throwing on Bergman's *The Virgin Spring* and leaving the room.

They may even have a good time. As mentioned earlier, I took a completely random flier one afternoon with *The Seven Samurai* (see chapter 1), playing it for Natalie and Eliza because I was writing an article on Kurosawa and had loaded up on his DVDs. The girls were six and eight, and you'd think they'd have

been out the door to the backyard in sixty seconds, but to the
astonishment of both Lori and myself, they were engrossed
from the get-go. It wasn't even raining. I read the subtitles to
them as if the movie was a Golden Book, pausing when war-
ranted to explain what was going on. The action was thrilling;
the actual violence minimal; the number of main characters just
enough to provide mastery without descending into confusion.

A few weeks later, emboldened, I showed them *Ohayo*, aka
Good Morning (see chapter 1) by the great Japanese master Yasujiro Ozu, and its gentle, extremely funny kid comedy won them
over; multiple viewings were requested and ensued. So the
groundwork was laid, and I realized that certain foreign-
language movies—ones with simple plots, a good heaping of
action or comedy, and if possible the presence of kids themselves—work extremely well with children. Grown-ups think of
the gold-plated classics of foreign film as rich in emotion and
meaning, short on plot—we think of Fellini, Antonioni, Truffaut, and other filmmakers whose work wrestles with questions
many kids don't need to ask yet. Fine; let them discover those
movies on their own. Showing them the ones in this chapter
will make it easier down the line.

There are windows of opportunity that open and close,
according to development and interests. My girls are older now
and can do the reading themselves, yet they're still at the stage
where switching back and forth between subtitle and picture
can be hard. Not surprisingly, foreign-language movies have
moved to the back burner. Eliza allows that some of them are
"*boring*," and from her point of view she's dead right. But please
allow me to point out that, immediately after saying this, she
asked if she could watch Renoir's *The Golden Coach* again. (All
right, that one's in English, but it plays like a Renoir film. Incidentally, this brings up the question of dubbed versus subtitles.
My parental stand is: dubbing if we must, subtitles preferred.
The girls went through a deep *Crouching Tiger, Hidden Dragon*

phase that included both options, depending on their mood and energy level; at the very least they came out with a clear understanding of the pros and cons of each.)

Why even force the issue? Think of it this way: If modern American kid culture never lets children out of the Disney/Nickelodeon/Britney box, their parents' culture is equally self-absorbed. It's a vicious cycle: We don't care about other cultures because we don't see other cultures, and we don't see them because the chefs who create our homegrown corporate media diets want to keep it that way. But we don't *see* other cultures, so how can we care about them? See?

It's a small world. It's getting smaller. It's good to understand people in other places so we can talk to them instead of waging war on them, because sooner or later the world will get so small that we'll be waging war on ourselves. Looking at our movies and TV shows and music, maybe we already are. If the popular culture a country creates forms a mirror of that country, then we are a nation of narcissists who cannot look away from the mirror—from our dreams of celebrity, from the fast buck, from the easy laugh, and from the quick-fix "personal growth" messages that are attached to so many American kid flicks like Minimum RDA emotional content.

Foreign movies are a window instead of a mirror: You often come out knowing more about the world than when you went in. I fail to understand how this could be considered anything but an asset in a growing human being.

Some of the following are for the little ones, again, to be read out loud. Others are for the more wayward older kids who think they've seen it all. If your children respond to a particular national cinema—and God knows they probably already understand more about Japanese culture than you or I ever will—push further down that path. If they like *Seven Samurai*, point out that the same director's *The Hidden Fortress* (1958) has the characters on which George Lucas based R2-D2 and C-3PO (they're peasants here, rather than robots). If they go for *Small Change*, move on to *The 400 Blows*, Truffaut's tough-minded portrait of a kid falling through the cracks. Keep it light. Don't make it homework. Show them the world.

LA BELLE ET LA BÊTE (B&W, 1946)

Directed by: Jean Cocteau

Starring: Jan Marais, Josette Day

Ages: 3 and up

The sell: Beauty and the Beast, before the Disney elves got hold of it

The plot: A man stops during a journey at a ruined castle and plucks a rose; the Beast (Marais) who is master of the castle sentences him to death, but the youngest of the man's three daughters, Belle (Day), agrees to take his place. Can a woman truly love a beast?

Why it's here: If you want to show your kids the power of both foreign-language films *and* black-and-white movies, toss on this stunner—a film stuck halfway between fairy tale and surrealist fancy. They'll be surprised to notice how much material Disney mined from this *Belle* for its own animated version, but they also stand to be swept up by an experience that runs far deeper, almost into the subbasement where we keep the archetypes. There are many layers to this movie, only one of which is available to children; what does it mean, for instance, that Marais plays both the Beast/prince and the movie's Gaston figure? That all men (and all boys) have both a hideous hero and a handsome jerk inside them?

Director Cocteau was a major French poet and playwright,

and he roots the thing in poetry—once you've seen the film, you can never forget Belle's journey through the castle, the living arms protruding from the walls with candelabras. At the same time, he shot the movie just after World War II had ended, and it's a plea for simplicity and gentleness, for a romantic world of "once upon a time" that then (as now) seemed far away. So it's exquisite, but be prepared: *Belle* is more potent than Disney ever dares and may be a shock for those who haven't been weaned.

Home video notes: Look for the restored edition released by Criterion in 1998.

What next: Check out Jacques Demy's *Donkey Skin* (1970), which is like a cross between *La belle et la bête* (to the extent of having Jean Marais play the evil king) and an episode of the old psychedelic Saturday morning TV show *H.R. Pufnstuf*. If your kids seem to go for French films of this period, try the much more ambitious *Children of Paradise* (1945), a sumptuous two-and-a-half-hour epic of life, romance, and the theater. Many consider it the greatest French film of all time.

THE GOLDEN COACH (COLOR—AND HOW—1953)

Directed by: Jean Renoir

Starring: Anna Magnani

Ages: 8 and up

The sell: Is life like a play? Or is a play like life?

The plot: An Italian traveling theatrical troupe arrives in a small town in Spanish South America, where the lead actress, a tempestuous diva named Camilla (Magnani) is torn between three men: a bullfighter, a pampered viceroy, and a soldier. Whom does she choose? What does it matter?

Why it's here: There are more famous Jean Renoir movies to choose from—warhorses like *Grand Illusion* and *The Rules of the Game*. They're great, but this is the one to start children on: It's in English and the colors come straight from their best box of paints. Magnani is the whirlwind at the film's center, a lovable, fascinatingly ugly beauty—a true *jolie laide*—who sees life as her best if most problematic role. What tickles children about this movie, besides the real children of the theater troupe tumbling over each other like monkeys, is the way everyone acts like a big kid, especially the men vying for Camilla's love. (The politics surrounding the viceroy, a playboy who orders the carriage of the title and pays for it out of the government till, are a comic variant on the entitled greed that still makes headlines.)

The music is by Vivaldi, the vibe playfully Baroque and baroque, and the director frames things so you're sometimes unsure whether you're watching a play or "real life." It's a Harlequin of a movie, often hilarious but with an unspoken awareness of the brevity of things. Renoir may have been the wisest person to have ever stepped behind a movie camera, and this one entertains children and adults while leaving a lasting taste of bittersweet.

Home video notes: Look for the Criterion DVD, which restores the colors to almost mind-bending potency.

Pause-button explanations: You'll have to help out with some of the political machinations.

Useless trivia: The director was the son of the Impressionist painter Pierre-Auguste Renoir. Maybe that explains the colors.

What next: Any of Renoir's great works: the antiwar war film *Grand Illusion* (1937), the social tragicomedy *The Rules of the Game* (1939), the nearly Buddhist *The River* (1951), the scruffy and extremely funny *Boudu Saved from Drowning* (1932). Obviously, these are for older and more ambitious viewers, but rewards are there.

PATHER PANCHALI (B&W, 1955)

Directed by: Satyajit Ray

Starring: Subir Bannerjee

Ages: 9 and up

The sell: You think *you've* got it hard? You think *you* could endure?

The plot: Life as seen through the eyes of a poor family in Bengal, India. The father (Kanu Bannerjee) is a Brahmin from a well-to-do family who has fallen on hard times, living in what's left of the family country estate with his wife (Karuna Bannerjee), adolescent daughter Durga (Uma Das Gupta), young son Apu (Subir Bannerjee), and incredibly old Auntie (Chunibala Devi). Apu and Durga, brother and sister, are protective of each other, even as their mother despairs that her husband will ever make ends meet. Tragedy strikes when Durga sickens and dies, and when we last see the family, father, mother, and son are moving on to the city.

Why it's here: Screening one of the great depressive works of post–World War II neorealism—a film with next to no plot, with subtitles, found-object actors, and barely a glimmer of hope—to two preadolescent American girls in 2006? Surely I must be off my meds.

Actually, I'm beginning to think watching *Pather Panchali* with E. and N. the other night may have been the payoff for this whole book. Satyajit Ray's 1955 debut film is rightly one of the classics of world cinema: a devastatingly humane record of survival and even joy in the face of squalor and poverty. It should be seen at least once by anyone who thinks they're really serious about movies. But watching it with *kids*? Even if the central character is a kid himself?

Eliza is eleven now and already world-weary about stories she knows are going to end badly: She rushes to predict who'll die so she won't have to feel hurt. Natalie is nine and, as ever, rolls with the narrative punches; nothing much fazes her, but bruises occasionally show up days or even weeks later (and she's happy to talk about them). They settled into this black-and-white foreign-language movie on the request of their dad, who left the rec-room door open and the remote at the ready. Bail if you feel like it, dears; no skin off my nose.

Pather Panchali begins with a girl about their age, so they locked in. The aged auntie shook them up, if only because they had never seen anyone so *old* in a movie before and because the film doesn't sugarcoat the infirmity: Auntie seems an inhuman monster until you understand she's the mellowest person here. Then Apu comes along and quickly grows into a saucer-eyed observer, and in him Eliza and Natalie saw any number of little brothers plaguing their friends. With the parents arguing about money, the girls were brought up short, because who thinks to put that in a movie when you can get it for free at home?

The pace is slow enough that a twenty-first-century child can get the fidgets, and both girls mentioned at different times that this was pretty boring. "Okay, I'll turn it off," I offered. "No, no—a little longer." We stopped halfway through for bedtime (to whining) and the next day they insisted we finish it off, metabolisms at last slowed down to the appropriate lope. When we got to the sequence in the wheat field, stalks glowing in the sun like alien life-forms and Durga bringing Apu to see the train pass by, the girls knew they were seeing something elemental and very special—life with the fat trimmed away. The final

scenes are unforgiving, and by then they were hushed and attentive; sad, too, but not floridly weeping as if this were a Bette
Davis movie. The girls felt the earth turning beneath the characters and themselves as Ray meant them to.

They want to see the next film in the *Apu* trilogy now, but I
think I want to let them catch their breath first.

What next: The other films in Ray's classic trilogy: *Aparajito*
(1957) and *The World of Apu* (1959). From here it's an easy jump
to more commercial, modern Bollywood films such as *Lagaan*
(2001), etc. Committed little neorealists might want to move on
to *The Bicycle Thief* (1948), the Italian postwar classic that galva-
nized more global filmmakers than just Ray, but that's a hard,
hard movie for a parent to watch with the kids.

SMALL CHANGE (COLOR, 1976)

Directed by: François Truffaut

Starring: Geory Desmouceaux, Philippe Goldmann, Jean-
François Stevenin

Ages: 10 and up

The sell: How kids live

The plot: Nothing much: just a few months among the boys of a
school in the town of Thiers, France, and, by extension, among
their parents, teachers, and friends. Sensitive Patrick (Desmouceaux) cares for his wheelchair-bound father, lusts after his best
friend's mother, but gets nervous around girls his own age. New
kid Julien (Goldmann) lives in squalor and hides a secret. Little
Gregory falls out a window and lands unhurt and laughing. After
Sylvie's parents leave her alone in the apartment, she manages to
both embarrass them and get a big Sunday dinner airlifted down

to her. Schoolteacher Richet (Stevenin) awaits the birth of his first child and tries to impart a little wisdom to the boys.

Why it's here: Made in 1976, so I'm not sure it counts as a genuine oldie, but it's certainly a classic—one of the few films to look at the life of young people from their own eye level. It's fiction, but it plays close to the documentary line: Truffaut cast locals from Thiers as themselves, and the children know how to play children. The ease of the cast in front of the cameras does your heart good.

There's no plot, per se, although there are recurrent stories we peek into from time to time: Patrick's attempts to come to terms with girls (which reaches its nadir in a movie theater scene where a friend makes out with both his own date *and* Patrick's), Richard's growing friendship with the teacher who has moved into the apartment downstairs, the sad tale of Julien, who is saved (perhaps) at the last moment. The adults go about their lives preoccupied with their own problems, and, honestly, that's fine by their children.

Small Change is about the lives that young people live apart from the grown-ups—the secret society they share with each other and no one else. (The tragedy of Julien is that neglect has made him isolate himself from this greater kid community.) Parents aren't invited in, loved as they may be, but certain teachers are.

Truffaut drops touches of whimsy into the movie: Please remind your young viewers that Little Gregory couldn't *really* fall nine floors with a happy gurgle. And the humiliation visited by Sylvie upon her errant parents is more satisfying than any Hollywood pratfall, but just as unbelievable. No matter. *Small Change* gets the rhythms of kid life—the exaggerations, the fears, and the pleasures. It's timeless and stateless and could possibly shock your children with its applicability to their own lives.

When I saw it in 1976, at the age of nineteen, it was like looking back through the doorway of a house I had just moved out of.

Pause-button explanations: There's a brief bit of nudity when two of the boys use binoculars to spy on a neighbor woman taking a shower. Look, it's a French film.

What next: If the Truffaut bug bites and they can handle a much darker story (based on the director's own childhood), send them to *The 400 Blows*. But a better bet might be *28 Up*, Michael Apted's great documentary in which he interviews the same handful of British men and women every seven years, starting in 1963 when they're seven. (He keeps going back, too; the latest version, *49 Up*, aired on British TV in 2005.) It's like watching time-lapse photos of human life.

THE UMBRELLAS OF CHERBOURG (COLOR, 1964)

Directed by: Jacques Demy

Starring: Catherine Deneuve, Nino Castelnuovo, Anne Vernon

Ages: 6 and up

The sell: What if life really were a musical?

The plot: Cherbourg teenager Geneviève (Deneuve) works in an umbrella shop run by her mother (Vernon) and falls in love with Guy (Castelnuovo), a young garage mechanic. Her mother disapproves, but they continue to meet, and after Guy is drafted into the army it turns out Geneviève is pregnant. Two years later, she hasn't heard from him so she accepts an offer of marriage from diamond dealer Cassard (Marc Michel), as Maman has urged. By the time Guy finally returns, it's too late for these two. Life goes on.

Why it's here: That plot may not sound like much, especially for younger kids, but here's the thing: Every word in *Umbrellas of Cherbourg* is sung. The music's by Michel Legrand and is very *franche*, sad even when ecstatic and vice versa. The entire movie evolves with such grace, melodicism, and movement that it lifts the purposefully "average" dialogue and plotline into a privileged realm. Then there's the cinematography by Jean Rabier that turns rainy Cherbourg into a candy box of colors. Perhaps this *is* what the world seems like to a seventeen-year-old girl in love. If so, how nice that someone—the gifted, slightly nuts Jacques Demy—captured it on film.

Demy grew up in France but grew up *on* Hollywood musicals, and *Umbrellas* runs with the marvelous idea at the center of the genre—that the most precious moments of our lives sing and dance. That includes both bitter and sweet, and younger viewers spoon-fed happy endings may be taken aback by the fact that all does not work out perfectly here. But the movie's honest about why (the things we owe to others and sheer bad timing) and kids seem to appreciate that honesty.

Ours did, anyway. Eliza and Natalie watched Demy's follow-up first, 1967's *The Young Girls of Rochefort*, because it has an aging Gene Kelly in it, as well as Deneuve playing opposite her real sister, Françoise Dorléac, who would die later that year in a car accident at twenty-six, another of the cinema's stupid early deaths. It's a crazier but lesser film than *Umbrellas*, and once the girls saw the latter, that's the one they asked for. Some adults hate *Umbrellas* with a passion, though—it's garish, they think, a celebration of the banal. I guarantee you that children will have seen nothing like it: insanely romantic while remaining oddly real, and offering people in place of heroes and villains.

Home video notes: Get the 1997 Fox Lorber DVD, with the restored print.

Pause-button explanations: You'll probably want to show this to kids who can handle the notion of out-of-wedlock pregnancy. Scratch that; they can probably handle it just fine, but can you handle explaining it to them? Also, good luck reading the subtitles to children without bursting into song yourself. I found myself blurting them out quickly, sotto voce, so we could hear the singing; the lyrics are simple enough that older kids will be able to follow along easily.

What next: *The Young Girls of Rochefort*

ZAZIE DANS LE MÉTRO (COLOR, 1960)

Directed by: Louis Malle

Starring: Catherine Demongeot, Philippe Noiret

Ages: 9 and up (with reservations)

The sell: Childhood is anarchy. Or it *should* be.

The plot: Demonic twelve-year-old Zazie (Demongeot) stays with her wacky uncle (Noiret) in Paris while her mother takes a weekend off to be with her boyfriend. The girl soon enough peels off on her own and has encounters around the city with various oddballs, all of whom she outwits. What Zazie really wants to do is ride on the metro, but the subway workers are on strike until the very end.

Why it's here: This may be the most subversive movie in the entire book—*Eloise* as translated by Salvador Dalí. It's filmed in a style that can only be called high *Road Runner*, with all sorts of camera gags and cartoony bits that echo silent-movie slapstick and prefigure Richard Lester's Beatles movies while standing knee-deep in the French New Wave. And it's often neck-snappingly funny, especially since little Demongeot is so unflappable.

Not to mention rude, foulmouthed, crafty, and empowered. She's, in short, a kid with none of the superego that parents consider it their business to spackle on over the course of childhood. There will be some mothers and fathers who'll find *Zazie* an affront to all that is good and right in this world, even as their children will think it's the most liberating thing they've ever seen.

Of course, some children may be shocked, too. Eliza blanched when the first "*merde*" popped out of the heroine's mouth—helpfully translated by the subtitles—while Natalie let out a yawp of blindsided laughter. The movie bends the frame of what movies about kids are supposed to be, just as so many of its gags seem to bend the law of physics. *Zazie* makes the chaos of modern kid movies and TV shows look toothless and sold-out; it says, in essence, that if kids ruled their own lives (or the movies, or the world), the resulting chaos would hurt—and hurt good.

I've probably talked you out of it, and, sure, the movie's a bit of a mess (that's the point). Even if you don't want to let your children within ten kilometers of the thing, though, know that it's out there: the anti–*Home Alone*, or *Amélie: The Early Years*.

Home video notes: Unavailable on DVD in this country, but the VHS tape can still be found online and in artsy-fartsy vid-shoppes.

Useless trivia: Based on a novel by the playful, uncategorizable French writer Raymond Queneau, whose book *Exercises in Style*—the same odd anecdote told ninety-nine different ways— makes a good gift for any budding writer you might know.

What next: Hmm. As mentioned above, *Zazie* points backward to the Keystone Kops and forward to *A Hard Day's Night*; it also leads older viewers to other New Wave directors like Godard (*Breathless*, 1960) and Truffaut (*Small Change*, *The 400 Blows*). And the movie's wayward, relaxed Paris-in-the-summer vibe is echoed in the cult Jacques Rivette film *Celine and Julie Go Boating* (1974), a very strange, very terrific movie that plays like *Alice in Wonderland* on tranquilizers.

9

. . . .

THE PEOPLE WHO MADE THEM

THE STARS

UP TO NOW, this book has been organized in a way that's hopefully practical to parents: movies to watch by age group, movies to watch by genre. As with so much that grown-ups try to teach kids, this goes against the grain of how we actually use movies. The history of film in America is the history of stars: We go to the movies to see the people in them. I can't imagine a young person who is taken with, say, Fred Astaire who doesn't immediately want to know more, and for some kids watching the Astaire and Rogers films becomes like collecting Pokemon cards—gotta have 'em all. Eliza treats Katharine Hepburn movies like notches on a gun; if William Powell's in it, Natalie will watch it. And so on, and why not?

Movie stars are our archetypes of behavior, and for a child they serve a similar function that the gods did for an ancient Greek. What happens if you break the law with abandon? Cagney tells you. What are the things women can and can't get away with? Joan Crawford, Bette Davis, and Katharine Hepburn are still hashing it out somewhere. Is goodness possible?

Look to Jimmy Stewart, who says the answer is not as simple as you think. Is grace possible? Look to Cary Grant, who answers, Yes, at a cost; or to Audrey Hepburn, who simply answers, Yes.

As usual, the essays below wander hither and yon, maybe too hither and far too yon, but they all work roughly out from a central consideration of what these actors and actresses might say to a child, in their bearing, in their biographies, in their choices of films. I don't know: What *does* Humphrey Bogart have to convey to a nine-year-old boy in the early twenty-first century? If he doesn't want to think about it—and he's nine, let him just watch the movies—it couldn't hurt for you to.

I haven't included nearly everyone I could or should have. The comedians are mostly dealt with over in the comedy chapter, and plenty of others have fallen through the cracks. You're right, maybe Spencer Tracy was the best actor of the bunch, but his screen persona was never as sharply defined as Gable's or Cooper's or Grant's, and he's of lesser interest as a personality to a child. Start with the demigods below and move forward.

After each essay, the performer's best films are briefly discussed; feel free to treat them as recommendations. Full filmographies can be found at the Internet Movie Database at www.imdb.com.

FRED ASTAIRE

You need to start a twenty-first century child on Astaire early. There's a fairly small window of psychological availability from, I don't know, ages three to eight, followed by increasing skepticism, then full-on doubt. The movies are old, for one thing— the great run of Astaire and Rogers musicals are seven decades in the past and undeniably quaint—but it's more than that. The *context* for Astaire, the common vocabulary needed to describe him, has vanished. There is nobody remotely like him now.

To be fair, there was nobody like him then. But there was a place he fit into, a social archetype Astaire could take as his own. The society dandy, forever in evening clothes, was as much a stereotype of the Roaring Twenties as hippies were of the '60s and slackers of the '90s. Astaire brought this figure into the Depression years—kept it alive for audiences who desperately needed it—and burned off its self-indulgent aspects. All that's left of the cliché is its Art Deco outline, and Astaire filled that up with dance: tap, ballroom, swing, up the wall, across the ceiling, and back down again (if you think I'm kidding, rent *Royal Wedding*).

Dancing in movies is often presented as a romantic, even sexual activity, but Fred will have none of that; not because he's a prude but because he simply doesn't care. Ginger, God love her, is there because we need him to dance *with* somebody if he's to avoid the self-seriousness that eventually overtook Gene Kelly. Fred's game for that; he understands the rules. Throw anyone next to him: Rogers, Cyd Charisse, Rita Hayworth, even poor two-left-feet Joan Fontaine in the perfectly titled *A Damsel in Distress*. Fred will adapt and make his costar look great and maybe even convince you his character is in love. But, really, he needs her like the candle needs the moth.

Small children roll with this intuitively—they recognize Astaire as a trickster, a figure with one foot in fairy tale. He's like Paul Bunyan or Davy Crockett; did he really exist? Does it matter? Not when they watch *Swing Time* or *Funny Face*, his own versions of tall tales. Biography is moot with Fred Astaire. Believing in him isn't exactly like believing in the Easter Bunny, but, after a certain age, it requires a similar credulousness—a stated willingness to believe.

So, older kids, not so much. Anyway, the heroes of current teen culture and tweener culture are all sexualized on one level or another—once you outgrow *Blue's Clues*, it's mostly about fronting—and the thing about Astaire is that he has no sexuality at all. He's not macho. He's not swish. He is simply and only about the movement. To a callow teenager, or an insecure one, that makes him a candidate for ridicule, and this is easy because Astaire makes dancing look easy. You have to read books to learn about the insane amount of practice the man put in, about Rogers's feet bleeding from filming the final sequence in *Top Hat* over and over, about the hard, hard work needed to make these movies appear insubstantial.

With every step he takes, Astaire insists that books and background stories aren't the point—what's up there on the screen is the point, and it's the only point. Dance, art, beauty, are their own rewards and as such don't require plot or even meaning to be meaningful. Again, this is a seed best planted early.

Top Hat *(B&W, 1935)* It feels like a delightful toy, from that weensy Art Deco Venice to the manifold Freds of the climactic title number. The most emblematic Astaire-Rogers movie: mistaken identity plot, Irving Berlin tunes, and a one-take version of "The Piccolino."

Swing Time *(B&W, 1936)* And this may be the best of the Astaire-Rogers, even if Fred dons blackface for the Bill "Bojangles" Robinson tribute (explain the cultural context, if you dare). George Stevens directs and the Jerome Kern–Dorothy Fields songs are sublime.

Easter Parade *(color, 1948)* Gene Kelly broke his leg and Astaire was called out of retirement to star opposite Judy Garland in a sly backstage love story with smart Berlin songs. The stars as bums singing "A Couple of Swells" are great fun.

The Band Wagon *(color, 1953)* Hilarious backstager about song-and-dance folk forced by an artsy-fartsy director to mount a pretentious musical "Faust." Astaire dances opposite Cyd Charisse in this one and Oscar Levant is his dyspeptic old self. Make sure the kids see the "Triplets" number, with the stars dressed up as babies.

Funny Face *(color, 1957)* Late, late in the afternoon, Astaire was paired with Audrey Hepburn for a wistfully lovely tale of a fashion photographer and the Greenwich Village beatnik he makes over. Tremendous Gershwin songs and, yes, that's *Eloise* author Kay Thompson singing "Think Pink."

HUMPHREY BOGART

Humphrey Bogart is not your typical movie star, and a kid instantly senses this. He's funny looking, with the face of a constipated basset hound, and he's *mean* more often than not—a Bogart smile is not an invitation to join in the fun. But here is what makes him special: He does not back down. The lives of kids are full of people telling them what to do, where to go, what to wear, playground bullies who exact tribute in lunch money or dignity, and Humphrey Bogart does not back down.

He doesn't even get ruffled. If Cary Grant is the male role model for ease and Jimmy Stewart for watchful goodness and John Wayne for indominability, then Bogey is here for the fact that he never loses his cool yet is always poised to react, with force if necessary but more often through the patient application of seasoned intelligence. I've seen children left utterly at sea by *The Maltese Falcon*, with its crosses and double-crosses, games within games, but they sit there fascinated because Bogey is the one true thing piercing the murk. He acknowledges something parents don't like to admit but kids know anyway—that people can be selfish and two-faced and small—and by his acknowledgment he overcomes it.

Bogart teaches mastery.

Not surprisingly, he's the only one of the old gods who came to stardom in middle age, and part of the attraction was what he had picked up along the way. This is an argument for leaving actors outside to weather for a decade or two; it's certainly Bogart's experience that sets him apart.

Before he settled into his hangdog features, the movies didn't know what to do with him. Born to a wealthy New York family in 1899, Bogart had a preppie upbringing (he was kicked out of Andover), and he's clearly more Humphrey than Bogey in the small film roles he picked up in the early 1930s. Fame and typecasting came with his vicious Duke Mantee in *The Petrified Forest* (1935) on Broadway and on-screen, but Bogart continued to languish in second-tier gangster parts until the one-two punch of *High Sierra* and *The Maltese Falcon* in 1941. After that, he was simply Bogart, and his wooing and winning of Lauren Bacall around the time of *To Have and Have Not* (1944) was a classic Hollywood love story.

He was gone much too soon. Bogart smoked on-screen with more attractiveness, more *wit*, than any other actor, and it killed him. He died of cancer of the esophagus, after several operations and a horrible final few months, at the age of fifty-seven. This irony may be worth a little conversation or two.

The Maltese Falcon *(B&W, 1941)* The stuff private-eye movie dreams are made of. He's detective Sam Spade, caught in a viper's nest of intrigue, and which side is he on? Great absurdist gallery of supporting players; director John Huston's first film. If you like this, also see the wilder and woolier *The Big Sleep* (1946).

Casablanca *(B&W, 1942)* You'll have to lay down a little World War II history before watching this one, but it's worth it. The best movie of all time? Certainly the best example of the studio system working at peak efficiency.

To Have and Have Not *(B&W, 1944)* Bogart meets Bacall in a twisty action-mystery from Howard Hawks. You know how to whistle, don't you?

The Treasure of the Sierra Madre (B&W, 1948) Tough-minded drama of greed and paranoia, with the star playing one his roughest customers in Fred C. Dobbs, ugly American panning for gold in Mexico. For the young Bogart adept who wants to broaden his or her palate.

The African Queen (color, 1951) Probably the best Bogart for younger kids, since it costars Kate Hepburn and both play enjoyably larger-than-life. She's a prim missionary, he's a drunken mail boat captain, and they have to get down an African river before the German army or the leeches get them. Bogart's one and only Oscar.

JAMES CAGNEY

My God, the energy of the man. Take a nine-year-old, put on *Footlight Parade* or *Angels with Dirty Faces*, and watch him or her be mesmerized by an actor who in many ways seems like a stylized kid—a confident cartoon bad boy. Cagney started out a Broadway hoofer but came to fame playing gangsters, and the huge appeal of him is that he conveys charm and malice in equal measure—you're never sure whether he'll reach for the girl or the gun (or the grapefruit).

Alone of the tough guys of early-talkies Hollywood, he had the smell of the streets on him; while Bogart was getting booted out of Andover, Cagney was coming up on the East Side of Manhattan, working odd jobs before plugging his electricity into the vaudeville circuit. Some of his earliest roles were female-impersonating "chorus girl" bits, and that makes sense, too: His characters often have a fey precision to them that verges on gay camp.

But they can also be cruelly irrational, delighting in anarchy. No matter that in real life Cagney was one of the gentlest guys in the business, on-screen the motor never idles and occasionally pins into the red. *The Public Enemy*, the 1931 gangster film that made him a star, is testimony to the brutal pleasures and short, sharp comeuppance of the thug life; seventeen years later, the astonishing *White Heat* shows the Cagney gangster in a harsher yet more elegiac light, as a mother-loving psycho. No wonder children can hardly look away from the guy.

When he's not playing a gangster, Cagney is a consistent, high-spirited comic joy. He won his Oscar in 1942 for playing *Yankee Doodle Dandy*'s song-and-dance man George M. Cohan, but his filmography is studded with forgotten happy occasions: 1940's *Torrid Zone*, with Jimmy on a banana plantation romancing oomphy Ann Sheridan and holding bandito George Tobias (the future Abner Kravitz of *Bewitched*) at bay; 1933's *Picture Snatcher*, in which he plays an early paparazzo; Billy Wilder's manic *One, Two, Three* (1961), Cagney's final film before retirement; the thoroughly demented *Lady Killer* (1933), in which he plays a gangster who makes good in Hollywood—shades of *Get Shorty*'s Chili Palmer—and goes *Public Enemy* one better by dragging Mae Clarke around by her *hair*.

An aside. When I was young and growing up outside of Boston, my elementary school class contained mostly well-behaved, dutiful children—luck of the draw, I suppose—until fifth grade, when a kid named Sam transferred in from another school. Suddenly we had a devil-eyed bad boy: he'd sass the teachers and play with matches, he used all the swears we'd heard of and many we hadn't, he knew about sex and what he didn't know he gleefully made up. It's an understatement to say we were fascinated by him, and that went for the teachers as well. Some of us joined up for mild debauchery—I recall tossing water balloons off Sam's apartment house roof at passersby, an activity I would have previously equated with looting a church—while others watched from a safer distance. Somehow, in this, lines were drawn that set and held for adulthood.

Eventually, of course, we grew up and embraced our own inner bad boys and girls. Sam survived; many of us expected him to be found in a Dumpster by his twenty-first birthday, but there he was at an informal thirtieth reunion, smiling and prosperous and married. There seemed nothing very dangerous about him anymore, and the rest of us were mildly disappointed. And then, two months later, I glanced at the police blotter in the newspaper, and there he was again, getting arrested for tossing his six-year-old son in the trunk of his car after the kid wouldn't stop pestering him from the backseat. A woman in the car behind him phoned 911 in horror, the son turned out to be fine, not even upset, but is what Sam did the definition of a bad boy right there—acting on what the rest of us only threaten? Is this the siren song of Jimmy Cagney, the devil-eyed boy of Warner Bros.' back-lot Manhattan? That he uses the grapefruit the rest of us only contemplate?

The Public Enemy *(B&W, 1931)* The rise and bloody fall of a tough little hoodlum named Tom Powers, *Enemy* set the pattern for everything from *Scarface* (1932) to *Scarface* (1983). Scalding at the time and still surprisingly gritty, this is the one where Cagney smacks Mae Clarke in the kisser with the citrus.

Footlight Parade *(B&W, 1933)* Typically baroque Busby Berkeley musical in the *42nd Street* tradition has Ruby Keeler, Dick Powell, and Cagney as Broadway producer Chester Kent, a rat-a-tat dynamo who can mount three shows at once and do some song and dance too.

A Midsummer Night's Dream *(B&W, 1935)* Cagney plays Bottom—ass head and all—in this top-heavy but remarkable all-star Hollywood Shakespeare.

Yankee Doodle Dandy *(B&W, 1942)* Extremely entertaining patriotic wartime corn about now-forgotten showman George

M. Cohan (he wrote "Over There"), this broke Cagney once and for all out of the gangster box.

White Heat *(B&W, 1949)* He returned for this psychologically acute but no less gonzo postwar gangland drama. Cagney's bad guys always threatened to explode, and in this one he finally does.

GARY COOPER

Cooper is old Hollywood's face of American nobility, of stoicism under pressure, and that image comes almost exclusively from two films: 1942's *The Pride of the Yankees* and 1952's *High Noon*. In the first he plays doomed New York Yankee Lou Gehrig, in the second an Old West lawman abandoned by the townspeople he has sworn to protect. Both films make the most of Coop's celebrated minimal style of acting—directors would watch in despair as he did *nothing* in front of the camera, then they'd get the rushes and be floored—and both trade on the mournfulness that lay in wait beneath his weathered, plainspoken persona. The longer Cooper was around, the sadder he seemed, as if this simple Montana boy slowly understood something he didn't want to admit. *High Noon* was created as a conscious metaphor for the moral cowardice of the Hollywood blacklist era, but the star's gravity seems to come from an even deeper and more mysterious well. What let Gary Cooper down? There's no answer, or none worth placing before a child just starting out on life.

Simplicity is the key to Cooper and his greatest meaning to younger audiences. By all accounts he was as we see him onscreen: easygoing, not especially articulate, aware of the responsibilities of fame, intent on acting honorably. A good man. Also a serious Hollywood playboy for decades; Cooper's star rose in the silent era, crossed over to early talkies—he moved even less than the microphones did—and with Gable he was one of the heartthrobs of the 1930s. His offscreen reputation as a ladykiller belies his on-screen solemnity and hints at an anarchic spark few movies exploited.

The ones that did were comedies, and Cooper, much like Henry Fonda, may be best encountered for the first time in comedy (unless your kid's into baseball, in which case cue up *Pride* right away). In a movie like *Ball of Fire* or *Mr. Deeds Goes to Town* Cooper isn't quite the butt of the joke—rather his gentle, dreamy squareness *is* the joke, and you sense he's in on it too. Especially in his early years, he was a serious man comfortable enough to play around a little, and that's increasingly unheard of in our reflexively cynical culture. Cooper makes common decency seem as attractive as the most jaded irony; of the old gods, only Gregory Peck comes close.

Peter Ibbetson *(B&W, 1935)* A little-seen but unique fantasy romance in which jailed Cooper and childhood sweetheart Ann Harding literally create a parallel universe for their love. If you can find the film—available only as part of Universal's five-film "Gary Cooper Collection"—it's a weird little gem for kids willing to roll with it. Eliza watched this almost by accident and ended up falling for it hard.

Mr. Deeds Goes to Town *(B&W, 1936)* Is Longfellow Deeds crazy for giving away his money, or is he a hero? Frank Capra's delightful semi-screwball comedy is perfect for children, since it trades on the doubts about wealth they themselves have.

Ball of Fire *(B&W, 1941)* Crazy-funny Howard Hawks screwball remake of *Snow White*. Barbara Stanwyck plays a stripper on the run from the mob who hides out with seven fuddy-duddy professors of language. Cooper's the cute one, of whom Stanwyck says, "I love him because he's the kind of guy who gets drunk on a glass of buttermilk."

The Pride of the Yankees *(B&W, 1942)* Coop as the then recently departed Lou Gehrig, playing opposite the real Babe Ruth, among others.

High Noon *(B&W, 1952)* Spare your kids the blacklist backstory for the time being and let them take this as a straight-up tale of doing what's right even when no one backs you up.

JOAN CRAWFORD AND BETTE DAVIS

Since alphabetical order has the malicious nerve to put these two next to each other, I might as well treat them together: the Great Star and the Great Actress. One can almost hear Crawford whimpering, "If only I weren't in the book at all . . ." and Davis catcalling back, "But ya AHH, Blanche, ya AHH!"

That's a tip of the hat to *Whatever Happened to Baby Jane*, the 1962 horror film and camp classic that finally put the two legends together after dueling careers of striving and rivalry. It's a great, Grand Guignol time for teenagers and up, and it works nicely off the stars' larger-than-life personas (Joan the tight-lipped martyr, Bette the smart, reckless hellion), but it's also a shallow gloss on what they each accomplished in their primes and what they have to say to audiences coming to them for the first time.

Crawford is an example to the little girls, and a warning. Her career trajectory says you can make it if you really *are* willing to sacrifice everything except the work: name, identity, other people, your own children. By the 1950s she was the only star from the silents still at the top of the Hollywood pile, and nothing in her stare or shoulder pads led audiences to think that was by accident. Although her first film roles came in 1925, when she was nineteen, Crawford had slowly worked her way toward Hollywood as a waitress, shopgirl, café dancer, possibly shading into more desperate areas, briefly morphing from her birth name of Lucille LeSeuer to Billie Cassin and back again.

She prospered in Los Angeles. MGM's Harry Rapf took her under his wing and sponsored a fan magazine contest to come up with her new name: Crawford's celebrity is thus entwined with her audience's desires at a genetic level. Her first starring roles were as flappers and party girls, and, as the talkies kicked in, she specialized in ambitious, starry-eyed lower-class women. By 1940 the persona had hardened into the husband-stealer of *The Women* and clearly something had to change.

Leaving MGM for Warner Bros., Crawford won an Oscar for *Mildred Pierce* and embarked on a run of melodramas that match her slightly lunatic air of intensity and make up her best and most florid work. By the '50s, however, the movies had become unintentional comedies, a fact of which the star seemed oblivious. She slowly sank into self-parody even as she maintained her quivering celebrity until the very end.

Could Crawford act? To be brutally honest, no, not really. That doesn't hurt a movie like *Humoresque*; you could argue that the star's bullheaded self-pity makes the film work. She seems canny rather than intelligent—in the way Demi Moore had going for herself back in the 1990s—and her best movies are variations on the theme of a nervy, misunderstood woman taking on a capricious world. What you can say is that she excelled at playing her best idea of herself, as a true star should. But there is also the sense that in six decades of public life, Crawford's eyes never once left the mirror—here is the warning to younger viewers, and it slips with ease into discussions of modern-day celebrity and its discontents. Crawford made herself—rather, Lucille LeSeuer made herself—in the same fashion that, say, Madonna Louise Ciccone or Jennifer Lopez or Christina Aguilera have made themselves: with conscious forethought and as an end in itself. And when she *had* made herself, she found there was nothing much more to say and so just gripped stardom tighter and tighter.

Bette Davis, on the other hand—well, you couldn't shut her up. The difference was that she had talent and brains as well as ambition, all three meant to draw attention away from the fact that she wasn't conventionally pretty. Initially Davis was to Warner Bros.' streetwise piss-and-vinegar as Crawford was to MGM's satin sheets, and then Jack Warner realized to his terror that she could act, too. Davis fought to go over to RKO for *Of Human Bondage* (1934), which made her name, then came back to fight the Warner front office over roles in movies like *Dangerous* (1935), which won her an Oscar that many people discounted as payback for not getting one for *Bondage*.

By 1938, after filing suit, fleeing to England, and being forced by her contract to return, Davis began her great run of roles: a second Oscar for *Jezebel* (1938), *Dark Victory* (1939), *The Letter* (1940), *The Little Foxes* (1941), *Now, Voyager* (1942), *Mr. Skeffington* (1944), and, late in the day, *All About Eve* (1950). *The Letter* might be too strong medicine for younger viewers—that incredible opening shot of Davis shooting down her lover in cold blood is a prelude to serious moral funkiness—but all the others are recommended to thoughtful older kids, and not only because the star is so much fun to watch.

A Joan Crawford movie is about the world sticking it to Joan. A Bette Davis movie is about Bette sticking it to the world. Which would you rather a child see and toss about in the crannies of his or her mind? Think about it for a moment. A heroine who is ennobled through her victimization, or one who acts before she can be ennobled, who risks the results of her own agency?

Davis heroines make wrong choices—sometimes, as in *The Little Foxes*, horrifically wrong—but at least they make them. Charlotte Vale in *Now, Voyager* transforms from a grown child emotionally abused by her mother to a woman confident enough to forgo her lover and care for a surrogate daughter. Mildred Pierce, by contrast, is a woman who makes the mistake of kicking her two-timing husband out and is punished for it with an abusive daughter and a leech of a boyfriend. *Mildred Pierce* is a hell of a movie but it's a closed loop; you take nothing away from it other than a fear of Ann Blyth. *Now, Voyager*, hunk of women's-weepie tosh that it is, gave something to my daughters they'll keep for a long time. Both Crawford and Davis spoke volumes to the women in the back row of the Bijou, but where Joan was about a woman's will thwarted, Bette was about the strength behind the will and about the ecstatic danger of letting it loose.

JOAN CRAWFORD

Dancing Lady *(B&W, 1933)* Early talkie Crawford that pairs her with Clark Gable in a sassy backstage musical, with both Fred Astaire *and* the Three Stooges milling around in the background.

Mildred Pierce *(B&W, 1945)* The female film noir that saved Crawford's career, it's an intensely watchable murder-mystery-meets-women's-melodrama, with an appealing Crawford suffering, suffering, suffering.

Humoresque *(B&W, 1946)* Unhinged society dame Crawford becomes the patron/lover of striving violinist John Garfield. Over-the-top soap opera is excellent nevertheless.

Torch Song *(color, 1953)* The movie to jump-start your cynical teen's love affair with bad late-period Joan Crawford movies. If they can make it through the "Two-Faced Woman" blackface number without their little eyes popping out and rolling around the living room floor, they need more help than this book can offer.

Johnny Guitar (*color, 1954*) Just your basic Freudian anti-McCarthy feminist Western, shot in flaming color by director Nicholas Ray. Great fun for weisenheimer older kids and budding auteurists, but was Crawford even in on the joke?

BETTE DAVIS

Jezebel (*B&W, 1938*) The competition was heating up for Scarlett O'Hara in *Gone with the Wind*, so Davis made her own antebellum melodrama just to show she looked good manipulating men in a hoopskirt. Won an Oscar for it, too.

The Private Lives of Elizabeth and Essex (*B&W, 1939*) Davis as Queen Elizabeth I: typecasting or what? Errol Flynn plays Essex, and for once he looks at a loss for words.

Dark Victory (*B&W, 1939*) Society girl Judith Traherne stops living the shallow life when she gets a brain tumor. A full-on weeper in the grand tradition, with Humphrey Bogart—just before he crossed over to the big time—as the Irish stablehand who loves Davis.

Now, Voyager (*B&W, 1942*) Ugly duckling Charlotte Vale becomes a swan and learns to stand up to her fearsome mother (Gladys Cooper) with the help of a kindly shrink (Claude Rains) and a tortured married man (Paul Henreid).

All about Eve (*B&W, 1950*) Perhaps the best backstage movie ever made, it features Davis playing an outsize version of herself. Huge if chatty fun.

MARLENE DIETRICH

You could think of Dietrich as the anti–Bette Davis: She doesn't force herself onto her movies so much as float mysteriously on the surface of them, another visual element along with the lighting and sets. With Garbo, she's proof of the unknowable, and, like Garbo, she came to Hollywood under the wing of a strong-willed director. But Josef von Sternberg was more than just Dietrich's mentor. The seven films they made together from 1930 to 1935 blur together into a unique and delirious cinematic expression of love, betrayal, and production design, and if you have a kid that likes one of them, he or she will probably like all of them. In her long post–von Sternberg career Dietrich occasionally threatened to dwindle into hotheaded exotica, but she refused to ever go away, and in truth her life may have been more interesting than her movies. Which is to say that when Eliza caught a documentary about the actress on TV one afternoon, she watched it with as much interest and dramatic payoff as a feature film.

Shanghai Express (B&W, 1932) "It took more than one man to change my name to Shanghai Lily." So says Dietrich as the train leaves Peking with a motley assortment of characters aboard. The best introduction to the von Sternberg/Dietrich films, with supporting actress Anna May Wong making up for a musty Clive Brook as the romantic lead.

Blonde Venus (B&W, 1932) Another von Sternberg, less coherent than the above but more visually dazzling, with Cary Grant in an early role and Dietrich dancing in a gorilla suit. The back half is Marlene on the lam with her young son: kind of a downer for kids.

Destry Rides Again (B&W, 1939) Excellent comic Western that revived Dietrich's career. She plays a saloon dancer named

Frenchy opposite Jimmy Stewart as the timid gunfighter of the title; Mel Brooks saw and remembered her when it came time to cast Madeline Kahn as Lili Von Schtupp in *Blazing Saddles*.

Golden Earrings *(B&W, 1947)* Underrated—all right, completely forgotten—World War II suspense romance about an Allied spy (Ray Milland) in Germany who's helped by a gypsy (Dietrich). Sounds preposterous, but director Mitchell Leisen comes through again.

Witness for the Prosecution *(B&W, 1957)* Billy Wilder's courtroom mystery pulls a late-career performance out of Dietrich that's more complicated than it first appears.

HENRY FONDA

Gary Cooper with a college degree? That does a disservice to both men, but Hank's steady all-American decency does have a more articulate, even pedagogical urge behind it. Which is to say a Fonda movie can teach you things: Okies are good, lynching is bad, the American judicial system works, but only if you tend to it. He made more than his share of Hollywood pap, but the urge to enlighten pops up consistently and increasingly in his filmography. There are conversations to be had, good ones, with your kids after seeing a Fonda movie. Perhaps there's also a conversation to be had, when they're older, about how a good actor and solid citizen can make a lousy father himself. But save that for after *On Golden Pond*.

Young Mr. Lincoln *(B&W, 1939)* John Ford's portrait of the future president as a young country lawyer is grand, simplistic Americana—cynics need not apply. Fonda is surprisingly good.

The Grapes of Wrath *(B&W, 1940)* Ruthless tale of the Great Depression, based on John Steinbeck's novel, with the star pared of actorly affectation as Okie Tom Joad. John Ford directs with all stops out.

The Lady Eve *(B&W, 1941)* Like Cooper, Fonda could do sly work in comedy, and he's a prize boob in Preston Sturges's farce about a con woman (Barbara Stanwyck) and the naive beer heir she fleeces and flummoxes.

The Ox-Bow Incident *(B&W, 1943)* Sober, underplayed drama about the dangers of vigilante justice in the Old West that puts its message across in provocative fashion.

12 Angry Men *(B&W, 1957)* Intensely watchable one-room drama about a Brooklyn jury ready to send a young man to the chair until one juror (Fonda) decides to speak up. Surprisingly suitable for all ages.

CLARK GABLE

They called him "the King"—they needed one just then. If every era gets the masculine ideal it deserves, then the 1930s were lucky to find him, but what does it say about the current generation that Gable has largely faded away while Cary Grant, Jimmy Stewart, John Wayne, and Humphrey Bogart retain almost as much cultural currency as they did in their heyday? Has Gable's easygoing macho become dated? Has he lost his potency in an age of Brad Pitt? Or is the answer simpler—that he was an immensely charismatic but not particularly complicated figure, and that his career never had a second act, never matured the way Grant's and Stewart's, Wayne's and Bogey's did.

Throughout the 1930s, though, Gable was Hollywood's own Jove. He was casual, solid, impulsive, funny, terrifically sexy— above all, he was very, very male, and that in itself was a change after the limpid drawing-room sheiks of the 1920s. The Depression called for, among other things, a sudden end to bullshit; the pretensions of the Jazz Age were simply not affordable anymore, financially or psychologically. Gable walked in like the delivery-man who you suddenly realize has more firepower than anyone else in the room.

He made twelve movies in 1931, the year he hit it big—*twelve movies*! Tom Cruise would need a defibrillator just to keep up—and by the end of the year he was so ubiquitous that the hip put-down was, "Who do you think you are, Clark Gable?" What was his secret? All of it: the lick of hair tumbling forward and the mocking, pursed lips; the broadness of his shoulders, his hands, his *head* (those ears for years a liability and suddenly a crucial part of the whole package); the sense women had that he might smoothly reach out and swallow them whole. For a while, Gable *was* sex.

He had one transcendent decade—the miracle year of 1931, an Oscar by 1935, the coronation as Rhett Butler by 1939—and everything that followed was an echo of that decade. Nobody seemed to notice or mind that the King looked increasingly lost after his wife, the adored Carole Lombard, died in a 1943 plane crash, that the postwar years passed by him in a rush. What he meant in the 1930s was more than enough to last. In his final film, 1963's *The Misfits*, he played opposite Marilyn Monroe, and she told a journalist, "Can you imagine what being kissed by him meant to me?" In this she spoke for millions of girls and women in the dark looking up at the screen of their shared fantasies.

What does Gable have to teach children? That vitality exists, that it can matter on a mass scale, and that film preserves it even after the rest of the world has moved on. And that the world does move on and will always do so.

Red Dust *(B&W, 1932)* Released during the first flush of Gable-mania, this saucy adventure pic casts him as a rubber plantation he-man driving ladylike Mary Astor and tough dame Jean Harlow dizzy with lust. It's as racy as it sounds, so keep the little ones away and use it to shock the teens.

It Happened One Night *(B&W, 1934)* The premiere screwball comedy, the first film to win the five major Oscars (actor, actress, director, writer, picture), the movie that sent the undershirt industry into a tailspin (Gable didn't wear one)—and it almost didn't happen.

Mutiny on the Bounty *(B&W, 1935)* The star's an impetuous, rippled Fletcher Christian going up against Charles Laughton's brutish Captain Bligh.

Gone with the Wind *(color, 1939)* It's Vivien Leigh's movie, and Gable's Rhett Butler is offscreen much of the time, but he still dominates it. No other actor could have done that.

Teacher's Pet *(B&W, 1958)* Gable's best postwar movie (even counting the lovely but flawed *Misfits*), this very funny light comedy pairs him with Doris Day as battling journalists. Imagine *Pillow Talk* with Rock Hudson replaced by an aging, still agile lion.

GRETA GARBO

She didn't say "I want to be alone," actually. She said "I want to be *left* alone," and the difference is between someone who prefers solitude and someone who actively dislikes other people. The mystery of Garbo—and mystery is her gift to us—is how someone so interesting to watch has no interest in returning the favor. She is the star who keeps her back to us. It's as though Garbo understood that movies are the cheapest approximation of human emotion to be had—a tin can for holding orchids—and so indulged them, and us, until it wasn't worth the bother.

The things that can't be said outnumber the things that can, so close up shop, pull down the broad-brimmed hats, become Hollywood's ghostly rebuke to itself. That she quit stardom only made her celebrity seem larger, because we never get over the lovers who get over us.

Why did she bother? Why should we bother with her? For the brief, incandescent moments when this sour-faced woman forgets the world is out there and comes alive—glows, smiles, is transfigured. And for the knowledge she holds (a promise, really) that the happiness never lasts. At such moments, Garbo is closer to the heart of things than any actress who worked the system, and one mourns the fact that she threw in the towel before the great European directors of the 1950s came to prominence. Can you imagine what her countryman Ingmar Bergman might have done with her?

Or maybe not. Garbo was brought over from Sweden by MGM and Louis B. Mayer, who made her a star during the silent era; in many ways her silent films remain her most powerful. Certainly they seem to take place in a privileged world, and perhaps her disenchantment stems from the disappearance of that world (and of her lover John Gilbert's career with it). "Garbo talks!" said the ads for 1930's *Anna Christie*, but the screenwriters never gave her anything to say that was as real as the looks she gives Gilbert in *Love* (1927) or her magnificent heartlessness in *Flesh and the Devil* (1926). Her secret smile in *Camille* (1936) seems directed at the smallness of the movies she found herself in; her empty stare from the bow of the ship at the end of *Queen Christina* (1933) seems to shame the talkies themselves. And those are her two best sound films. After 1941's *Two-faced Woman*, a drab embarrassment of a modern-dress comedy, Garbo just walked away like an adult from a childhood suit of clothes.

Can a child get his or her mind around this? Intuitively, yes, I think so. Other celebrities sell themselves with abandon, divulge their innermost secrets, talk the banal language of recovery, shake their various tatas in the culture's face. Garbo insists on privacy and, better, unknowability. Look but do not touch, she says, for when you touch something it becomes ordinary.

Flesh and the Devil *(B&W, 1926)* Not the first Garbo to try but a pretty amazing follow-up. It's silent and dated in some ways, not at all in others: Garbo herself, as the woman who comes between John Gilbert and Lars Hanson, is as timeless and cruel as the Sphinx.

Queen Christina *(B&W, 1933)* Parboiled Hollywood history about the sixteenth-century Swedish ruler who abdicates for love, it gives Garbo and Gilbert one last fling, a moving scene of bedroom memory, and a totally Zen final shot.

Anna Karenina *(B&W, 1935)* Again, more Hollywood than Tolstoy, but it's excellent Hollywood. Garbo is the adulterous heroine ennobled by motherhood and bad love, though who these days would take Fredric March over Basil Rathbone? Extremely well directed by the underrated Clarence Brown.

Camille *(B&W, 1936)* Garbo's single best sound film, and she's at her least forbidding as the doomed courtesan ("Armand . . . cough . . .") in love against all common sense with boy-toy Robert Taylor. Director George Cukor brings out the star's gentle side; would they had worked together more.

Ninotchka *(B&W, 1939)* "Garbo laughs!" the ads said, and so she does, though not terribly convincingly. Still, the Ernst Lubitsch comedy about a dour Russian (Garbo) who falls for a dapper American (Melvyn Douglas) is well loved and easy to take.

JUDY GARLAND

Children come to Garland through Dorothy Gale in *The Wizard of Oz*, but they inherently sense in that movie the sadness that fueled her and overtook her: the movie's a fractal, containing all sides of the actress's past, present, and future. I suppose all her movies are like that. Shirley Temple came close to getting the role, but can you imagine her singing "Over the Rainbow"? Can you imagine anyone *but* Garland singing it? She invests the trite lyrics with aching hope and unbearable loss; the song feels weighted with nostalgia for something that hasn't yet happened, that may in fact never happen.

She was sixteen and already whipsawing between the sleeping pills and uppers the MGM studio doctors prescribed to keep her working; when a year's rest was recommended, an executive said there was $14 million tied up in her, so, sorry, no. The young Garland never seriously resisted, because this was show business and she had been onstage since the age of three. She was born Frances Gumm and was part of a vaudeville act with two sisters, but Mama put her money on the one with talent and moved to Hollywood. A renamed Judy got her break singing "You Made Me Love You" to a photo of Clark Gable in *The Big Broadcast of 1938*, found love with Andy Hardy, went to Oz. She may have felt she already lived there.

Her subsequent life was a train wreck—five husbands, drug-induced weight problems, missed days of shooting, paranoid outbursts, disappearances—and yet she was loved intensely by coworkers as well as audiences, and all you have to do is look at the movies to understand why. There has rarely been anyone so vibrantly *there* on-screen. Garland burned bright and she burned fast: When an exasperated MGM dumped her in 1950, she was only twenty-eight. In *A Star Is Born*, in which she plays a rising actress but seems to carry centuries of accumulated show business wisdom on her shoulders, she was thirty-two. At her death in 1969 from an overdose of pills, she seemed a creature from a bygone age, and she was forty-seven.

Garland has different things to say to grown-ups and to children. To the adults who respond to her—the Stonewall boys who rioted in the streets when she died, anyone who feels that joyful pit in their stomach when she sings—she acknowledges that artifice, the *show* of show business, is the only worthwhile escape from the disappointments of the real world. That if you turn the knob to 11, maybe you can even drown out the real world and pretend it doesn't matter, an act both futile and necessary.

To children, she offers hope, sisterhood, caution. Judy was Eliza's first old movie star crush—we hopped with her from *Wizard* to *Meet Me in St. Louis* to *The Pirate* to *The Harvey Girls* and played a best-of CD on car trips until Lori and I couldn't take it anymore. We briefly theorized our daughter might be a gay man trapped in the body of a five-year-old girl. The key, in the end, was Garland's voice. Some kids come out of the womb singing and Eliza is one of them; from an early age she has been able to keep up an improvised flow of melody that first charms and then, after about ten consecutive hours, has adults within earshot begging for the mercy of a quick death. But the kid *can't* stop, and I think at some critical point in Eliza's brain development Garland gave her reason not to.

Listen to "Have Yourself a Merry Little Christmas," from *Meet Me in St. Louis*, a song sung with a wistfulness that belies its fragile, essentially benign lyrics. It's a nostalgic song in a nostalgic movie, but Garland makes the loss present tense; she both cherishes and mourns the moment in the same exhaled breath. "Have yourself a merry little Christmas *now*," she sings, as if the listener will never, ever have another chance to, and it's possible she knew the truth of that better than you or I. Sing now, advises the singer—sing while you can.

The Wizard of Oz *(B&W/color, 1939)* Just think—"Over the Rainbow" almost got cut from the movie.

Meet Me in St. Louis *(color, 1944)* Delightful, plangent musical about a bygone America—although it was to audiences of the day what a movie set in the 1960s would be to us—with Garland and Margaret O'Brien in effortless sync.

The Clock *(B&W, 1945)* No singing, but you don't mind. Vincente Minnelli directed this love story about a two-day romance between a Manhattan girl (Garland) and a soldier on leave (Robert Walker) and ended up marrying his star. It's a little-known but thoroughly charming miniature.

The Harvey Girls *(color, 1946)* Garland as a wholesome waitress in the Old West? Sounds ridiculous and it kind of is, but my girls love it, from the star singing "On the Atchison, Topeka, and the Santa Fe" to Angela Lansbury oomphing it up as a dance hall girl.

A Star Is Born *(color, 1954)* Long, problematic, unmissable if only for Judy singing "Born in a Trunk" (she practically was) and "The Man That Got Away." James Mason plays her falling-star husband but no one who sees this movie doubts who the true victim is.

CARY GRANT

I'll keep this simple: Cary Grant is proof that human grace is possible.

Not the sort of physical agility perfected by Fred Astaire, nor Cagney's ball-bearing strut, nor Audrey Hepburn's elegance—those are different forms of grace and in some ways lesser ones. Grant contains them all and adds something further: moral aplomb.

That's a word that doesn't get much of a workout these days: "aplomb." *Brewer's Dictionary of Phrase and Fable* says it "means true to the plumbline, but is generally used to express that self-possession which arises from perfect self-confidence. We also talk of a dancer's aplomb, meaning that he is a perfect master of his art." Grant was never a dancer, but in his youth he worked as a tumbler and a stiltwalker, and his career is an infinite expansion on the idea of balance.

By the time of *North by Northwest* (1959), he could play a callow playboy deepened by espionage and love—and he'd get you to go along with the game, knowing it was a game—but in truth one felt as if there was nothing Cary Grant hadn't already seen and didn't already know. This is true even as early as *The Philadelphia Story* (1940), and what's truly odd is that this accumulated wisdom lightened him, gave him a playful ease other stars never remotely approached. Some observers mistook this for the lightweight, as if Grant was merely about the twinkling bon mot and the empty tuxedo. That's a simpleminded notion, and a simple viewing of *Notorious* is enough to dispel it: There his character loses control of the situation and turns bitter and endlessly, understandably cruel.

Grant was also the rare leading man to excel at comedy—to ground the silliest of farces with timing and joy. The man had *fun*, knew the real, worldly depths of pleasure that could be had from fun, and can you say that about Cooper, Fonda, Stewart, even Gable? Grant went drag in *I Was a Male War Bride* (1949), played a fuddy-duddy in *Bringing Up Baby* (1937), acted like a five-year-old in *Monkey Business* (1952), and never seemed to stoop to conquer; rather, he raised the material to his level, just as *His Girl Friday* (1940) lets him rev the motor and find out just how fast, how mean, how funny Cary Grant can be.

How much of this did he himself understand? There's evidence, distressing as it may seem, that Grant was a man both less complicated and more so than the star he created. Born Archie

Leach in England, he lived a rough-and-tumble early life that brought him to America as part of a boy's acrobat troupe; he worked his way to Hollywood and languished in handsome-stick roles for Paramount in the early 1930s. Mae West invited him to come up and see her sometime in *She Done Him Wrong* (1933) but he grinned and seemed too nervous to take her up on it.

He was loaned out to RKO and George Cukor for *Sylvia Scarlett* (1935), opposite Katharine Hepburn, and the film was a scandalous flop—yet in it Cary Grant was suddenly and finally Cary Grant: raffish, sexy, confident. He somehow managed to sign a joint contract with both RKO and Columbia and within two years was a superstar. The persona gelled, primarily due to films he made with Hitchcock and Howard Hawks, but the sense that he had discovered himself and was firing on all cylinders is unmistakeable.

But. The money quote is—has to be—this one: "I have spent the greater part of my life fluctuating between Archie Leach and Cary Grant, unsure of each, suspecting each." Offscreen, Grant married five times and some of the divorces were ugly. He experimented extensively with LSD under a psychiatrist's care before the drug was declared illegal in the 1960s; the notion of that plummy voice saying, "Oh, wow, look at my *hand*" cannot be contained by the human mind. There is a story Dyan Cannon told after their marriage had foundered of she and Cary watching the Oscars at home and Grant jumping up and down on the bed in a rage at forever being passed over. He was right, of course.

So he was human. But not on-screen, never on-screen—that's the weird genius of the thing. Grant somehow created a human type tweaked just enough so the imperfections can't be seen and then sent him out to play. I like what Kate Hepburn said about him once, that Cary Grant was "a personality functioning." Which is another way of saying: grace.

I've written elsewhere in this book of the dangers of showing Cary Grant movies to young girls—no living man they will ever meet can measure up. But it is an imperative, even a parental duty, that young boys see the movies listed below. As they grow older, their culture will urge them toward greater and greater crassness—will insist on the vulgar as more honest and therefore worthier. And you know what? Sometimes it is. But Grant, simply by being Grant, refutes this argument. He holds out the possibility of style, of balance—of aplomb—and he dares you to emulate him.

Bringing Up Baby *(B&W, 1938)* Rollicking screwball about a daft heiress (Kate Hepburn) and a nerdy zoology professor (Grant) who loses his bone. Manic, nearly perfect.

Only Angels Have Wings *(B&W, 1939)* Grant as a tersely competent mail pilot in South America, scrapped over by Jean Arthur and Rita Hayworth. Howard Hawks fanatics adore it, others find it dated; kids will think it's a solid adventure movie and soak up the unstated messages about respect and professionalism without flinching.

Gunga Din *(B&W, 1939)* The PC police are all over George Stevens's Kipling adaptation, and, yes, the white actors in Hindu shoe polish and the cartoonish Kali cultists are embarrassing today. It's still an intense, well-made boys-own-adventure flick, with thought-provoking ideas of sacrifice and duty.

Monkey Business *(B&W, 1952)* Achingly funny farce about married scientists Grant and Ginger Rogers who stumble across a youth potion. A young Marilyn Monroe figures into it somehow. Silly but immensely enjoyable, and kids love it.

North by Northwest *(color, 1959)* Could anybody but Cary Grant run from an attacking crop duster with panache?

AUDREY HEPBURN

The other Hepburn and as quietly poised as Kate is a jangle of eccentricities. Audrey came to the ball late—her breakthrough was 1953's *Roman Holiday*—and left early, more or less retiring after 1967's *Two for the Road*. Her impact is much larger than her filmography, though, and she offers some of the same lessons to girls that Cary Grant offers to boys: that class and balanced elegance are qualities to be imitated, that less can and usually does mean more.

Where Grant built a movie personality from the timbers of Archie Leach, Hepburn was by all accounts very much as we see her on-screen, and naturalism is a large part of her appeal. Her characters are girlish in a thoughtful, European convent-raised sort of way, and they bloom into worldliness on their own terms, with the aid but not the necessity of men.

That said, too many of Hepburn's movies pair her with old Hollywood goats like Bogart and William Holden (*Sabrina*), Cooper (*Love in the Afternoon*), Astaire (*Funny Face*), Grant (*Charade*), and Rex Harrison (*My Fair Lady*). She was the first newly minted star of the postwar generation, and so Hollywood lined the previous generation's men up like duffers at a stag party while shipping Joan Crawford and Bette Davis out on ice floes of melodrama. The only movies in the above list that aren't queasy in the playing are *Funny Face* (because Astaire was always more interested in dancing with his costars than in kissing them) and *Charade* (because Cary Grant was ageless and because it was like casting two members of the same species—swans, perhaps, or eland).

Roman Holiday retains the magic, though—Hepburn seems freshly found (in fact she'd been working in films a few years and was coming off a Broadway success in *Gigi*, discovered and cast by Colette herself) and Gregory Peck is both reasonably close to her age and appropriately courtly. There are other fine vehicles too, but there's also the sense that, as with Marilyn Monroe, the persona overshadowed the individual movies. Hepburn was not nearly as well served by Hollywood as she could have been—because she was born too late for the dream factory? Or because she simply outclassed it? Amid the painted dolls and ballroom backdrops she was the real thing, and eventually she saw no reason to stay.

Roman Holiday *(B&W, 1953)* What screen royalty looks like.

Funny Face *(color, 1957)* Astaire and Hepburn at play in Greenwich Village and Paris. Unlike *My Fair Lady*, that's her real singing voice, and it has a wobbly-colt loveliness. The last of the great MGM musicals (made at Paramount, ironically enough).

Breakfast at Tiffany's *(color, 1961)* Save this classic comedy-drama until the kids are older or you'll have to explain (a) what Holly Golightly does for a living and (b) why Mickey Rooney is playing a Japanese guy. For certain people, though, *Tiffany's* is a watershed experience; hum a few bars of "Moon River" and watch them burst into tears.

Charade *(color, 1963)* Hepburn and Grant in the best Hitchcock movie Hitchcock didn't make.

My Fair Lady *(color, 1964)* About as spry as a two-ton block of concrete, but you can't miss it, even with Marni Nixon dubbing Hepburn's singing voice when she probably should have dubbed Rex Harrison's.

KATHARINE HEPBURN

It was late June 2003, and the rumor was that she wasn't going to make it through the weekend—that Kate the Great was finally leaving us after ninety-six years. On the way home from work I stopped at the video store and rented *Bringing Up Baby*—again—and watched it—again—with my daughters, Natalie guffawing when Hepburn rips Cary Grant's evening jacket up the middle, Eliza covering her eyes when the couple takes off after the wrong leopard, and all of us getting happy chills from Kate's burbling midnight laugh.

"Was she always tough like that?" Natalie asked when the credits came on at the end. That gave me pause. Hepburn's Susan Vance is a classic screwball heroine taking pratfalls in haute couture, but gangster-movie tough she isn't.

By "tough," it turned out, my daughter meant unladylike, headstrong, willing to mix it up with the boys—all salutary qualities to this particular kid. The answer then, of course, is yes, Katharine Hepburn was plenty tough—but more in her career than in her individual films, and it was a toughness that fought against the grain of both Hollywood and the moviegoing public.

Hepburn died a beloved institution, outliving fellow legends, lovers, front-office executives, and gossip columnists, so it's not surprising we've forgotten how problematic she was early on. Signed by David O. Selznick in 1932 on the strength of a splashy role in Broadway's *The Warrior Husband* (she played an Amazon princess who makes her entrance carrying a dead stag on her shoulders), Hepburn didn't take to Hollywood, nor it to her. She wore trousers, refused to play the town's social games, and taunted interviewers who wanted to know if she had any children by answering, "Yes, two white and three colored." Most people understood she was looking down her nose at them and hated her right back.

Yet her first film proved the doubters wrong. *A Bill of Divorcement* showed not only that the young Hepburn could steal a film from John Barrymore but that she was ravishing on-screen, a raw actress but an almost unearthly presence.

Hepburn didn't win a best actress Oscar for *Divorcement*, but her award two films later for *Morning Glory* (1933) was understood in the industry to be a make-good for the debut. She followed that up by playing Jo March in the end-of-the-year hit *Little Women*—the best of her early films and one of the most inspired matchings of actress and role in film history.

After that, the public soured on her eccentric airs. Trying to repeat the success of *Little Women*, RKO stuck her in a succession of hoopskirted women's films, most of which seemed deeply irrelevant to an audience struggling through the Depression. Some of them are charming (*The Little Minister*, *Quality Street*), most are dreadful (*Mary of Scotland*, *A Woman Rebels*), and the exceptions run hot and cold, from the four-star *Alice Adams* to the inspired dud *Sylvia Scarlett* to the unwatchable *Spitfire*, in which Hepburn wraps her Bryn Mawr accent around the part of an Appalachian hillbilly. By this point, her back-lot nickname was "Katharine of Arrogance."

What modern audiences forget is that *Bringing Up Baby* was a desperation move—the studio's attempt to jazz up Hepburn's image by throwing her into modern dress and letting her act goofy. The reviews were favorable, but audiences stayed away; shortly afterward, she and RKO parted ways, and an influential distributor ran a trade ad brandishing the star, among others, as "box office poison." Her career seemingly over, she returned to her family summer home in Connecticut in time to see it leveled by the hurricane of 1938.

Two things, and two things only, saved Hepburn's bacon: *The Philadelphia Story* and Spencer Tracy. The first was the play Philip Barry tailored to her personality; it became a Broadway smash and allowed her to return to Hollywood (and, this time, MGM) holding on to the film rights. The second was merely the love of her life; more important to her persona, the relationship with Tracy mellowed her in the eyes of the film industry and the public alike. The nine movies they made together are of varying quality—and they sometimes take too much delight in bringing Kate down a peg—but in all of them she is softened while staying essentially true to herself.

Behind the scenes, Hepburn endeared herself to Hollywood by caring for Tracy through his bouts of insecurity-fueled alcoholism; where the town once saw mannered egotism, they now saw talented selflessness. *The African Queen* (1951) was the movie that pushed the onetime pariah into legend: It proved Kate could hold her own against Humphrey Bogart on the screen and John Huston behind the camera, and it showed the studios she could handle as difficult a location shoot as could be imagined.

That she was in a hit without Tracy was important. In the two decades that followed, Hepburn carved out a body of work in which she was as challenging and difficult as her earliest films hinted, but now the acclaim was unanimous, at times overindulgent. *Summertime, Suddenly Last Summer, Long Day's Journey into Night, The Lion in Winter*—these are incredible performances, sometimes subtle, sometimes outrageously big, all coursing with the prickly, fully felt vitality of a woman unafraid to be herself.

Hepburn stayed true. She didn't come to us but waited, patiently and for years, for us to catch up with her. *That*, Natalie, is tough.

Little Women *(B&W, 1933)* Lovely Louisa May Alcott adaptation with a glowing young Hepburn. All girls should see this at some point in their lives, preferably early on.

Bringing Up Baby *(B&W, 1938)* Kate's at her most manic and mannered and funny—and, Jesus, look at her sink that putt.

The Philadelphia Story *(B&W, 1940)* Dazzling high-society fun for tweeners and up but it's a movie that seems richer the older you get.

Adam's Rib *(B&W, 1949)* The best Tracy and Hepburn, hands down.

The African Queen *(color, 1951)* Miss Hepburn, meet Mr. Bogart.

MARILYN MONROE

The life and death of Monroe was a better movie than any she made. That's cold, but it reflects the quality of the work, which now looks surprisingly poor. She's not necessarily to blame: By the time Monroe had any real clout in Hollywood and, more crucially, understood how to use it, her career was almost over. Death turned her instantly into a victim and prompted our reigning culture of necrology, the adoration of dead stars that insists Elvis, Jim Morrison, Tupac are alive somewhere out there beyond their fans' hearts. Marilyn was the first to die for our sins of celebrity obsession, and the grass of her memorial is kept green with crocodile tears.

The irony is that when it all clicked Monroe was marvelous—sexy, funny, moving. But surprisingly few of her thirty movies treat her as anything other than an erotic mutant. It was Marilyn's misfortune to be the reigning sex goddess of a decade profoundly screwed up about sex, and it didn't help that many of her films were made for that most provincial of studios, 20th Century Fox. To watch them now is to see her vital mix of lust and tenderness mocked and misunderstood—and every so often used to its fullest.

In 1946, Fox snapped up the successful magazine model but used her mostly for publicity stills; she then went to Columbia and bounced around as blink-and-you'll-miss-her baggage to Groucho Marx in *Love Happy* (1950). Two 1950 roles suddenly had critics and audiences asking, "Who's the blonde?" She was the bimbo bauble on George Sanders's arm in *All About Eve*'s party scene, but it was John Huston's *The Asphalt Jungle* that debuted the unnerving combination of sex and naïveté we came to know as Monroe. Fox signed her to a new contract and wasted her in tiny parts, but she got to play opposite Cary Grant in *Monkey Business* (1952) and had her first dramatic lead as the psychotic hotel babysitter of *Don't Bother to Knock* (1952)—a lulu of a role and a premonition of things to come.

Fox finally figured out it had a star on its hands and put her into A-list projects, but few of them showcased her very real gifts for comedy. *Niagara* (1963) is a dank suspense film, *River of No Return* (1954) a Western, *There's No Business Like Show Business* (1954) an old-school Fox musical with Ethel Merman blaring the hair off Monroe's head. There's the sniggering, one-dirty-joke embarrassment of *The Seven Year Itch* (1955) and the strident *Bus Stop* (1957), in which Monroe is at least allowed to act. And there's Howard Hawks's wonderful *Gentlemen Prefer Blondes* (1953), one of the two movies that figured out what to do with Marilyn and did it well.

The other, of course, is *Some Like It Hot* (1959), in which director Billy Wilder atones for the stupid ogling of *Seven Year Itch*. It's a guy movie, even if the guys are wearing women's clothing, so it makes sense that the one woman in it is Monroe, but the tenderness she displays, and that the movie displays toward her, is something new.

In *The Misfits* (1961), opposite Clark Gable, there was even the hint she might have gone on to do interesting and valuable work in the New Cinema of the 1960s if she hadn't killed herself (or been killed; pick your paranoia). Monroe had an adventurous streak; maybe she would have teamed up with Cassavetes or the young Coppola, or perhaps she might have relaxed and turned once again to comedy. Or maybe not: Maybe by now she'd be the Secret Square or be glimpsed like Elizabeth Taylor to the side of all-star charity events. She certainly wouldn't be the star she is today. Elton John wouldn't have written a song for her. Michael Jackson would probably still want to be her best friend, though.

What do you tell the children about Monroe? That she died because we only wanted her to be sexy? That we weren't good enough for her? That she illustrates the dangers of not having a good agent to watch out for you and of sleeping with the president (and the president's brother)?

No, you show them the movies and tell them she's not alive anymore. That's all. They'll pick apart the strands of the persona readily enough: the dumb blond routine that has a surprising number of floors to it, an on-screen confidence that never seemed to pick up momentum, a gathering sadness. And maybe they can start a culture of her life, of vitality, rather than a culture of martyrdom and death. Monroe might have even preferred it that way.

Monkey Business (B&W, 1952) A young Monroe as a secretary— her boss gives her a letter and says, "Find someone to type this"—playing patty-cake with Cary Grant after he drinks a youth potion. Delightful Hawks comedy uses her as the butt of the joke, but it's a very funny joke.

Gentlemen Prefer Blondes (color, 1953) Another Hawks comedy, but this time Marilyn is the lead, the joke, and in on the joke as dreamy gold digger Lorelei Lee. Her performance of "Diamonds Are a Girl's Best Friend" may be her finest moment on film.

Some Like It Hot (B&W, 1959) She manages to be both on the periphery of the action and central to it in Wilder's fizzy cross-dressing farce. Her two musical numbers are "I Want to Be Loved By You" and "I'm Through with Love," and her own tragedy, if you're looking for one, may lie between the two titles.

BARBARA STANWYCK

The glorious tootsie. Stanwyck wasn't beautiful but she has moments on-screen where she makes all the Hollywood lovelies look like frauds. She didn't exude sex appeal but rather a knowledge of sex—its joys and uses and abuses. Stanwyck's characters have been around the block, for good (*The Lady Eve*) or for ill (*Double Indemnity*), and she offers up the opposite of innocence as a possibility in life. She's one of the sneakier role models for a girl: Where many Hollywood starlets hide in the brawny arms of the leading man, Stanwyck leads him merrily by the nose into heaven or hell.

Her biography also teaches the virtues of professionalism. Hardworking, no-nonsense, a Brooklyn girl from the tips of her flats to the top of her head, Stanwyck was adored by everyone in the film industry as a smart, good-hearted trouper—one of the boys in a male-dominated business. She was pals with the director and the lowliest grip alike, and probably more with the latter than the former. She dealt straight with the audience, even when playing shady ladies: Fred MacMurray in *Double Indemnity* is a bigger sap for not seeing what any fool in the back row can see—that Stanwyck's Phyllis Dietrichson is a viper. And when Stanwyck plays it noble she can move you to tears, because you intuitively understand how far a Flatbush kid named Ruby Stevens, orphaned and in foster homes by age five, has to go to open her heart. Her characters know the value of wariness and they know when to give it up.

Baby Face *(B&W, 1933)* Amazingly blunt pre-Code drama has Stanwyck's ambitious office girl literally sleeping her way up the corporate ladder, floor by floor. Show it to the teenagers who think old movies are asexual, then have a little discussion about morality and gender.

Stella Dallas *(B&W, 1937)* Five-hankie weeper about mother love. Tacky Stanwyck divorces tony husband John Boles, but should she keep daughter Ann Shirley down too? The dated class angle is interesting but it's the crosscurrents of guilt and maternal feeling that make this work.

Remember the Night *(B&W, 1940)* Another little-known Mitchell Leisen gem, with a script by Preston Sturges, this pairs Stanwyck and Fred MacMurray as a shoplifter and the prosecutor who has to take her home over the Christmas recess. More light drama than comedy, but it sticks to the ribs.

The Lady Eve *(B&W, 1941)* Sturges writes and directs here, in what may be his single funniest film. Stanwyck is the con woman taking boob Henry Fonda to the cleaners; her second-half portrayal of "Lady Eve Sidwick" is delicious.

Double Indemnity *(B&W, 1944)* Again, one for the teens—a seedy, tawdry film noir about a slippery insurance man (MacMurray), the dame (Stanwyck) who lures him into murder, and the insurance man's suspicious boss (Edward G. Robinson).

JIMMY STEWART

Stewart is the most approachable of the old-time stars—the most like you or me—and his gentle stammer and lowered gaze suggest there's been some mistake, that he belongs down in the audience rather than up there on the screen. But then, gathering his courage, he'll look up and you can see the passion building steam, the brows knotting together, and he'll burst forth in panegyrics of righteous anger or love. Jimmy Stewart is the small-town kid who somehow became a movie star. He's our best friend, cousin, uncle, our best boy. Even Harry Truman said,

"If Bess and I had a son, we'd want him to be just like Jimmy Stewart."

That's how it was supposed to go, at least. That's how it did go until World War II, during which Stewart flew twenty bombing missions and came back both a changed man and a harder, more interesting actor. He drank a bit too much and watched his old movies until, in his own words, they made him want to vomit. Then he met Alfred Hitchcock and, more importantly for his short-term prospects, director Anthony Mann, who put Stewart into a run of Westerns notable for their depth and scalding violence. Before the war, Stewart's sole Western was *Destry Rides Again* (1939), a wonderful comic oater in which the idea of Jimmy the gunfighter is clearly a joke. Not so with the Mann films: When Stewart smashed villain Dan Duryea's head into the bar in 1950's *Winchester '73*, audiences couldn't believe what they were seeing.

The Naked Spur (1953) and *The Man from Laramie* (1955) are the best of the collaboration, and by this time Stewart's partnership with Hitch was paying off too, moving from the dud experimentalism of *Rope* (1948) to *Rear Window* (1954) and *Vertigo* (1958). *Window* is simply one of the greatest of all suspense movies, with endless things to say about what we look for when we sit in the dark and watch—either movies or the couple across the way. *Vertigo* is Hitchcock's most personal movie, more disturbing than entertaining but a masterpiece nonetheless. It's most tragic aspect is that Stewart, playing an obsessive, even cruel man, lets us see the sweet, simple, lost Jimmy of an earlier era buried under the neuroses. This is acting of a maturity none of his peers approached, and perhaps it's just a coincidence that he saw far more death during World War II than any other major Hollywood star.

What I'm saying is that Stewart is more complicated than is generally allowed, to his credit as a performer and a human being, and that it might be worthwhile to let your children grow up along with him. Younger children might start with his prewar films, the ones like *You Can't Take It with You* (1938), *Mr. Smith Goes to Washington* (1939), *Destry Rides Again*, and *The Shop Around the Corner* (1940), all films in which he burns his quiet way toward idealism. Then they could move on to *The Philadelphia Story* (1940), in which Stewart starts cynical and by the climax is drunk with champagne and passion.

Actually, my girls came to Stewart first through *Philadelphia Story*, and I was surprised how much they were initially put off by him. Eliza, then about eight, stomped around the house for a few days imitating Jimmy's wide-eyed glare of renewed purpose and judged that she found the man a little barmy. He won an Oscar for *that*? she wondered. A viewing of *Mr. Smith Goes to Washington* some months later put the man in proper perspective, and we've since fanned out across the filmography.

They haven't seen the Mann Westerns yet, though—they're more psychologically penetrating than a lot of grown-ups can handle—but *Rear Window* was a big hit, and, along with the lighter *North by Northwest*, it's probably the best child's-first-Hitchcock. *Vertigo*, when they finally saw it, deepened their love for the actor in ways they couldn't quite quantify; the girls intuitively understood it as a tragedy in which Jimmy Stewart goes terribly wrong.

And then there's *It's a Wonderful Life* (1946), which is both unavoidable and a film more fraught with unhappiness than most people realize. This is a movie that for most of its running time says life is one crushing disappointment after another and that any sane man—that is to say, Jimmy Stewart—would consider suicide as an option.

Then it pushes the matter even further, contemplating the total negation of self and the unimaginable idea of what your world would be without you. All the angels and happy endings in Hollywood can't erase the harsh taste of where *It's a Wonderful Life* goes, and it is Stewart rather than Capra who takes it there. So, sure, show it to the kids on Christmas Eve, but don't be surprised if they're unusually quiet afterward.

Mr. Smith Goes to Washington *(B&W, 1939)* On the short list of all-time four-star family classics, though these days only a child would be fooled by its political optimism. All the more reason to show it to them now and give them some ideals to work from.

The Shop Around the Corner *(B&W, 1940)* One of the wisest, warmest, wittiest romantic comedies to come out of Hollywood, with the oft-paired Stewart and Margaret Sullavan as coworkers who hate each other by day and pen aching anonymous love letters by night.

The Philadelphia Story *(B&W, 1940)* Stewart won his Oscar as Macaulay Connor, the cynical reporter suddenly bathed in Tracy Lord's chilly upper-class light. A beautifully written and subtly intelligent comedy of manners, with Cary Grant pulling strings from the sidelines.

Harvey *(B&W, 1950)* Stewart as Elwood P. Dowd, a gently deluded man convinced that his best friend is a six-foot-tall invisible rabbit named Harvey. The adaptation of the long-running stage comedy is solid if not up to its reputation as one of the star's best, but it's good fun for kids.

Rear Window *(color, 1954)* Did Stewart's neighbor across the way kill his wife? The hero, apartment-bound with a broken leg, uses camera and binoculars to pry and spy, and the results are as gripping as anything Hitchcock did. Bonus points if your kids notice that every one of the windows in the apartment complex is its own mini-movie.

SHIRLEY TEMPLE

Young children see Temple as a peculiar but fascinating doll, one that can't be played with but that magically moves and talks of its own accord. She can be a powerful figure if you're small and coming to movies for the first time: There are all these grown-ups on the screen and then suddenly there's someone just like you. Even better, she's the center of events, the adults snapping to attention around her, and she acts like this is meet and her due. It's the bubbly self-confidence of Temple that astounds seventy years later—her belief that the world is her playpen and she's more than happy to share it with you if you're willing to remember your lines.

Seriously. Alice Faye, one of Temple's adult costars, said, "She knew everyone's dialogue, and if you forgot a line, she gave it to you. We all hated her for that." Can Temple be blamed for acting like she owned the entire film industry? For a few years, she did. Shirley saved 20th Century Fox from bankruptcy and brought audiences back into movie theaters during the worst days of the Depression—it's not an overstatement to say that this six-year-old girl, playing her own little self on-screen, was a psychic lifeline to millions of Americans, proof that open-faced good cheer was even possible.

She was sacred. When writer Graham Greene, then a British film reviewer, wrote snidely that her male admirers were essentially pedophiles, the publication he was writing for was sued and went out of business. When Temple lost a tooth in an on-set accident, Fox head Darryl Zanuck panicked and ran out of a meeting with John Steinbeck. There was a story of her sitting in the lap of a department-store Santa Claus who asked for her autograph. Her father was inundated with letters from women wanting to sleep with him, hoping against genetic hope to sire another Shirley, even as mothers across the land burned their daughters' hair with curling irons, forced them into tap lessons, and coaxed them to learn the words to "Animal Crackers in My Soup."

But Temple was irreproducible, most of all in her self-possession. This is the quality any viewer, and especially a young one, takes away from the movies: that Shirley belongs where she is and is where she belongs, and why, she wonders, can't everyone be like that? There's a surprising amount of darkness to her movies—parents dying or lost to poverty, a creepy molester who keeps trying to snatch her away in *Poor Little Rich Girl* (1936)— but Temple's ironclad certainty conquers all. Asked to play fear or unhappiness—asked to act—she was unconvincing. When she became a teenager and then an adult, she was a fresh-faced ingenue no better or worse than thousands of others who hadn't once been Shirley Temple. But at six, in one of the eleven movies she made in 1933 (she worked as hard as that other Depression angel, Clark Gable), Temple was as steady and as natural as a healthy pulse, a child using the adults for a grand game of dress-up. There are worse things to learn than assurance.

Little Miss Marker *(B&W, 1934)* Temple's her father's gambling IOU, winning over a motley assortment of Damon Runyon mugs in the film that made her a star. The setting is surprisingly seedy and adult; it would be awhile before her movies became childlike.

The Little Colonel *(B&W, 1935)* The Civil War as pure corn, but Temple and Bill "Bojangles" Robinson have their first dance together. Yeah, it's a scene top-heavy with racial/racist iconography—and Robinson was one of this country's greatest dancers. Figure it out for yourself.

Heidi *(B&W, 1937)* Johanna Spyri's Swiss miss, leaving the Alps for adventures in the big city. It may have been the role Temple was born to play.

Wee Willie Winkie *(B&W, 1937)* John Ford's grand Indian adventure has all the Hollywood/Raj clichés—it's like *Gunga Din* with Shirley Temple wandering through the foreground, brokering peace between the British soldiers and native rebels. In other words, weird but fascinating.

The Little Princess *(color, 1939)* Her last big hit, a solid Technicolor adaptation of the Frances Hodgson Burnett classic.

JOHN WAYNE

Kids are lucky for coming to John Wayne in the twenty-first century, long after the culture wars around him have died down. There are still adults who refuse to watch his movies and there are other adults who refuse to watch anything *but* his movies, and both sides cheat themselves. The problem is that Wayne embodies certain American qualities so well that one's response to him is political by default. Was he morally certain or a pigheaded reactionary? A leader of men or a bully? Was he a man of few words or just someone who couldn't think of more than a few? You will never get a straight answer from anyone who was alive when Wayne was, because Wayne is transparent—you see right through him to what you want to see.

Children are thankfully, blessedly, apolitical, and so they can see John Wayne in his contradictions. God knows they're there. Born Marion Morrison, he was a cowboy hero who grew up in the suburbs of Los Angeles. He was an overnight phenomenon in *Stagecoach* (1939) after eleven years and sixty-four movies. He was a star of Westerns who didn't much like horses, and a patriotic star of war films who spent World War II trying awfully hard not to get drafted (in the end he never served). And he was a self-made man, literally creating a screen persona from the scraps of what he found and saw. "When I started," Wayne said late in life, "I knew I was no actor, so I went to work on the Wayne thing. It was as deliberate a projection as you'll ever see. . . . I practiced in front of a mirror."

So what we call "John Wayne" was a false Western front; nothing in that makes him different from any other celebrity and probably more honest than most. But what makes him interesting, to a child or anyone not hamstrung by ideology, is how consciously Wayne addresses his own paradox in his best work. Movies like *Red River, The Searchers*, and *The Man Who Shot Liberty Valance* explicitly wonder what it takes to be a hero in America, and whether the ruthlessness needed to conquer a country can function—should be allowed to function—once conquering is done and civilizing has started. Wayne knew and explored the twin pitfalls of power and obsession, and his filmography is studded with as much bitterness (1945's *They Were Expendable*) as strength (1959's *Rio Bravo*). Whether or not he was a hero in life is endlessly debatable. Few people think of him simply as an actor, but that is what he was, and a more thoughtful one than he gets credit for.

Here's what I'd suggest: Show the five movies below to your children and then ask *them* who John Wayne is. I'll bet they have a clearer picture than either you or I do.

Stagecoach *(B&W, 1939)* John Ford set out to make a consciously old-fashioned Western with all the myths in place, and Wayne was the freshest myth of all, gliding before a vast rear-projection vista like Venus on the half-saddle.

Red River *(B&W, 1948)* The first of Wayne's sadistic and bitter patriarchs, goading surrogate son Montgomery Clift across Howard Hawks's cattle-drive epic.

The Quiet Man *(color, 1952)* Some people think this droll romantic comedy about an American boxer (Wayne) and the Irish lass (Maureen O'Hara) he woos is one of John Ford's most charming films ever. Others find it a piece of irredeemable chauvinist piggery. Worth watching with the older kids and talking it over.

The Searchers *(color, 1956)* Ethan Edwards (Wayne) loses his brother's family to the Comanches and spends years tracking the one survivor, turning into a bitter, racist ghost of a man along the way. One of the hardest but most moving Westerns ever made, it's Ford's and Wayne's crowning achievement.

Rio Bravo *(color, 1959)* His best Western with Hawks, by contrast, is a high comic picaresque about a sheriff stuck with a bunch of misfits (Dean Martin, Ricky Nelson, Walter Brennan) when bad guys come to town. Made as a conscious rebuttal to *High Noon*, it's a lot more fun than that sounds.

THE DIRECTORS

Do kids really care who made the movie? Nope, and yet there's an argument to be made that teaching them *someone* did is worth the effort. Movies don't make themselves—they're stories fashioned with conscious craft and art by an army of people, and while it's often going too far to say that one person sets the tone for a film, in the case of the nine directors below, it's mostly correct.

Personality, in other words, is not reserved to the space in front of the camera. Once they understand this, your kids may begin to see and hear the language of the movies they watch, the grammar that includes camerawork, music, costumes, design. They may detect cinematic accents that change from one filmmaker to the next. And they may understand that films aren't just dreams that unfurl in front of them, magic stories that move, but the result of human creativity and hard labor. At the very least, teaching kids about directors prompts them to be alert for the times when movies and media fudge the truth, and that's a lesson that can never be learned too soon.

The first old-time director most kids learn to distinguish is Hitchcock, of course. For one thing, he keeps popping up in his own movies like a game of Whack-a-Mole; for another, his films have such a unique style and voice that Hitch is their biggest star, even bigger than Jimmy Stewart or Cary Grant. The others on this list don't loom quite as large in a child's frame of reference—ask my daughters to name a few directors and they'll rattle off Hitchcock and Steven Spielberg, then *maybe* Howard Hawks only because their dad's a fanatic, and then they'll run out of gas ("Tim Burton!" Natalie pipes up in disagreement. "Clint Eastwood!").

But that's okay: There'll be more than enough time if they're interested. For your purposes, the filmmakers below are consistent and surprisingly foolproof—wells you can return to again and again until the kids learn to chase their own auteurs.

FRANK CAPRA

Capra arrived in steerage from Sicily when he was six, and his movies see America from the rail of a ship coming into harbor. All that bigness that can celebrate an individual and still swallow him up; all the things that could go horribly wrong before going right.

In his optimism and naïveté, he's the most childlike of golden age directors, and the one whose movies hew most closely to a child's idea of how the world should work. In other words, Capra movies lie—at their best, wonderfully well—and before they lie, they dance close to the edge of the pit.

Mr. Smith Goes to Washington is the movie from which the others all radiate: If you buy into its vision of homespun faith in democracy surviving the rack (and why wouldn't you when

Jimmy Stewart is up there giving the performance of his life and Jean Arthur is looking on with tears in her eyes and even the vice president of the United States, standing in for Abe Lincoln, is giving the hero a supportive wink?), then Capra will soothe your fears. His movies insist that believing will make it so, and perhaps it will, and, really, who wants to take that possibility away from a child?

A grown-up might observe that Stewart gets a happy ending only because Claude Rains cracks and confesses all on the floor of the Senate, and that this is asking an awful lot of a U.S. politician, even a fictional one. But happy endings don't just happen in Capra movies; they're embraced in an orgy of emotionalism, *It's a Wonderful Life*'s George Bailey hugging Zuzu, his wife, all of Bedford Falls, the entire universe to his breast while tears of joy fall. The director's need to make things right bends the laws of probability and very nearly the laws of physics, like the walls of Jericho tumbling at the end of *It Happened One Night*. So much seems at stake, including life itself; there is more suicide and attempted suicide in Frank Capra's films than in the canon of any other major director, and yet he always ends up affirming the world, even when you don't believe him.

For an adult, it takes willingness for these movies to work— or at least the ability to set one's cynicism aside for two hours— and that's an easier process with a kid sitting next to you. The idealism we constantly cut to fit the compromises of daily life children are still growing into, and a case could be made that Capra movies help build strong bones, like a slightly hysterical glass of milk. The core films—*Mr. Smith*, *Mr. Deeds*, *Wonderful Life*—go surprisingly far into despair, and 1941's *Meet John Doe*, Capra's most self-important movie, barely makes it back alive. But they do, they all do, on the backs of their individualist "little guys" fighting the system (which system includes the crowds that idolize the heroes only to turn on them; Capra distrusts the mass far more than he loves it) and on the strength of the director's sheer need to believe.

There's more to Capra, though; there has to be. Before he started buying his own press, the man made entertainments, and you could argue that they're the better movies. Show *Mr. Smith* to your kids early on, but maybe loosen them up with 1934's *It Happened One Night*, the first film to sweep the major Oscars and a comedy that still has the pizzazz of a lucky fluke. Or go further back, to Capra's first feature directing job after years of struggling, the 1926 silent comedy *The Strong Man*, featuring a strange little man named Harry Langdon who was once the box office equal of Chaplin, Keaton, and Lloyd, and who is now almost entirely forgotten. Try the Broadway stage farce adaptations *You Can't Take It with You* (1938) and *Arsenic and Old Lace* (1944), both a little creaky and both enlivened by their casts.

Especially try the films from the early '30s, when Capra was getting serious but hadn't yet hammered his populism into public statuary: *Platinum Blonde* (1931), which made a star out of Jean Harlow; *The Miracle Woman* (1931), with Barbara Stanwyck playing a two-faced evangelist; *American Madness* (1932), in which the director makes his bid to be taken for a Great Director; and the unique and maddening *The Bitter Tea of General Yen* (1933)—brilliantly directed romantic melodrama, plea for racial equality, and a film that stars Swedish actor Nils Asther in yellowface as a Chinese warlord in love with Stanwyck.

Capra went into World War II with a camera, and the films he made in the *Why We Fight* series are models of documentary propaganda. The things he saw during the war that didn't make it into those films are just out of sight in *It's a Wonderful Life*—a film that went so far into the dark that 1946 audiences recoiled. It was his last halfway decent movie, with the director holding on to his homilies in mounting panic before they finally slipped away forever. Capra needs to be seen before belief fades.

It Happened One Night *(B&W, 1934)* Rich brat Colbert and snappy reporter Gable on the road in Depression America, laughing and flirting. The first screwball comedy and an Oscar juggernaut that inaugurated plot conventions we're still living with.

Mr. Deeds Goes to Town *(B&W, 1936)* Longfellow Deeds, a piece of droll Vermont oak played by Gary Cooper, was the first and lightest of Capra's plainspoken common men. He inherits a fortune, the city slickers come calling, and Deeds shows them what's what. It's great fun for kids.

Mr. Smith Goes to Washington *(B&W, 1939)* If Capra hadn't cast Jimmy Stewart, do you think this would have worked? Me neither.

Arsenic and Old Lace *(B&W, 1944)* Cary Grant mugs a little too heavily (even he thought so) but this adaptation of the stage farce about two sweet old ladies who poison lonely old men is funny/scary in just the right mix.

It's a Wonderful Life *(B&W, 1946)* Everyone thinks it's a Christmas classic, but, face it, this is one spiked cup of eggnog until the angels fix everything. The littlest audiences won't get what's going on here at all. All others: must-see.

GEORGE CUKOR

He was known as a "women's director," which meant, of course, that he was gay. That was the code, but Cukor was better than the code, even in the few instances where it may have hampered his career.

Cukor was, simply, a tremendously gifted choreographer of human emotion—light and dark, male and female—because he understood emotion to be the primary clay from which movies are made. He wasn't a show-off with the camera; rather, characters, and the actors playing them, were his focus. You pay attention to the people in a Cukor film, to what they want and how they go about getting it, and you pause often to admire the performances, but you rarely notice the direction, because Cukor's is an art that never calls attention to itself. This is more than mere "elegance" (another code word) but, rather, a willingness to trust narrative momentum and to only frame it appropriately. Cukor served a handful of great actresses—ten films with his discovery, Kate Hepburn; also Garland and Garbo, Ingrid Bergman and Audrey Hepburn—but he served the story first.

There are no great Cukor themes or prototypical camera shots like Ford's sunlit corridors; he has no discernible filmmaking "accent." We recognize a Hitchcock movie by what's there: a camera angle that changes everything, a gleefully half-glimpsed body part. Cukor, by contrast, is identifiable by subtraction—by who he's not—or by inference. At worst, he's a director who teaches tastefulness; at best (and this is immeasurable), he teaches taste, which is a lesson most children don't understand until years after they've seen the movies. When it is time for them to know who George Cukor is, they'll realize they already do.

There are five films to start with below, but Cukor was a workhorse, and he had a higher rate of return than most. *Dinner at Eight*, *Camille*, *Holiday*, *The Philadelphia Story*, *Gaslight*, *A Double Life*, *Adam's Rib*, *Les Girls*, and (last, stodgiest, and most popular) *My Fair Lady*—any one of these movies would liven up a filmography. That they and the titles below are the work of one man is a fact history still hasn't properly judged.

Little Women *(B&W, 1933)* Cukor never read the Louisa May Alcott novel, a fact about which Hepburn teased him constantly. But he had in her a Jo (which is to say an Alcott) with deep taproots in nineteenth-century New England, and the film has a sense of place and of values astonishing for a movie shot in 1933 Hollywood.

Sylvia Scarlett *(B&W, 1935)* A bomb that today looks like a high-spirited lark. Hepburn dresses like a boy, Cary Grant finally comes into his own, and at one point the whole cast decides to start a music hall troupe called the Pink Pierrots. Why? Who knows?

The Women *(B&W, 1939)* Adapting Clare Booth Luce's Broadway comedy, Cukor rounds up an all-woman cast that includes Norma Shearer suffering teddibly in the lead and Paulette Goddard, Rosalind Russell, Mary Boland, Joan Fontaine, and Phyllis Povah giving her merry hell. Off in the corner, husband-stealer Joan Crawford sharpens her talons.

Born Yesterday *(B&W, 1950)* Judy Holliday delightfully re-creates her stage role as Billie Dawn, dimbulb gangster's moll who becomes intellectually and romantically (and even patriotically) enlightened when tutored by newspaperman William Holden.

A Star Is Born *(color, 1954)* A flawed masterpiece—overlong, then injudiciously cut back by the studio, and Cukor is clearly uneasy with the new CinemaScope frame—but it is to the end of Garland's career what *Wizard of Oz* is to its beginning: the rainbow, mourned.

JOHN FORD

Like Capra, Ford was studio-era Hollywood's idea of an auteur: a reliable and gifted (if ornery) filmmaking talent whose personality carried over to the bones of his movies. There is no mistaking a Ford film, and with four Oscars for directing, he was celebrated for it. He was a household name and, in a very real sense, the Spielberg of his day—the standard to which the rest of the industry aspired.

This is no longer the case. The problem with being the standard is that you quickly become that from which the culture moves on. Ford is still treasured by film buffs and academics, by lovers of Americana and John Wayne (you can't love the actor without loving the director), but his movies have dated in ways that those of, say, Hawks or William Wellman haven't. Overfamiliarity plays a part. Monument Valley, the location Ford discovered and used as a dramatic stage, now appears in car commercials, a trite visual signifier of "Americanness" that was rich and unplundered when the director invented it. What Ford the filmmaker codified, Ford the automaker now sells.

Mostly, though, John Ford has fallen afoul of political correctness. When I studied film in college in the late 1970s, he was far out of fashion, a figure to be held at arm's length and dealt with rather than enjoyed. His macho men and demure women had nothing to do with the gender roles we were busy reassessing and deconstructing. He was patriotic in ways easy to scoff at. Our beloved film professor had mostly rude things to say, and used Ford as a counterweight to exalt Hawks, a simple enough process given the unpretentiousness of the latter.

Ford *is* sentimental. He *does* lean too heavily on clichés he helped invent, most glaringly whenever he has to deal with mothers and relations between men and women (again, look to Hawks for a tarter take). He can be appallingly simplistic and self-consciously "poetic." And yet: Any child's consideration of American cinema has to come to grips with not only *Stagecoach* and *The Searchers*—the first a restating of the frontier dream and the second its brutal dismantling—but also *The Grapes of Wrath*, *Young Mr. Lincoln*, *How Green Was My Valley*, *My Darling Clementine*, the "Cavalry Trilogy" of *Fort Apache*, *She Wore a Yellow Ribbon*, and *Rio Grande*, *The Informer*, and the sweet, knuckleheaded *The Quiet Man*.

These remain beautifully made, gorgeously shot, often powerful movies—peak studio product—and worth watching with or without kids. And some (not all) are more complex than they're given credit for, in ways children intuit even as parents resist. *How Green Was My Valley* romanticizes the hardships of life in a Welsh mining village but only because its grown narrator (played by a young Roddy MacDowell) does so. *The Man Who Shot Liberty Valance*, Ford's last great film, says that "when the legend becomes fact, print the legend," and that line goes to the heart of the truth of the American experience, but does Ford really believe it? Should we? Or is he finally copping to the lies his movies can't live without?

Here is something to think about: Ford, like Capra, made movies for modern children to grow out of. Unlike Capra, you can grow back into them later down the line.

Stagecoach *(B&W, 1939)* In one fell swoop, Ford and screenwriter Dudley Nichols reinvigorated the Western—strictly a B-level genre in 1939—and moved John Wayne to the forefront of American icons. Based on, of all things, a Guy de Maupassant short story.

Young Mr. Lincoln *(B&W, 1939)* Lovely, plainspoken Americana, with a mysteriously calm lead performance by Henry Fonda. A movie that prints the legend, expertly.

The Grapes of Wrath *(B&W, 1940)* The flip side of the gentle pieties of *Lincoln*: an unyielding saga of the Depression dispossessed, from the Steinbeck book. Nobody wanted the movie made, but what looked like blowtorch realism then has its share of blarney now. Still, a landmark in screen pessimism and a solid history lesson for the kids.

They Were Expendable *(B&W, 1945)* One of the best studio-era World War II movies, it's a dark, emotionally honest retelling of U.S. troops in the Philippines in the early days of the war. Robert Montgomery and John Wayne have rarely been better.

The Searchers *(color, 1956)* Ethan Edwards (Wayne) spends years tracking the survivors of an Indian massacre, becoming his own worst enemy in the process. A movie that simultaneously celebrates and debunks ideals of Old West heroism.

HOWARD HAWKS

Hawks liked to say that a successful movie has at least three good scenes and no bad ones, that a successful director is one who "doesn't annoy you." People in his dramas hardly talk at all, or they speak directly to the task at hand. People in his comedies rarely stop talking.

He worked, and worked brilliantly, in every genre Hollywood had to offer, and was paid well for it while receiving shockingly little critical praise. But that makes sense: Hawks wasn't an artist but a professional, and the art that hides in professionalism—often more lasting than the art that declares its name—takes time to emerge. His friend and rival John Ford was the great cinematic poet of his time, with four Oscars on his mantel. Hawks had one nomination, for 1941's *Sergeant York*, and no wins until he received an honorary award in 1975, two years before his death.

In between he was rediscovered and celebrated by the young French critics who would become the filmmakers of the New Wave—Jean-Luc Godard, François Truffaut, the rest of those aching smarty-pants—and Hawks indulged them with interviews and tall tales, even as he scratched his head at the complicated analyses the French boys came up with. These were just movies, weren't they? Hawks is the test case for the auteur theory: His personality and values show up in almost everything he did, not because he consciously put them there, but because he couldn't do otherwise.

The first thing a kid learns, even before he learns who Hawks is, is that certain films are fun. Not just enjoyable, but really *fun*: devilishly smart, crackling with focused playfulness. *Twentieth Century*, *Bringing Up Baby*, *His Girl Friday*, *Ball of Fire*, *To Have and Have Not*, *I Was a Male War Bride*, *Monkey Business*, *Gentlemen Prefer Blondes*, *Rio Bravo*, and *Hatari!* are some of the most blissfully good times Hollywood ever released. Pauline Kael called *Baby* an American equivalent to Restoration comedy, but the comment could go for the whole lot.

The dramas, by contrast, are moodier and obsessed with work. A Hawks hero is defined by the job to be done, and grandstanding only gets you killed. The mail pilots in *Only Angels Have Wings*, the cattlemen in *Red River*, the soldiers in *Sergeant York*, the scientists in *The Thing from Another World* (directed by Christian Nyby with a major assist from producer Hawks), the private eye in *The Big Sleep* all want to get it over with, get paid, go home. Doing the job to the utmost of one's abilities is by definition part of the deal. If Hawks's career made a virtue of professionalism, his dramas make it their subject.

In these films, certain stars assume the stature by which we still remember them. You could argue that no one used Cary Grant better, even Hitchcock—the actor's persona expands in surface poise and moral depth in the movies he made with Hawks. Bogart in *The Big Sleep* and *To Have and Have Not* is a much harder nut than in his other films, while Hawks's John Wayne is a more problematically confident figure than Ford's.

And the women. A through line in all of his movies—a major part of the Hawks pleasure principle—is that men are inherently conservative animals and women are the free radicals, the upsetters of apple carts. Mr. Orthodoxy, meet Miss Catastrophe. Hepburn in *Bringing Up Baby* is a Hepburn no one else imagined was even there. *Gentlemen Prefer Blondes* is Marilyn Monroe's best starring vehicle and the only film to find more than one sniggering level to her sexpot persona. Carole Lombard (*Twentieth*

Century), Barbara Stanwyck (*Ball of Fire*), and Rosalind Russell (*His Girl Friday*) keep up with the boys and even outstrip them (although it should be pointed out that Cary Grant in *Friday* has the role Hawks usually assigns to women). Hawks loves the battle of the sexes; it's what people do for relaxation when the work is done. And the women almost always win, because entropy always wins.

To kids, he's an invisible director, unlike Hitch or Ford or a glorious screwup like Orson Welles. My daughters know Hawks only because I regularly pointed out his name until they were able to do the math. What his films insist upon—again, without ever seeming to—is that (A) a job well done is the only reasonable way of coping with a chaotic universe and (B) giving in to the chaos is the only reasonable way of knowing we're alive.

Twentieth Century *(B&W, 1934)* Carole Lombard as a spoiled Broadway star and John Barrymore as her spoiled director trying to woo her back on the cross-country train of the title. Like watching two hams kiss or two big babies giving each other the hotfoot. Barrymore, the greatest Hamlet of his generation, imitates a camel.

Bringing Up Baby *(B&W, 1938)* "The love impulse in man frequently reveals itself in terms of conflict."

Only Angels Have Wings *(B&W, 1939)* Get past the toy airplanes and you have Hawks's greatest drama of men doing what they have to do and women banging their heads against the wall in frustration.

Gentlemen Prefer Blondes *(color, 1953)* Hawks's greatest comedy of women doing what they like to do and men banging their heads against the wall in frustration.

Rio Bravo *(color, 1959)* Rollicking Western picaresque—a picnic with serious undertones—about a sheriff (John Wayne) facing down villains with a patchwork crew of drunks, kids, and gimps.

ALFRED HITCHCOCK

The story Hitchcock liked to tell about himself was when he was six and his father sent him round to the local constabulary with a note. The child had done something wrong—wandered too far from home, he recalled—and the officer on duty read the note, nodded, and led the offender to a cell. "This is what we do to naughty boys," he said, and locked Hitchcock in for five minutes. To a frightened six-year-old, it felt like several hours. For the rest of his life, policemen filled him with anxiety.

Or so he said. With Hitchcock the telling of the tale is always as important as what the tale tells. In everything he said and did, there is the tension between the pit in the stomach and the pulling of the leg. So: Is this anecdote the source of all those charming, hateful murderers—all those naughty boys—with whom we identify in his movies? My daughter Natalie watched Bruno straining to reach the incriminating lighter in *Strangers on a Train*, urging him on sotto voce—"Come on . . . *come on* . . ."—then looked at me and said, incredulously, "What am I doing?" You're doing what Hitch wants you to do, honey: smudging the thin line between hero and villain, pondering when and how and why and *if* you might crisscross it yourself. It's safe. It's only a movie. But wade too far and the bottom drops out.

Or is that childhood story just Hitchcock messing with our heads again, playing the ghoulish uncle he knew we wanted him to be? By his own admission, the director was an intensely shy man, and his public persona was as much an inspired invention as any moment in his movies. Why did he bother? Was it because the films already possessed a more distinctive personality than those of other directors and it was therefore natural for the public to want to put a face to that personality? What we thought of as "Hitchcock" was a great cartoon, made of cartoon bits: the slow, plummy diction; the pear-shaped body and head (like draftsman's ovals with the barest minimum of details); the deadpan assurance that blood will out. He gave himself so readily to the silhouette and to our expectations of fear and delight.

And that's what Hitchcock is to a young viewer: the first understanding that being scared can be not only scary but fun. What a discovery! Liberation from monsters under the bed! But: Does it harden tiny sensibilities to shock and cruelty? Does it lead eventually to your children spending your hard-earned money on *Friday the 13th XXVII*? Three answers: It depends upon which Hitch you show them; These are the risks parents take; No, Hitchcock is not a gateway drug to splatter movies because he sets the creative bar high and asks you to notice. Maybe he treated actors like cattle, but he never thought of audiences as sheep.

With a handful of exceptions, his films say it's possible to master anxiety by aestheticizing it, by putting it in ironic quotes that let a viewer indulge the fear while standing outside it. ***North by Northwest*** (1959) is the ideal first Hitchcock movie for children: a grand Tinkertoy contraption in which no one's in real danger of getting hurt, either by a murderous crop duster or by falling off Mount Rushmore.

The other key introductory films are ***Rebecca*** (1940, more demented Gothic women's melodrama than suspense, although there's plenty of the latter), ***Rear Window*** (1954, great premise and just enough gruesomeness—more talked about than seen—to give a kid pleasurable willies), and ***Suspicion*** (1941), in which only a child would believe Grant could possibly be a wife-murderer. Also, the entire run of early British sound films, which have an engaging air of make-believe: ***The Lady Vanishes*** (1938), ***The 39 Steps*** (1935), ***Young and Innocent*** (1937), ***Secret Agent*** (1936), ***The Man Who Knew Too Much*** (1934). The exception here is ***Sabotage*** (1936), in which the heroine's little brother unknowingly carries a bomb that detonates, along with him, on a midtown bus. Even Hitchcock realized he'd gone too far with that one.

From there, on to Hitchcock 102: *Strangers on a Train* (1951), in which a most disagreeable young woman is murdered, and her murderer is a sociable if psychotic gent; thank goodness Hitch gives us boring old Farley Granger as a good guy to fall back on and one of the most suspenseful tennis matches in the movies. *Spellbound* (1945) and *Saboteur* (1942) fit here too, both classic wrong-man plots, with the former having the added attraction of Gregory Peck and Ingrid Bergman at their most youthfully beautiful and dream sequences designed by Salvador Dalí. *To Catch a Thief* (1955) and the 1956 *Man Who Knew Too Much* remake are extremely watchable but a little too harmless.

Notorious (1946) would seem to go here as well, but it's one of Hitchcock's most emotionally unforgiving films—underneath the Ingrid-Bergman-marries-a-Nazi-spy suspense plot is a harrowing drama about romantic trust and bitterness. In other words: boring, at least to a kid, although there is that incredible crane shot from a balcony overlooking a party all the way down to the key clutched in Bergman's fist. *Notorious* is perhaps Hitchcock's most grown-up film, and arguably his best; save it for the more attentive older children and for yourself. The same could be (and has been) said of *Vertigo* (1958), which kids can certainly watch and enjoy but probably won't get any real meat out of until they're older. That particular movie is the Hitchcock gift that keeps on giving—it says so much about the director's own obsessions and about the way we try to mold the people we love into the people who never loved us back. It's Natalie's single favorite movie by the way.

Then there are the movies to steer clear of until your kids are on the edge of adolescence. *Psycho* (1960) goes to the head of this class, obviously, and it's the one Hitchcock film that refuses to play patty-cake, that forgoes the ironic quote marks and shoves you into that shower with Janet Leigh. *The Birds* (1963) as well, for that shot of the corpse with its eyes pecked out and its sense of inexplicable apocalypse—like your kids don't get enough of that when they read the newspaper. (This isn't specific to the post-9/11 era. I remember my mother forbidding me to watch the film when it aired on TV in the late 1960s— like I didn't get enough of that when I read the newspaper.) *Shadow of a Doubt* is earlier Hitchcock, from 1943, and it's gore free, but it also involves a girl's beloved uncle who turns out to be a serial killer—proceed at your own risk and understand that it was the director's own favorite of his films. (And note that Eliza, at eleven, had no problem with it at all; if anything, she identified with the heroine's growing resourcefulness.)

Then there are the misfires—*I Confess* (1953), *Stage Fright* (1950), *Torn Curtain* (1966), *Mr. and Mrs. Smith* (1941)—and oddities like *Rope* (1948), *The Wrong Man* (1956), and *Lifeboat* (1944). There are solid middle-of-the-roaders like *Foreign Correspondent* (1940) and *Dial M for Murder* (1954), and there is *Marnie* (1964), which doesn't seem to belong anywhere. For the kid who discovers Hitchcock and is industrious enough to pursue him across an infinitely rewarding filmography, the director is first evidence that movies can speak the language of a person who made them. Hitch, in fact, prompts us to look for the people behind *everything*.

MICHAEL POWELL

A gifted British eccentric, like Hitchcock but not as universally celebrated, Powell deserves to be a household name, at least in your household. His movies—made on his own and in partnership with Emeric Pressburger as "The Archers"—are startling, felicitous excursions into fancy, often shot in colors as pure as

dreaming. Even at their most realistic, they show how imagination and longing can disorder people's sensibilities: In *I Know
Where I'm Going!* a hardheaded young woman is seduced by the
remoteness of the Scottish coast into giving up her dreams; in
Black Narcissus, an order of nuns in the Himalayas find themselves going crazy from high altitudes and repressed lusts. In *The
Red Shoes*, the line between ballet and life, fairy tale and reality is
smudged until it's invisible, and the heroine dances right off the
table. Powell is an odd customer, but his films can take your
breath away. They hold out to a first-time viewer the possibilities and perils of fantasy—of what can be gained and lost when
you think up something unheard of and then give in to it.

The Thief of Bagdad *(color, 1940)* Producer Alexander Korda went
through six directors, so who knows what Powell contributed?
Except that the riotous Technicolor photography and dream-
land Arabian Nights sets do seem his handiwork.

The 49th Parallel *(B&W, 1941)* Nazis on the run—in *Canada*.
Made before the United States entered World War II, this excellent, suspenseful chase film follows the crew of a destroyed
U-boat as they cross the Great White North trying to get into
neutral America. Laurence Olivier, Leslie Howard, and Raymond Massey show up as locals they encounter.

I Know Where I'm Going! *(B&W, 1945)* Wendy Hiller is off to marry
the industrialist of her dreams but gets stranded by the Scottish
mist and whirlpools. A lovely, funny, borderline surreal classic
about how the magic of a place can break down all best-laid
plans.

Stairway to Heaven *(B&W/color, 1946)* RAF pilot David Niven was
supposed to die in a plane crash, but his angel escort missed him
in the fog—now Niven has to argue his case before the heavenly
court. Similar to Hollywood fantasies like *It's a Wonderful Life*
and *Here Comes Mr. Jordan* but smarter and more affecting.

The Red Shoes *(color, 1948)* The best movie ever made about the compromises life makes with art, and about the work and camaraderie that go into the creative act. The "Red Shoes" ballet, wonky and lifting off from realism into a Technicolor fever state, is worth the price of admission.

NICHOLAS RAY

Ray is for thoughtful tweeners and teenagers who have begun to wonder how much of the world is arrayed against them. He's to the cinema what J. D. Salinger is to literature, and not just because *Rebel Without a Cause* (1955) is the closest film equivalent to *Catcher in the Rye* (1951). Ray's characters are victims of society and of themselves, and they roil with emotions that mark them as outsiders, that doom them, and that are proof they're more alive than anyone else. You may know someone like this living under your roof.

If you're unsympathetic to this sort of thing, a Ray movie may only smell like self-pity. More likely, if you're feeling bruised and misunderstood, the director will become the one adult who knows your secrets, and his circle of heroes—Dean and Natalie Wood in *Rebel*, Bogart in *In a Lonely Place*, Farley Granger and the incandescent Cathy O'Donnell in *They Live by Night*, James Mason with his God complex in *Bigger Than Life*— your comrades on the midnight bus. Ray's movies are company when company is needed.

They Live by Night *(B&W, 1949)* Two young lovers on the run from the law. It's like an incomparably tender blueprint for *Bonnie and Clyde*, and good luck finding it: It's not on video yet and only occasionally shows up on TV.

In a Lonely Place *(B&W, 1950)* Bogart as a troubled screenwriter with a penchant for violence and an unfortunate soft spot for the lady next door (Gloria Grahame, whose marriage to Ray was busting up during shooting). The one film to get under the ugly side of the Bogey persona.

Johnny Guitar *(color, 1954)* Magnificently insane Western in which the women wear the pants and everyone's out to crucify Joan Crawford. The closest Ray came to comedy, although the joke appears to have been lost on the star.

Rebel Without a Cause *(color, 1955)* Still the best movie about growing up privileged and directionless in America.

Bigger Than Life *(color, 1956)* Is schoolteacher James Mason going crazy because of his addiction to prescription drugs, or because the lockstep conformity of the 1950s is squeezing his head until it pops? Another rare one worth locating.

PRESTON STURGES

Everyone falls on their ass in a Preston Sturges movie; his is a democracy of pratfalls. Sturges doesn't even let himself off the hook: Playing Hollywood filmmaker John L. Sullivan in *Sullivan's Travels*, Joel McCrea is handed one humiliation after another, and you can almost hear the *wah-wah-wah* of the director's raucous offscreen laughter.

Aside from Hitchcock and Capra, Sturges was the rare Hollywood director with such a distinctive "voice" that even folks in the back row picked up on it. Certainly kids get the continuity—the sense that these comedies go further, with more rude, intelligent joy, than most of what passes for funny in old movies. Sturges found *people* funny, and his films are studded with lumpy character actors who surround the leads and jostle them until they give into the madness.

The filmmaker had a biography as delicious as any of his movies. Born wealthy, he was pampered and ignored by a high-living mother, who stowed him in European boarding schools while she swanned around with Isadora Duncan and other aesthetes (Duncan's fatal scarf, in fact, was a gift from Mother Sturges). He invented a kiss-proof lipstick, wrote a play that was a hit, and then wrote several that were not, forcing him to go to Hollywood to replenish his bank account. There he was so annoyed at the screenwriter's footstool status in the industry that he bullied his way into directing, starting with *The Great McGinty* in 1940.

That movie, about a bum (Brian Donleavy) who rises to become state governor, is still hilariously frank about what it takes to get elected to high office in this country—money and groveling to special interests—but the director's love of farce keeps it far from didacticism. Not for Sturges the gentle idealism of Frank Capra; in fact, *Sullivan's Travels* is still the final statement on the foolhardiness of message pictures. (Are you listening, Woody Allen? Of course you are; you swiped *Sullivan's* ending for *Hannah and Her Sisters*.) People want to laugh, Sturges knew, but he also knew they could take their laughter with a sting if the jokes were funny.

He loved giving it to big business: *Christmas in July* (1940) thumbs its nose at the advertising industry and his script for *Easy Living* (1937, directed by Mitchell Leisen) pulls the rug out from under Wall Street. The pomposities of institutions as varied as the army (*Hail the Conquering Hero*, 1944) and American motherhood (*The Miracle of Morgan's Creek*, 1944) attracted his happy lance. The latter film, about a small-town girl named Trudy Kockenlocker who gets drunk with some soldiers one night and ends up pregnant, is as envelope-pushing a comedy as was made during the studio era—where was the Paramount brass, out at a bond rally?

There is no social agenda to these movies other than that people who take themselves too seriously deserve a good old-fashioned Bronx raspberry. To that end Sturges stuffed his movies with blue-collar character comedians until the edges of the screen threatened to burst. This could turn merely manic, and in truth *Hail* and *Miracle* are often more noisy than funny. The earlier films—*Sullivan's*, *Palm Beach*, above all *The Lady Eve*, which plays like a Howard Hawks screwball comedy with extra-strength moxie—are the best places to start. The lesson of Sturges's brief flare of a career is that talent is lucky to find its moment: After World War II, he made few movies (mostly bad ones) and died at loose ends, as though the kiss-proof lipstick had finally worn off. The lesson of his movies is that too much is never enough.

The Lady Eve *(B&W, 1941)* Barbara Stanwyck, as a smart, gum-snapping con woman, meets her match in idiot beer heir Henry Fonda, of whom she says, "I need him like the ax needs the turkey."

Sullivan's Travels *(B&W, 1941)* Joel McCrea plays Sturges, for all intents and purposes: a Hollywood director of comedies (cf., "Hey Hey in the Hayloft") who decides he wants to make "art" and goes out to meet "the people." The people meet him back, but not like he expected. A useful film for introducing kids to the enchanting, short-lived phenomenon that was Veronica Lake.

The Palm Beach Story *(B&W, 1942)* Something about Joel McCrea and Claudette Colbert as a husband and wife who love each other but can't live together, a cross-country train filled with drunken duck hunters, and the apotheosis of (wait for it) the Weenie King.

Hail the Conquering Hero *(B&W, 1944)* Shrimpy 4-F Eddie Bracken becomes an instant war hero when a bunch of marines lie about his exploits to please his mother. There's a lesson here about fibbing if you can stop laughing long enough to deliver it.

Unfaithfully Yours *(B&W, 1948)* Sturges's only worthwhile postwar comedy is a gem about a symphony conductor (Rex Harrison) who believes his wife is fooling around and who dreams up three different ways to deal with it—including murder—scored to three different classical pieces. The bit with the recording machine is paralyzingly funny.

BILLY WILDER

Wilder expects the worst of people and is rarely disappointed. With the exception of *Some Like It Hot*, this is probably not a message you want to share with your youngest child, the one with heart of lambskin and eyes that gaze with faith upon the world. Wilder is for the older, harder kids who suspect the cosmic joke at the back of things. Because of when and where he worked, his movies are often saddled with happy endings insisted on by the studio or provided by Wilder, who knew on which side his career was buttered. Those endings are as believable as a smiley face at a poker game, and this is one of his few flaws; still, children hold on to them.

Anyway, you expected sunshine from a man who got out of Germany the moment Hitler came to power? There were those who stayed, expecting the thing to blow over, and there were people like Wilder who understood the beast had been loosed and that a sensible person might want to get a head start. And there were those who couldn't get out, like his mother, who died in a concentration camp.

He landed first in Paris and then Hollywood—not speaking a word of English—and bunked with Peter Lorre while he traded on his reputation as an ace screenwriter in Weimar-era Berlin to scrape together script assignments. By 1938, he had found

Charles Brackett, the first of his two great writing partners, and they worked their way up from Deanna Durbin musicals to scintillating Mitchell Leisen comedies (*Midnight*) and dramas (*Hold Back the Dawn*), Lubitsch's *Ninotchka* with Garbo, and Hawks's *Ball of Fire*. Hugely rewarding films all, yet Wilder chafed to direct, never forgiving Leisen for caving in when *Dawn* star Charles Boyer refused to shoot a scene in which his character talks to a cockroach.

Wilder's first film as director was 1942's *The Major and the Minor*—Ginger Rogers pretending to be a little girl, and as funny/borderline creepy as it sounds. *Double Indemnity* (1944) was the first true Billy Wilder film, a sordid yet impressively sardonic, even funny tale of greed, adultery, and murder, with the audience cued to root for Fred MacMurray and Barbara Stanwyck while hating their guts. *The Lost Weekend* (1945) was a groundbreaking treatment of alcoholism for its time, but *Sunset Blvd.* (1950) was the first real evidence of how far Brackett and Wilder, and Wilder in particular, was willing to go. Hollywood avoids its own history assiduously, but here the director dug up the bodies and placed them at the head of the table (and in the swimming pool), and a lot of people took years to forgive him for it.

There is good '50s Wilder for boys (*Stalag 17*) and girls (*Sabrina*), and there are also duds: *The Seven Year Itch* is the shallowest Marilyn Monroe of them all, and whoever hired the most cynical director in the business to make *The Spirit of St. Louis*—and cast forty-nine-year-old James Stewart as the young Charles Lindbergh—didn't get a Christmas bonus that year. By now, though, Wilder was writing his scripts with I. A. L. Diamond and the results were more frank and often mind-blowingly funny: *Some Like It Hot* (1959) is genius and suitable for all ages. *The Apartment* (1960) is close to its equal and *not* suitable for all ages, with its acid portrayal of corporate executives shagging their secretaries in Jack Lemmon's flat.

Wilder grew more ribald as the '60s kicked in—or coarser, depending on where you sit—and if *One Two Three* (1961) and *The Fortune Cookie* (1966) are raucous, *Kiss Me Stupid* (1963) is just amazingly lewd (and, as such, highly recommended to thirteen-year-old boys). His filmography, seen in the long view, tracks the decline of the studio system's steel-belted good cheer and the rise of a new distrust, in everything from institutions to human nature, that would flower with the hippie counterculture. Wilder helped make the New Hollywood of Coppola and Spielberg and De Palma possible, but he himself had no idea what to do with its freedoms. He is the last director listed in this book because a child who embraces his films is ready to leave childhood behind.

Double Indemnity *(B&W, 1944)* Lovingly sleazy murder melodrama, with Fred MacMurray and Barbara Stanwyck as two L.A. vipers in lust and Edward G. Robinson as the good guy—MacMurray's insurance adjustor boss who smells a rat. Key protonoir for kids who get on that wavelength.

The Lost Weekend *(B&W, 1945)* Ray Milland (who won an Oscar, as did Wilder) staggers through Manhattan trying to pawn his typewriter for a drink—and that's before the hallucinations kick in. Grueling landmark treatment of alcoholism is worthwhile for the older bunch, but even they won't believe the happy wrap-up.

Sunset Blvd. *(B&W, 1950)* Absolutely essential Hollywood ghoul show, with silent star Gloria Swanson playing a demented version of herself and has-beens like Buster Keaton dragged out of mothballs. Plus a monkey funeral.

Some Like It Hot *(B&W, 1959)* Lemmon and Curtis in drag, Marilyn in that dress, and the audience in stitches. Wilder and Diamond's finest two hours.

The Apartment *(B&W, 1960)* Wilder's second best director Oscar came for this mordant, surprisingly heartfelt tale of a corporate schnook (Lemmon) who lends his flat to his bosses for their afternoon delights, only to fall for a cast-off elevator girl (Shirley MacLaine).

AFTERWORD

. . . .

TOWARD A REASONED DEFENSE OF BLACK AND
WHITE IN A MULTICOLORED WORLD

I'M NOT SURE what this is doing all the way back here. If you're uninterested in black-and-white movies, you've already put this book back on the bookstore shelf and moved on. If you are interested in black and white, you need no convincing.

Your children may, though. It depends on who they are, and when they are. There are adults, too, who sharply push anything but the full rainbow away with varying emotions: impatience, frustration, boredom, annoyance. But a story is a story, isn't it? What does it matter whether it's in color or not? On the other hand, does black and white even have relevance in the twenty-first century? Or do its pleasures belong in a museum, the real world rushing by outside?

Black and white has almost entirely slipped away, but it used to be the way we fixed the world for keeping. This was not choice but chemistry, a by-product of early photography's inability to record colors. Silver halides only turn black when you expose them to light, and nothing Louis Daguerre or William Henry Fox Talbot did could convince the molecules otherwise, so the new medium was both more realistic and less "real" than the genres of landscape and portrait painting it replaced as the final word in fidelity.

Civil War soldiers wore blue or gray, then, and they bled red, but we can only think of them as colorless daguerrotypes—we can't *not* think of them in black and white, tinted, perhaps, with a modest blush on each cheek. And so it went. Little Alice Liddell and Julia Margaret Cameron's fairy princesses, Gilded Age barons, Jacob Riis's urchins, Edison's unlovely kissers, anarchists, flappers, the Depression's forgotten men, the Art Deco cross-stepping of Astaire, the thundering dolly shot that introduced John Wayne (after sixty-odd films) to the world in *Stagecoach*, the *Hindenburg*, Hitler, all the family snapshots left behind in the ghettos: all black and white. All missing a crucial element of perceptual reality and, because they're the only evidence we have, accepted as that reality. It hurts the head to think of the Depression in color.

Thus, for the longest time, color was a gimmick, at best a hope for the future. Its crudeness parodied the real world in the way little girls put on their mothers' makeup. Unable to replicate natural tones through photographic means, early filmmakers and distributors tinted the celluloid strips by hand, frame by frame, or ran entire sequences through a dye bath so that night scenes would be all blue, outdoor scenes all yellow, and so forth. As early as 1903, the gunshot at the end of *The Great Train Robbery* flashed an unexpected red, a promise to audiences that more might possibly come, someday.

It took a while. Black and white passed for reality only because color was for so long the greater artifice—more expensive, more technologically bedeviling—and was understood as such by both the film industry and the average moviegoer. A company called Kinemacolor, run by an Englishman named C. Albert Smith and an American named Charles Urban, produced the first color film to get a serious theatrical release, 1911's *The Durbar at Delhi*, but the technology broke down too often and the company was stymied in the United States by Edison's Motion Picture Patents Trust. Two Americans, Herbert

Kalmus and Daniel Comstock, came up with the Technicolor process as early as 1915, and their two-component approach (a special camera exposed alternating frames of black-and-white film through red and green filters; the resulting frames were separated, dyed the appropriate colors, and sandwiched into one film) found initial favor in silent-era Hollywood starting with 1922's *The Toll of the Sea.*

Epics like *The Ten Commandments* (1923) and *Ben-Hur* (1926) used the process for individual scenes, and Douglas Fairbanks's 1926 swashbuckler *The Pirate* was the first film entirely shot in two-component Technicolor. I've written above of taking the girls to see a print of the Lon Chaney *Phantom of the Opera* that used every color trick available in 1925: full-frame dye coloring, two-component Technicolor (for the Bal Masque sequence only; Natalie said the red and green color scheme made her think of peppermints), and a special hand-tinting process for the Phantom's billowing red cape in the nighttime rooftop sequence, a scene that is now burned into our collective memory. And still this was mere showmanship, a reference to the thing but not the thing itself.

With the Depression, the studios backed off from the expensive Technicolor system until the company came up with a superior approach in which a camera prism split the image onto three color-sensitive negatives from which a single positive "matrix" was made. That literally meant a special camera that exposed three pieces of film running side by side and, in the early days, three projectors strapped together to show them. Walt Disney tried it out first, with 1932's *Flowers and Trees* and *The Three Little Pigs*, but the first feature to be shot in three-strip Technicolor was 1935's *Becky Sharp*. There followed (among others) Disney's *Snow White* (1937), *The Adventures of Robin Hood* (1938), *The Wizard of Oz* (1939), and, the commercial pinnacle, *Gone with the Wind* (1939).

And still the vast majority of movies remained black and

white, and with it our consensual mediated reality. The primary reason was economic: Technicolor cost three times as much to shoot, develop, and print. It required ridiculous amounts of lighting for the three film stocks to properly expose. Black and white was also easier on the various craftsmen and craftswomen behind the scenes, since lighting designers, gaffers, makeup artists, and lab technicians didn't have to worry about matching hues from shot to shot.

And there was the underlying fact that Technicolor wasn't so much real as hyperreal, a splashy, ersatz imitation of life that had its own very real beauties (see Powell and Pressburger's *The Red Shoes* or *Black Narcissus*, or the lavish, kinky melodrama *Leave Her to Heaven*, or the gonzo Busby Berkeley musical *The Gang's All Here*) but that never seriously competed with black and white as a representation of the prewar world. Technicolor was the banana split with the whipped cream *and* the cherry on top. Life itself wasn't that rich—was it?

After World War II, itself black and white in the cultural memory banks, the world divided in two. The movies increasingly opened up like a rainbow fan: As the '50s settled in and the industry panic over TV grew, more and more films up and down the food chain burst into color. Technicolor, its three-strip negatives finally sandwiched into one piece of film by the 1940s, got competition from Kodak and other companies. Black and white gradually changed from the norm to a statement— consider the dark moral codes of film noir, unthinkable with tints and color charts—and, finally, to an admission of poverty. By the early 1960s, black and white only meant you couldn't afford to shoot it in color, unless you were Hitchcock (but, then, everything about *Psycho* was a calculated affront to the senses). By *The Last Picture Show* in 1971, black-and-white photography had become the aesthete's choice, a representation of *un*reality.

That was on one hand. On TV and in newspapers, the world

remained black and white for a while longer. The Zapruder film—so grainy it backs into modern art, with JFK's head exploding into a pink mist of Kodachrome II ink on celluloid canvas, like a Seurat or Roy Lichtenstein's Zipatones—the Zapruder film was the door that opened onto Vietnam's oranges, greens, and reds on our new color TV sets. And perhaps that's it. Perhaps once audiences have seen the color of real blood, there's no turning back. Black and white becomes a lie, and a damaging one.

But even that was forty years ago. What's black and white now? The photos on the inside of the newspaper, one or two channels your kids surf quickly past on their way to the Cartoon Network. A mistake; evidence of the past in a world addicted to the present. Proof that our grandparents were once young, which is the same as saying that we'll someday be old. Black and white is the bad news.

So asking children to watch a black-and-white movie today is like asking them to swim upstream against human evolution. Worse—it's an invitation to consider the distant past in a kiddie culture that distrusts even yesterday and that tars those who break the taboo of modernity, of constant lockstep coolness, with the closest insult at hand. Or, as I once saw posted on an online bulletin board by an exasperated teenage old-movie freak, "All of my friends in school think black and white is totally gay."

Well, baby, maybe they're just scared. For a lot of younger audiences—and I've asked my daughters and their friends about this—black and white represents an unsettling lack, and not just of color. Compared to the pounding sugar shock induced by media aimed at children, old movies can seem disturbingly empty. The pace is unhurried, the action irregular, the dramatic payoff uncertain or, worse, corny and predictable. Kids thrive on knowing the rules and feeling superior to them, and entertainment corporations are slavish about catering to those inter-

ests if only to close the sale. One false move and you've lost
them, literally so in the home video environment, which is the
only place most kids watch old movies and from which their
entire shiny lives beckon them to come away if they're bored for
a nanosecond.

At the same time, an unbroken field of black and white is
almost *too* full—or, rather, it's missing a crucial visual element
that allows a modern viewer to gain traction. In 1941, someone
watching *Citizen Kane* knew where to look, even given the
novelty of Welles's and cinematographer Gregg Toland's com-
positions. In 2005, a similar someone doesn't have the media
training to read those same images as easily. Natalie once
offhandedly told me, "When I look at black and white, it all just
looks like the same thing." Color in movies has become one of
the most important ways of telling us where to focus our attention, and to take that away from a kid can be bewildering, like
suddenly pulling out a crutch. Unlike everything else they see,
black and white doesn't curry favor. You have to meet it halfway.

Some do—some children just take to other languages—and
in so doing they discover a world of different visual pleasures
and lost high-spiritedness. In many ways it's a simpler world, and
there's something to the notion that loving black and white for
its own sake is a conservative urge, not in any political sense but
as a willful retreat from modernity's perceived noise and vulgar-
ity. Eliza's early love of black and white, in other words, was not
unrelated to her distaste for all things Britney, and it wavered
once she found Avril Lavigne, a pop singer she and her fourth-
grade friends could agree upon. (This slammed to a halt the day
Lavigne appeared glammed up on the cover of *Cosmo* and my
daughter learned that celebrities can betray you as easily as
friends or family.)

Eliza's friend Sally, on the other hand, groans with profound
annoyance when Eliza suggests a black-and-white film during
playdates; they've had little tiffs about it, followed by ugly com-

promises. I love Sally—she's a deep, deep file, with an active and troubled curiosity about the way the world happens, and maybe black and white is just too much *work* for her and not blessedly mind-numbing enough. It may be a reminder of everything she's supposed to do. Whereas for Eliza it's a refuge from same.

Natalie, like most kids, lives in the middle. She prefers color because that's how the world looks, but she understands there's meat to be had from the nutshells of black-and-white movies and she's willing to crack them, especially if they're funny or rough. So I have one kid who will watch anything with the Marx Brothers or tommy guns, and another who pines for Cary Grant and swoons with Bette Davis. For the first child, black and white is not reality but an acceptable simulacrum—one version in the broad media bazaar of choices offered to her. For the second child, black and white is a *response* to reality, and a potentially favored one.

I'm sympathetic to Eliza, even as I recognize the dangers and seductions of a silvery world where everyone dresses beautifully and says exactly the right thing. When the virus hit during my adolescence—when I saw that late-night airing of *Duck Soup* and started haunting Boston's old-movie revival houses and buying up books with titles like *They Had Faces Then* and *The Parade's Gone By*—it was with a clear sense that this cave of Aristotelian shadows was different from the polyester early '70s I was living in. Better, too: easier, more direct. You could understand it, and you knew when and most likely how it was going to end. The enjoyment was in the journey.

It could also be intensely beautiful, the more so because the images were the size of a wall. I recall seeing the 1933 Warner Bros. production of *A Midsummer Night's Dream* at Boston's old Park Square Theater, next to a downtown Continental Trailways bus depot that also no longer exists, and getting lost in the movie's crazy back-lot Rousseau visuals, the young Mickey Rooney as a howling Puck and Cagney with the ass's head the best thing in the whole overstuffed movie. Or *The Devil Is a Woman*, von Sternberg's last film with Marlene Dietrich, in which the star is almost completely swallowed up by decor and patterns of light, just another jigsaw piece in the world's unbearable sensuousness. *Devil* is a movie that needs to be big; a coffee-table jewel on TV, it's a beautiful nightmare when projected.

The prints at the revival houses were iffy—this was before film restoration had acquired cachet and funding, before (more to the point) there was a commercial market for the best possible version of a film. That came later, in the late 1990s, with DVD and the studios' understanding that Turner Classic Movies junkies would gladly buy a bunch of Garbo films if you promised them clean prints, trailers, and a nice-looking box. Thus what was once a communal experience—an audience of strangers staring together at dreams on the inside of a building—increasingly becomes a collector's experience, and more often than not a solitary one.

But movies are to be shared. At the revival houses I went to in Boston and, later, in New York, there was a camaraderie of viewership that hovered—again, like the aftermath of a dream—as we spilled back onto the sidewalks. This was during that brief countercultural window between TV's *Million Dollar Movie* and the rise of home video, when paying to see an old film in a theater was socially acceptable, even desirable. You met like minds of all ages and genders, and conversations always led off toward other movies, older, newer, unheard of (*You've never seen* Battle of Algiers? *It's playing next week at the Brattle*).

At the same time, these movies were an intensely private pursuit, if only because the mainstream culture was charging ahead into the disco era. On the personal front, I developed an odd double existence: I grew my hair long and baked out on Yes records like any self-respecting 1974 suburban teenager—but then I'd retreat to the cave to absorb *The Grapes of Wrath* and Rita Hayworth, to freak out over W. C. Fields in *International*

House, to pine for Isabel Jewell as the little seamstress at the end of MGM's *A Tale of Two Cities*.

I'm not kidding about the cave, either. It was a basement rec room into which my mother never ventured, with pale stucco walls that sweated moisture in the summer. The furnishings were several retired easy chairs, an out-of-tune piano, and an old living room TV set on which I watched 1930s movies deep into the night, lights off, happily stoned, enveloped in flicker. The prints the local stations aired were awful, and this somehow made the experience all the more precious, as though I were peering at relics through a ruined church window.

Strangely, I experienced the same aesthetic shock to the system, and for some of the same reasons, when I discovered punk rock a few years later. Here was another medium of almost binary simplicity, of *sonic* black and white, only it was happening right now. But old movies remained for me a first love, the one you never get over, and when I got to college I found I had company. I also found there were even more movies to see, in color, from other countries, from the present, that concretely or obliquely cleared the decks as expertly as the Ramones' first album or Cagney in *White Heat*.

Yet there was something about the old films, the black-and-white ones, that made my college coterie of hairy film junkies lapse into devotional silence. Some people flee from evidence of the past; we embraced it. Reasons were varied: to fool ourselves into believing we could master a subject, because the screenplays were better (smarter, more literate), because Joan Bennett in *Scarlet Street* kept us up at night, because Jean Renoir made us cry, because if I watch Cary Grant enough I may possibly become him—may even step into the frame like Buster Keaton in *Sherlock Jr.* and never look back. Because life frightens me. Or because these movies show me parts of life I never knew were there, and now I see them everywhere.

Today, when I'm channel surfing and I glimpse black and

white, I still stop and check it out, the same way that 99 percent of the world hurries on, searching for the color that is their birthright. I may find one of those inky chiaroscuro master-pieces like *Sweet Smell of Success* or *The Third Man*, or Astaire the human swizzle stick, or the bleak grays of Italian neorealism, or the hard slash of film noir, or Karloff's shoe-box head looming out of the shadows.

Is it too much to want one's children to stop and look, too? Or does the desire itself skew the test results, the lab mice look-ing uncertainly over their furry shoulders at Professor Heisen-berg and saying "*Nah*, we'd rather watch *Barnyard*"? I go back and forth about this. Of my daughters, Natalie has the greater preference for harmless modern junk—the *Cheaper by the Dozen* remakes, *The Suite Life of Zack and Cody* on TV—and outside of setting reasonable media-inhalation limits, who are my wife and I to say no? But then, suddenly, she breaks into a chorus of "Shanghai Lil" from *Footlight Parade* or insists to one of her play-dates that *Strangers on a Train* is the best Hitchcock movie and what do you mean you don't know who Hitchcock is? I am finally understanding that what was for me a vast unknown country to explore and escape to is for her a familiar neighbor-hood among other familiar neighborhoods, and home is always close by. I suspect that this book has been more about home than about movies.

As I was writing this chapter, I had lunch with a friend in her late sixties, a much-loved editor for a small Boston newspaper. Kay and I had a history: Her husband had been both a teacher and a mentor to me in grammar school, I had babysat their chil-dren as a teenager, and then Kay and I had reconnected when I returned to Boston to work at the local paper. We had lunch two or three times a year in the old style: several hours long, with Kay lavishing care on a martini while I, a weenie of my generation, watched from the far side of a glass of seltzer.

This lunch was different, though, because Bill had died two

months earlier and Kay was having a terrible time of it. She wanted to talk about everything except sorrow, and we did, occasionally brushing against the bruise and moving on. I told her about this book and why I wanted to write it, and the conundrum of black and white in a color world. With a short, scornful laugh, Kay said she preferred color, always had. Color was special when she was young—color was the future! In the 1980s, her daughter had majored in film studies at college; the professors insisted black and white was morally superior, so the daughter would rent old movies to watch with Kay, who was Just. Not. Interested.

"I loved . . . *Technicolor*," Kay said with the tone of a woman confessing sins, and she told me of a night in her teens when she went to see *Easter Parade* at the local movie palace in Marblehead, Massachusetts, where she grew up. She had gone alone. It was a double bill—"you always saw two movies back then, always"—and the only things she remembers about the first film are that everyone in it was elegant and that the heroine had a white telephone. What kind of person has a white telephone? Only in the unspeakably wealthy stratosphere of suffering movie heroines. I mentioned that there was an entire genre of World War II–era Italian films derisively labeled "white telephone movies" by the young neorealist directors then coming up (kids with names like Fellini and Rossellini), and I asked her if she would have remembered that telephone if the film had been in color. "No," she said, after a pause. "No, I wouldn't have."

But what Kay really wanted to tell me about was *Easter Parade*, or rather the rapture of being surrounded by its heightened rainbow. *This* was the anomaly, the phoenix come to ground in Marblehead and bursting into flames again. Astaire and Judy Garland and Irving Berlin were secondary to the sheer sensation of it; everything else was suddenly just . . . movies. In my own mind's eye I saw a young woman—the age Eliza and Natalie will be in a few years—in a darkened theater, the spectrum reflecting off her face as she looks at the screen and somehow, impossibly, *through* it, like Dorothy Gale gazing through the sepia doorway of her farmhouse at the colors of Oz rioting just beyond the threshhold. Looking toward—what? The promise of adulthood? Everything that hasn't yet happened? The infinite hues of life's possibilities? Movies hint at so many different kinds of paradise when we're young. How can the real world ever measure up?

Like this: When she came out of the theater, Kay said, it was night and snow was falling. The snowflakes, big as moths, thudded softly to the ground under the streetlights, and she walked the twenty minutes home alone in an ecstasy of confusion. It seemed, she said, as though she were walking between artifice and reality, and I shivered with her, there at the restaurant table fifty-eight years later. What did it mean, she wondered, when a movie was in color and the world could be so perfectly black and white?

ACKNOWLEDGMENTS

. . . .

I OWE MANY thanks to the folks at Cinemasmith in Coolidge Corner, Brookline, Massachusetts, for letting me keep two-day rentals out for five weeks and not forcing me to mortgage my children in return. Best selection in the Boston area, too, and, yes, that's a plug.

My agent, Sarah Burnes at Burnes & Clegg and the Gernert Company, understood the idea of this book right away and provided the enthusiasm, advice, and forward drive necessary to help get it over the hump to reality and to a publisher.

Peter Smith, a good friend and better writer, led me to Sarah and offered solidarity and support. His late father, A. O. Smith, was a mentor to me in both grammar and life, as were Walter McCloskey and Paul Monette. David Thomson showed me more movies than I had dreamed existed and pointed me toward new ways of thinking and writing about them; I owe my voice to his. Phil Rosen taught me not to be ashamed of melodrama. Richard Dohanian taught me the proper way to cook a steak and an appreciation for the genius of Bill Evans, both long-view exercises that better prepare a person for fatherhood.

Four women closer to home have been my larger inspiration:

Eliza and Natalie, of course, without whom this book would not be possible.

Lori Yarvis, my wife, first reader, and this book's silent partner (law firm of Hungadunga, Hungadunga, Hungadunga, and McCormack), without whom Eliza and Natalie would not be possible, nor the author's career, sanity, equilibrium, joy.

Marjorie Jane Tice Burr Rowell, without whom the author would not be possible and who led me to consider a movie when I was fourteen that led to other things, including this book, even if she lived only long enough to know it was being written and to hear the beginning of the thanks I tried to write into every line.

INDEX

. . . .

THE BEST OLD MOVIES FOR CHILDREN
(Organized by Age Group)

The page numbers below refer to the main discussion of each movie. In some cases, where a movie is worth watching because of the director and/or one or more stars, more than one page number is included.

To Watch with Your Tweener

To Watch with Your Teenager

The Graduate Course: For Committed
Film Junkies

WGRL-HQ NONFIC
31057010167271
791.4375 BURR   0007
Burr, Ty.
The best old movies for
families : a guide to watching

Burr, Ty.
WEST GA REGIONAL LIBRARY SYS

DISCARD